# Clash of Powers

The US–China trade war instigated by President Trump has thrown the multilateral trading system into a crisis. Drawing on vast interview and documentary materials, Hopewell shows how US–China conflict had already paralysed the system of international rules and institutions governing trade. The China Paradox—the fact that China is both a developing country and an economic powerhouse—creates significant challenges for global trade governance and rule-making. While China demands exemptions from global trade disciplines as a developing country, the US refuses to extend special treatment to its rival. The implications of this conflict extend far beyond trade, impeding pro-development and pro-environment reforms of the global trading system. As one of the first analyses of the implications of US–China rivalry for the governance of global trade, this book is crucial to our understanding of China's impact on the global trading system and on the liberal international economic order.

KRISTEN HOPEWELL is an Associate Professor in the School of Public Policy and Global Affairs at the University of British Columbia.

# Clash of Powers

## US–China Rivalry in Global Trade Governance

**KRISTEN HOPEWELL**

*University of British Columbia*

CAMBRIDGE
UNIVERSITY PRESS

# CAMBRIDGE
## UNIVERSITY PRESS

University Printing House, Cambridge CB2 8BS, United Kingdom

One Liberty Plaza, 20th Floor, New York, NY 10006, USA

477 Williamstown Road, Port Melbourne, VIC 3207, Australia

314–321, 3rd Floor, Plot 3, Splendor Forum, Jasola District Centre,
New Delhi – 110025, India

79 Anson Road, #06–04/06, Singapore 079906

Cambridge University Press is part of the University of Cambridge.

It furthers the University's mission by disseminating knowledge in the pursuit of
education, learning, and research at the highest international levels of excellence.

www.cambridge.org
Information on this title: www.cambridge.org/9781108834797
DOI: 10.1017/9781108877015

First published 2020

*A catalogue record for this publication is available from the British Library.*

*Library of Congress Cataloging-in-Publication Data*
NAMES: Hopewell, Kristen, 1978– author.
TITLE: Clash of powers : US-China rivalry in global trade governance / Kristen Hopewell,
University of Edinburgh.
DESCRIPTION: Cambridge, United Kingdom ; New York, NY : Cambridge University Press,
2020. | Includes bibliographical references and index.
IDENTIFIERS: LCCN 2020007242 (print) | LCCN 2020007243 (ebook) |
ISBN 9781108834797 (hardcover) | ISBN 9781108819862 (paperback) |
ISBN 9781108877015 (epub)
SUBJECTS: LCSH: International trade–Political aspects. | Commercial policy. | United States–
Foreign economic relations. | China–Foreign economic relations. | Hegemony. | Balance of power.
CLASSIFICATION: LCC HF1379 .H6735 2020 (print) | LCC HF1379 (ebook) |
DDC 382.0973–dc23
LC record available at https://lccn.loc.gov/2020007242
LC ebook record available at https://lccn.loc.gov/2020007243

ISBN 978-1-108-83479-7 Hardback
ISBN 978-1-108-81986-2 Paperback

# Contents

v

# Figures

# Tables

# Acknowledgments

I am deeply indebted to the many trade negotiators and policymakers who made the analysis in this book possible by generously sharing their time and insights. This research was supported by a Future Research Leaders Grant from the UK Economic and Social Research Council (ESRC).

Thanks to those who provided helpful commentary, reactions, and feedback on the material in the book. They include Matthew Bishop, Fred Block, Paul Bowles, Shaun Breslin, Tim Büthe, Ana Célia Castro, Gregory Chin, Jennifer Clapp, Benjamin Cohen, Andrea Collins, Andy Cooper, Marieke de Goede, Peter Evans, Matt Ferchen, Rosemary Foot, Andrew Gamble, Nana de Graaff, Julian Gruin, Iain Hardie, Eugenia Heldt, Kathryn Hochstetler, Maria Johnson, Miles Kahler, Sandra Lavenex, Zakiya Luna, Matias Margulis, Emma Mawdsley, Li Mingjiang, Jens Mortensen, John Odell, Sigrid Quack, John Ravenhill, Charlotte Rommerskirchen, James Scott, Omar Serrano, JP Singh, Lynn Verduzco-Baker, Huang Renwei, Jue Wang, Matthew Weinert, Zheng Yu, and Ren Xiao.

I benefited greatly from the opportunity to present various parts of this project to policymakers, including at the Wilson Center in Washington, DC; the United Nations University World Institute for Development Economics Research in Helsinki; the UK Foreign and Commonwealth Office and Department for International Trade in London; and the BRICS Seminar on Governance held in conjunction with the 2017 BRICS Summit in Quanzhou, China.

I would also like to thank participants in workshops and seminars where I presented aspects of this work at the University of Cambridge,

Cornell University, the Center for Global Cooperation Research at the University of Duisburg-Essen, University of Geneva, Leiden University, London School of Economics, University of Manchester, University of Sheffield, and Federal University of Rio de Janeiro.

I am grateful to Robert Dreesen at Cambridge University Press for his support of this project, as well as to three anonymous reviewers of the manuscript for their very valuable suggestions and advice.

# Introduction

How is growing rivalry between the United States and China—the clash of a hegemon and its emerging challenger—affecting the governance of global trade? For over seventy years, the US has been the dominant state in the international system. The construction of the US-led liberal international economic order—the institutions, rules, and laws established to govern the global economy—has been a distinct and defining feature of American hegemony. Its central pillar has been an open and rules-based multilateral trading system to create stable conditions for international trade and facilitate global economic integration. The international institutions created and dominated by the US—such as the World Trade Organization (WTO)—enabled it to set the rules of the global economy, and thereby provided a vital means to reinforce and project its power globally. Yet after four decades of rapid and sustained economic growth, China has now emerged as the world's leading trading state and second largest economy. The rise of China is reshaping the global economy and the institutions charged with its governance, yet the nature and implications of these changes are only beginning to be understood.

There is heated debate about the impact of China's rise on the US-led liberal international economic order. Skeptics dismiss claims of declining American hegemony in the face of a rising China as exaggerated or overhyped. Certainly, while China has become a major economic player, it is still nowhere near on a par with the US. Given the American hegemon's vastly greater economic, military, and soft power capabilities, many argue that China is not an imminent challenger, and the US maintains its position as the world's sole superpower. Moreover, since China is now tightly integrated into the global economy and heavily dependent on international trade, and it has benefited considerably from the existing system of global economic governance that has enabled its rise, many expect that China will support the overarching goals and principles of the system and seek to sustain it. In short, the prevailing view is that the US maintains its dominance in the international system, China does not possess sufficient power to pose a real threat to US hegemony, and, even if it did, China would likely support rather than challenge the established global economic architecture that the US has created. This book, however, challenges each of these assumptions.

It does so by analyzing China's impact on global trade governance, which is at the heart of the US-led liberal international economic order. Contrary to those who insist that the US remains secure in its hegemony, I argue that the rise of China has sharply curtailed the US's "institutional power" (Barnett and Duvall 2005)—its power over the institutions and rules that govern the global economy. The US constructed the institutions of global economic governance, which served as an important channel for the projection of American power, and their rules have reflected its primacy. Now, however, even though China's economic and overall power capabilities remain far smaller than those of the US, I show that China's rise has significantly constrained the exercise of US power in global economic institutions. Amid the rise of China, the US's ability to dominate the governing institutions of the trading system and to write the rules of global trade has been severely weakened.

In contrast to the assumption that a rising China can be smoothly integrated into the US-led liberal international economic order, I argue that US–China rivalry has become the predominant dynamic shaping global trade governance, and it is creating serious problems for its functioning. The US and China are engaged in a struggle over the rules of global trade, with each seeking to shape the rules to reflect and advance its interests. China is refusing simply to be a rule-taker, or to accept the rules demanded by the US. As I will demonstrate, the confrontation between these two dominant powers has paralyzed global trade governance and led to a breakdown in rule-making. Not only is this undermining the institutions that are essential to ensuring stability and order in the international trading system, but it also has crucial implications for a broader set of issues, including efforts to promote global development and protect the environment.

This book is particularly timely as trade has become a flashpoint of conflict between the US and China. Trade tensions between the two powers have escalated dramatically, amid growing concerns about the

US trade deficit, allegations of unfair trade practices by China, and the use of protectionist measures by the US in retaliation, heightening the risk of a trade war between the world's two largest economies. However, while attention has overwhelmingly focused on the bilateral trading relationship between the US and China, this book analyzes a critical aspect of their growing rivalry that has been largely overlooked: their battle over the global institutions and rules governing trade.

At the heart of this battle is a conflict over how China should be treated under global trade rules. The *China paradox*—the fact that China is simultaneously both a developing country and a major economic heavyweight—has created significant challenges for global trade governance. China demands certain exemptions from global trade disciplines in light of its status as a developing country, but the US refuses to extend such special treatment to a key economic competitor and its chief hegemonic rival. Importantly, the effects of this conflict go far beyond US–China relations. China presents itself as a champion of the rights of developing countries, but the traditional North–South framing of global trade politics is increasingly problematic. As this book will show, in some areas China has now become a major impediment to pro-development reform of the trading system. In addition, by refusing to accept disciplines on its trade practices, China is also impeding efforts directed at "greening" the multilateral trading system by using global trade rules to promote important sustainable development objectives.

## AMERICAN HEGEMONY AND THE LIBERAL INTERNATIONAL ECONOMIC ORDER

A key aspect of American hegemony to date has been its dominance of global institutions. The US emerged from World War II with an overwhelming and unprecedented concentration of economic, military, and political power. The American hegemon wielded its power to forge a new and historically distinct international order that both reflected and reinforced its primacy (Arrighi and Silver 1999; Walt 2011). This American-led order—which some have termed the "American imperium" (Katzenstein 2005), an "informal empire" (Panich and Gindin 2012; Wood 2005), "consensual empire" (Maier 2002), or "empire of invitation" (Lundestad 1990)—was based on the US's position at the epicenter of global capitalism and institutionalized through an extensive system of global governance. The US, backed by other Western states, engaged in an extraordinary and unprecedented building of multilateral institutions, including the International Monetary Fund (IMF), the World Bank, the Organisation for Economic Co-operation and Development (OECD), and the General Agreement on Tariffs and Trade (GATT), which became the WTO. These institutions have served as the pillars of the US hegemonic order (Gilpin 1987; Keohane 1984; Ruggie 1996).

The era of American hegemony has been historically distinct in that, unlike previous hegemons, US power has been exercised in and through international rules and institutions. The US established and consolidated its dominance of the global order through these governance institutions, which served as a means for the US to advance its economic and strategic interests (Mastanduno 2009). The US "ran the system," providing leadership (or domination) and facilitating cooperation among states (Ikenberry 2015a). While a hierarchical order sustained by American economic and military power, the US-led liberal international economic order required the buy-in of other states (Lake 2009). Consequently, although international institutions served as a channel for the projection of American power, their rules and norms also served—at least to some extent—to rein in the arbitrary and indiscriminate use of power by the hegemon. The existing global governance architecture is thus deeply intertwined with US hegemony. In no prior period of hegemonic transition has there been such an extensive system of global governance in place, or such an elaborate corpus of international law, norms, and standards.

This is not to suggest, however, that the liberal international economic order was simply a beneficent creation of the American hegemon that worked equally well for all states. On the contrary, its constituent institutions and rules have always reflected underlying power asymmetries among states, and especially the overarching power of the US. For nearly its entire seventy-year history, developing countries have complained that the multilateral trading system, for instance, has failed to adequately address the needs and concerns of the Global South (Margulis 2017). The rules of the global trade regime were constructed by the US and a handful of other advanced-industrialized states and designed primarily to advance their interests and objectives (Hopewell 2016; Wilkinson and Scott 2008). As a result, the benefits of multilateral trade liberalization have been unevenly distributed and often bypassed the vast majority of developing countries (Ruggie 1982). Conflict between the Global North and the Global South has thus been a central fault line in the trading system, as evident from the Third Worldist movement of the 1950s to the 1970s to the more recent surge of developing country activism in the Doha Round of trade negotiations at the WTO.

## DEBATING THE EXTENT AND IMPACT OF CHINA'S RISE

In this context, understanding the implications of a rising China has become a central preoccupation of scholars and policymakers alike. While the rise of China is widely viewed as the most important geopolitical event of the twenty-first century, there are major debates about how to assess the extent, significance, and implications of its ascent. First, are we in the midst of a hegemonic transition from the US to China, or does the US maintain its dominance? And, second, can the US-led liberal international economic order adapt to, manage, and accommodate the rise of China?

### Debate 1: US Hegemony

The first issue of contention is whether we are, in fact, witnessing the decline of US hegemony and the rise of China as a new global hegemon. The remarkable expansion of the Chinese economy, and projections that China may soon surpass the US as the world's largest economy, have prompted assertions that China is in the process of overtaking the US as the world's dominant power (Acharya 2014; Jacques 2009; Rachman 2016). Measured at purchasing power parity (PPP) rates, China's GDP ($19 trillion) has already surpassed that of the US ($18 trillion).[1] China has replaced America as the top manufacturer and exporter, with export volumes that now vastly exceed those of the US ($2.3 trillion versus $1.5 trillion).[2] China has also become the largest market for many commodities and consumer goods, home to some of the world's biggest corporations, and a massive source of outward investment, aid, and lending. Some analysts, such as Arvind Subramanian (2011), thus conclude that "China's ascendancy is imminent" and its dominance "a sure thing"– based on its GDP, volume of trade, and role as a net creditor to the world, especially its large holdings of US debt.

Yet assertions that US power is being eclipsed by China have been met with a strong chorus of rebuttals. Many scholars refute claims of a power transition from the US to China, pointing out that China still remains far from parity with the US in its power capabilities (Beckley 2011; Cox 2012; Kagan 2012; Slaughter 2009). Even strictly in economic terms, despite China's gains, it is clear that the US maintains a preponderance of power. While the US share of global GDP has fallen from 40 percent in 1960 to 25 percent in 2016, the US still remains the world's largest and richest economy by far.[3] China, by comparison, accounts for just 15 percent of global GDP at market exchange rates, which arguably provide the most accurate measure of economic might. In these terms, the American economy is 65 percent larger than China's (with US GDP of $18 trillion compared to China's $11 trillion).[4] As Edward Mansfield (2014: 439) puts it, while large, China's economy is thus "currently nowhere near the size needed to challenge the US." Moreover, the US's economic power is further magnified by its dominance in global capital markets, its technological advantage, and the status of the US dollar as the world's most important currency (Hung 2015; Norrlof 2014; Wade 2017).

Many have also questioned predictions that China will overtake the US in coming decades, cautioning against extrapolating China's future growth trajectory based on its previous performance (Babones 2011; Nye 2012). China's growth has already decelerated and it faces a host of domestic economic challenges—including the threat of the middle-income trap, a rapidly aging population, high levels of public and private indebtedness, excessive investment and overcapacity, an asset bubble, and severe pollution—that are likely to slow the pace of its future growth (Lynch 2015). Skeptics frequently point out that similar predictions in the 1980s that a rising Japan would overtake the US proved unfounded: when the Japanese economy stagnated in the 1990s, it quickly ceased to be seen as a threat to American hegemony (Lake 2014). Speculation that China's economic boom may likewise go bust, or at least not persist indefinitely, has led to doubts about China's ability to continue its rise (Hung 2015) and suggestions that it may remain merely a "partial power" (Shambaugh 2013).

Much of the current debate has thus focused on sizing up and comparing the relative power capabilities of the US and China. Beyond its economic primacy, the US also maintains an overwhelming military advantage, with no prospect of China catching up anytime soon (Brooks and Wohlforth 2016; Kagan 2012). And the US benefits from an extensive network of allies and considerable soft power advantages (Brooks and Wohlforth 2016; Nye 2012). As Gregory Chin and Carla Freeman (2016) summarize: "the relative preponderance of power resources remains in the hands of the US... The US retains the advantage of superior power across all dimensions of national power (material, ideational, soft, hard, high politics, low politics)."

Accordingly, most accounts reject the notion that US hegemony is threatened by the rise of China, arguing that China is in no position to replace the US as a global hegemon. As Salvatore Babones (2015) puts it,

"There are few factual indications that American decline has begun—or that it will begin anytime soon." On the contrary, he argues that: "Putting aside all the alarmist punditry, American hegemony is now as firm as or firmer than it has ever been, and will remain so for a long time to come." In short, he concludes, "American hegemony is here to stay." Similarly, Brooks and Wohlforth (2016: 91, 97) argue that China "still has a long way to go before it might gain the economic and technological capacity to become a superpower" and thus conclude that "rather than expecting a power transition in international politics, everyone should start getting used to a world in which the United States remains the sole superpower for decades to come."

In sum, a narrow focus on comparing the relative power capabilities of the US and China has led many to insist on the enduring strength of American hegemony, concluding, in the words of Daniel Drezner (2011), that the US "still has a huge lead" and remains "vastly more powerful" than China. However, what this misses is that there are important ways in which China is already constraining US power—specifically its institutional or rule-making power. Institutional power refers to the ability to shape the rules of an institution to guide, steer, and constrain the actions of others (Barnett and Duvall 2005; Krasner 2011). It is, in short, the ability to set the rules of the game by which other actors must play. In global economic governance, rules and institutions are, of course, not neutral but reflect the distribution of power in the international system. One of the privileges of US hegemony has been an extraordinary power to shape the rules of the global economy in its favor. Global institutions, built and dominated by the US, have reflected its interests and preferences and played a major role in the stabilization and effectiveness of American hegemony (Hurrell 2004).

Many scholars argue that the US retains its dominance in global economic institutions, with China unable to translate its growing economic weight into effective political influence (Beeson and Bell 2009; Pinto, Macdonald, and Marshall 2011; Subacchi 2008; Vestergaard and Wade 2015). As Miles Kahler (2010: 178) argues, "national economic capabilities are not easily translated into influence over governance or institutions." For instance, despite its emergence as a major trader in the 1960s and 70s, Japan's influence in global trade governance has always lagged far behind its economic might. Today, according to Robert Wade (2017: 137–38), the US and other Western states "have successfully kept control of the commanding heights" and they "continue to set the global economic and financial governance agenda," while China and other emerging powers have exercised little real leadership or influence. Simply put, he argues, the US—and the West more broadly—"remains on top, economically and politically" (Wade 2017: 135).

This book, however, challenges the prevailing assumption that the US maintains its dominance in global economic governance. As I will show, China has become a central player in global trade governance. If the US and China are competing for economic dominance, they are also engaged in a pitched battle to set the rules of that competition, through institutions like the WTO. Each wants its own interests and preferences to be inscribed in the institutions and rules governing global trade. Rivalry between the US and China is not solely about amassing power resources; it is also a struggle over institutional power and setting the rules of the game. In contrast to those who argue that China lacks sufficient power to pose a real threat to the US, drawing on an analysis of the trade regime, I argue that the US's institutional power has been severely weakened by the rise of China.

Rule-making power is a crucial aspect of hegemony: a hegemon is powerful enough to maintain the rules of the system and "play the dominant role in constructing new rules" (Keohane and Nye 2011: 37). For the last seven decades, the American hegemon has had sufficient power to play the dominant role in writing and enforcing the rules of the global trading system, including driving forward the ongoing process of constructing new rules to govern international commerce. But its rule-making power has now been impeded by China, an emerging challenger that has been unwilling to defer to American hegemony in global trade governance. As the analysis that follows will show, existing trade institutions created under US hegemony are being undermined, and American efforts to construct new trade rules have been repeatedly thwarted by a rising China. The US and China are engaged in a struggle over the rules of the game—and specifically whether, and how, the rules will apply to China. Despite the US's superior power resources, China has been able to persistently block the US from achieving its objectives across a wide range of different areas of trade governance. To quote Christopher Layne (2018: 110), "in international politics, who rules makes the rules." China's rise, I argue, has profoundly disrupted the US's ability to make the rules and thus to rule. Accounts that emphasize the continuity and resilience of US hegemony in the face of a rising China therefore miss important dynamics of change currently taking place within global institutions.

## Debate 2: Global Economic Governance

The second, and closely related, subject of debate is how a rising China will affect the existing system of global economic governance constructed under American hegemony (Gray and Murphy 2015; Lesage and Van de Graaf 2015). Some are pessimistic and foresee conflict, based on the assumption that rising powers like China hold fundamentally different interests and agendas than established powers and are therefore likely to be system-challengers rather than system-supporters (Bremmer and Roubini 2011; Castañeda 2010; Kagan 2010; Kupchan 2014). The pessimistic view thus predicts that power shifts will weaken multilateral cooperation and destabilize the international economic architecture (Layne 2009; Patrick 2010). Others are more optimistic about the prospects for global economic governance to continue to function smoothly amid shifting power. The optimistic view expects that China and other emerging powers will be supporters of, and seek to maintain, the liberal international economic order that has facilitated and enabled their rise (Cox 2012; Nye 2015; Snyder 2011; Xiao 2013). Economic interdependence between the US and China, it is argued, will foster cooperation and lead them to find ways to jointly participate in the management of the existing institutional order.

Those who take a sanguine view of China's impact on the existing order assume that its objectives are fundamentally status quo oriented. Miles Kahler (2010: 178) argues that China's "preferences over institutional design and policies are unlikely to diverge from the status quo." Brooks and Wohlforth (2016: 100) similarly conclude that China's use of its growing economic clout on the international stage "will likely involve only minor or cosmetic alterations to the existing order, important for burnishing Beijing's prestige but not threatening to the order's basic arrangements or principles." Likewise, John Ikenberry (2015a) maintains that China and other rising powers are heavily invested in the existing order and therefore not radical revisionists:

[They] may not share all the values and interests of the United States and the other established stakeholders. But they are not, in reality, advancing revisionist ideas of global order. ... [T]hey are not putting forward ideas for international order that require a fundamental break with the existing system.

Certainly, in the case of trade, in particular, there is broad agreement that, as one of the prime beneficiaries of the liberal global trading order that has enabled the boom in China's exports and that has propelled its extraordinarily rapid economic growth and development, China has a keen interest in maintaining the multilateral trading system and is therefore clearly a status-quo rather than revisionist power (Breslin 2013; Gao 2015; Narlikar 2013; Quark 2013; Scott and Wilkinson 2013).

For many, a key factor in determining whether power shifts will result in conflict or cooperation is whether the US and other traditional powers adapt to the rise of new powers by integrating them into existing institutions and their decision-making structures. This means giving China and other emerging powers a seat at the table that reflects their economic weight and allowing them to assume a leadership role in global economic governance (Kahler 2016; Paul 2016b; Zangl et al. 2016). Many contend that the future of global economic governance hinges on the willingness of the US to redistribute authority, make room for rising states, and develop a system of shared leadership that accommodates the demands of rising powers for greater voice and authority (Drezner 2007; Ikenberry 2015a; Zakaria 2008). The liberal international economic order can be maintained, it is argued, if rising states are welcomed and incorporated into the power structures of its constitutive institutions. Much is therefore believed to rest on the US's willingness to make adjustments to accommodate rising powers: China will "actively seek to integrate into an expanded and reorganized liberal international order," provided that the US and other Western states act to reform global institutions to make room for China (Ikenberry 2011: 344). Indeed, many argue that liberal global governance can be renewed and strengthened by incorporating China and other rising powers, becoming more inclusive, representative, and legitimate (Vestergaard and Wade 2015; Warwick Commission 2008; Zoellick 2010). The dominant view is thus that if the decision-making structures of the existing system of global economic governance can be opened to incorporate China, it will readily integrate into and support the system.

To summarize, the conventional wisdom foresees China's rise having a minimal impact on global economic governance—either because the US maintains a preponderance of power capabilities or because it can lock-in China's support for the system by giving it a seat at the table, or because China lacks influence or supports the fundamental objectives of the system. Yet, I argue, what we see in global trade governance is that China's rise is in fact proving highly disruptive—both to US power and to the institutional order it created. This book challenges the argument that a rising China can be smoothly integrated into the US-led liberal international economic order because China has benefited from the existence of that order and has an interest in maintaining it. As I will show, although China may indeed be broadly system-supporting, its rise has nonetheless created serious difficulties for the functioning of the global trade regime. Even if China is not putting forward revisionist ideas for international order that represent a fundamental break with the existing system, as many claim, I demonstrate that its rise is nonetheless still having highly disruptive effects.

## THE ARGUMENT

This book analyzes the impact of China's rise on the governance of global trade. Its central contention is that China has become a pivotal actor, along with the US, in global trade governance, but this shift in power is proving to be far from smooth. While debates rage over whether we are in the process of a hegemonic transition from the US to China—which is likely unknowable at this point and only to be revealed through the passage of time—I argue that regardless of whether or not China will ever overtake the US as hegemon, its rise has *already* proven highly destabilizing for the system of global trade governance created under US hegemony. Growing rivalry between the US and China—the clash of a hegemon and its (potentially) emerging challenger—has become the predominant dynamic in contemporary global trade governance. And it is profoundly undermining global institutions and rule-making in trade.

Even if the US maintains a preponderance of power in the international system, its capacity to direct and steer global trade governance—which until now has been a defining feature of its hegemony—has been severely diminished. In other words, if the US once "ran the system," as Ikenberry (2015a) puts it, this book demonstrates the extent to which that has now been disrupted: China has proven a significant counterbalance to US power that has substantially weakened American control over the institutions governing global trade. In the realm of trade, the American hegemon's ability to exercise its power in and through global institutions has been sharply constrained by the rise of China. From the perspective of global governance, US hegemony—in the sense of its ability to dominate or lead global institutions—has been severely undermined by the rise of China.

This book analyzes China's impact on two key multilateral institutions for governing trade: the World Trade Organization (WTO) and the OECD Arrangement on Export Credit. The WTO is the primary forum for international cooperation on trade and the core institution created to govern the liberal international trading order under American hegemony.

It is viewed by many as the most successful post-war international organization (Allee 2012). As a key pillar of the US-led liberal economic order
(Ikenberry 2011), the WTO is a critical case for assessing the nature and
impact of China's rise. I analyze China's impact both during the Doha
Round of trade negotiations (2001–11) and in its aftermath. In addition,
the analysis goes beyond the WTO to consider China's impact on the
OECD Arrangement, which regulates the use of export credit (subsidized
loans and other forms of financing by states to promote their exports) in
order to prevent a global subsidy war. Although the export credit regime
has been comparatively neglected by scholars—likely because it worked
successfully and without incident for several decades—it has played an
essential role in maintaining the liberal trading order. Yet, as I will show,
China's rise has had significant consequences for the workings of both the
WTO and the OECD Arrangement.

The book focuses specifically on the impact of US–China rivalry on
global trade rule-making. A central function of the global trade regime is
the ongoing negotiation of new and expanded rules to govern trade. The
construction of global trade rules is an essential part of global economic
regulation, necessary to ensure the stability and functioning of global
markets. In addition, as several of the cases analyzed here highlight, global
trade rule-making also has implications for achieving other important
objectives such as promoting global development and protecting the environment. The global trade architecture is meant to be continually evolving
through the expansion and deepening of global trade rules (Das 2007).
This is explicitly stipulated in the mandate of the WTO (GATT 1994), and
it is also a core principle of the OECD Arrangement. However, I argue, the
primary function of the multilateral trading system—the construction of
rules to govern the global economy—has now been largely blocked due to
conflict between the system's two dominant powers, the US and China.
This analysis draws on field research conducted over an eleven-year period
between 2007 and 2018 at the WTO in Geneva and the OECD in Paris, as
well as in Washington, Beijing, Brussels, Tokyo, Brasilia, Sao Paulo, New
Delhi, and Ottawa, including over 200 interviews with trade negotiators,
senior government officials, and representatives of industry and non-
governmental organizations (NGOs).[5]

## The Limits of Incorporation

Existing scholarship has assumed that if rising powers are supporters of
established governance institutions and successfully incorporated into

their decision-making structures, then those institutions will continue to function smoothly and effectively (Ikenberry 2011; Paul 2016a). However, analysis of global trade governance challenges this view. This is an area of global economic governance where the US has actively sought to incorporate China: the US and other established powers welcomed China into the power structure of existing or new institutions, attempted to engage it in the process of global rule-making, and gave it a seat at the table that reflected its economic weight. The WTO represents a case of successful incorporation, in which China joined the institution and subsequently became part of its core power structure. It is also a case in which China is a system-supporter, rather than a radical revisionist: China strongly supports the rules-based system of the WTO, from which it has been a major beneficiary. Yet, China's rise has nonetheless proven profoundly disruptive to the multilateral trading system: a clash between the US and China has resulted in the collapse of the Doha Round, representing a breakdown of the institution's core negotiation function.

Since the Doha collapse, the focus at the WTO has shifted from seeking to conclude a broad-based, comprehensive trade round to trying to craft narrower, targeted agreements on specific trade issues, such as agricultural subsidies and fisheries subsidies. Yet, as I demonstrate, the same fundamental and intractable conflict between the US and China—which centers on how China should be classified and treated under multilateral trade rules—has persisted in the post-Doha context and continues to impede efforts to construct new and expanded rules for the international trading system. It is clear that changes in the distribution of power are thus having destabilizing effects—even when China is incorporated into global trade governance and is broadly supportive of its aims and principles, as in the case of the WTO.

Furthermore, as analysis of the OECD Arrangement illustrates, although China is generally a beneficiary and supporter of an open, rules-based trading system, it has actively resisted incorporation into some important aspects of the trade regime. There has been a concerted effort on the part of the US and other established powers to incorporate China into global rule-making on export credit; indeed, the US made this one of its top priorities in its economic relations with China. The US and other advanced-industrialized states have a keen interest in binding China to such rules, as China has become the world's largest supplier of export credit. But, despite considerable pressure from the US and other advanced-industrialized states, China has resisted US-led efforts to incorporate it into existing or new disciplines on export credit, which it views as contrary to its development interests. There are thus certain aspects of global trade governance where China has economic and strategic reasons to resist incorporation—and China has shown that it has sufficient power to successfully repel efforts by the US and other established powers to compel it to participate. The result, however, is that China's rise risks undermining the system for governing export credit that worked effectively for decades to prevent a competitive spiral of state subsidization via export credit.

Can the global trading system adapt to, manage, and accommodate increasing rivalry between the US and China? The evidence to date, I argue, suggests that this is proving extremely difficult. Growing tensions surrounding China's rise and its rivalry with the US are profoundly undermining the established system of global trade governance by eroding the efficacy of existing institutions and preventing the creation of new and stronger rules to govern global trade. In this analysis, I seek to go beyond a narrow focus on US–China relations to examine the broader, systemic implications of the power struggle between the US and China. The evidence presented demonstrates why US–China rivalry matters—not just for great power politics, or the relative weight or interests of those two states, but because it has critical implications for vital areas of global governance and policy. As I will show, the disruption of global rule-making in trade has significant consequences not only for the governance of global markets and trade, but also for efforts to use the trading system to address important global problems related to development and the environment.

The book analyzes five cases: (1) the WTO Doha Round, a broad-based, comprehensive trade round; (2) post-Doha WTO negotiations on agricultural subsidies; (3) post-Doha WTO negotiations on fisheries subsidies; (4) the OECD Arrangement on Export Credit, focused on industrial goods and services; and (5) new OECD Arrangement disciplines on export credit for coal-fired power plants. The negotiations analyzed here capture a diverse array of issue areas: a comprehensive trade round, agriculture, fisheries, industrial goods and services, and coal-fired power plants. The cases cover two distinct institutions with different institutional dynamics: the WTO—a formal international organization with near-universal membership that makes hard law that is legally binding on states; and the OECD Arrangement—an informal "gentleman's agreement" based on a form of club governance. The selected cases also capture variation in China's incorporation: the WTO represents a case in which China has been incorporated into global trade governance; the

OECD Arrangement is a case in which China has refused to be incorporated; and the negotiation of the new OECD Arrangement rules on export credit for coal power plants represents a case in which China was absent entirely from the negotiations. As the cases analyzed demonstrate, regardless of whether or not China has been incorporated into governing institutions, its rise is proving highly destabilizing across a wide range of different areas of global trade governance.

As the collapse of the Doha Round indicates, conflict between the US and China—centered on how China should be treated in the multilateral trading system, and specifically whether it should have access to the special and differential treatment granted to developing countries—has severely disrupted global rule-making in the realm of trade. Analysis of the post-Doha negotiations on agricultural subsidies and fisheries subsidies shows how this US–China conflict has persisted and has continued to block rule-making at the WTO. The agriculture and fisheries cases also highlight the wider consequences of this conflict, as these are issues of tremendous importance to much of the developing world, and in the case of fisheries subsidies also critical to advancing important environmental objectives. Both of these cases underscore the difficulty of treating China as a developing country and exempting it from trade disciplines, given that its policies have profound global implications. The case of export credit shows how China's understandable reluctance to participate in the regime, due to a clash with its development objectives, is nonetheless eroding an important set of rules intended to prevent a global subsidy war. Finally, the negotiation of new rules governing export credit for coal power plants—one of the first efforts to construct global disciplines on subsidies for fossil fuel industries—illustrates the challenge of crafting meaningful global rules in the realm of trade without China's participation. Like fisheries subsidies, this case also lies at the intersection of trade and environment and therefore underscores the broader implications of contemporary difficulties in constructing effective global trade rules.

### Peripheral Powers

The rise of China has radically changed the dynamics of global trade governance. US–China conflict has become the dominant feature in multilateral trade negotiations, across a wide range of different areas. Amid the central, gravitational pull of conflict between these two dominant powers, I argue that other major powers—even those that were once dominant players in global trade negotiations such as the EU—have been relegated to the status of "peripheral powers." This represents a significant shift. For much of the history of the trading system, it was the US and EU—the transatlantic "G2," along with Japan and Canada as junior partners— that dominated negotiations (Elsig and Dupont 2012; VanGrasstek 2013). The inner-circle of decision-making, centered on these four players, was known as the "Quad." Then, during the Doha Round, two emerging powers, Brazil and India—who played a far more active and aggressive role in challenging the dominance of the traditional powers and shaping the agenda of the round than China—displaced Japan and Canada from the inner-circle and formed a new "Quad" with the US and EU (Hopewell 2015). Now, however, the dynamics of power have shifted once again: other major powers, including the EU, Japan, Canada, India, and Brazil, have become largely secondary to the new G2 of the US and China. While these other states still play an important role in multilateral trade negotiations—and may exert influence in advancing or blocking specific issues—ultimately, as the following analysis will show, the principal dynamic now centers on the two most powerful players, the US and China.

We are thus seeing a realignment of the primary structure of global trade politics. In recent decades, the appearance of growing multipolarity in the global political economy has prompted a flurry of interest and excitement (Acharya 2014; Margulis and Porter 2013; Stuenkel 2015). Yet, in the realm of trade, the multipolar world associated with the emergence of the BRICS (Brazil, Russia, India, China, and South Africa) (Armijo 2007; Chin 2015; Cooper 2016) or the "rise of the rest" (Zakaria 2008) is collapsing back into a geopolitical system defined by two power players.

### This Time It's Different: The Japan Comparison

In debates about the impact of China's rise, skeptics frequently draw parallels to erroneous predictions that a rising Japan would bring an end to American economic dominance in the 1980s and early 1990s. To quote Edward Mansfield (2014: 439), two ensuing decades of Japanese economic decline and contraction "made a mockery of those predictions." Likewise, David Lake (2014: 445) argues, "one need only remember the fear of 'Japan, Inc.' in the 1980s—an overhyped trend that was followed by an American technological resurgence and two decades of stagnation in Japan" to know that predictions of power shifts can often be wrong. Ruchir Sharma (2012) confidently asserts in *Foreign Affairs*:

"in due time, the sense of many Americans today" that China is swiftly overtaking the US "will be remembered as one of the country's periodic bouts of paranoia, akin to the hype that accompanied Japan's ascent in the 1980s." Many thus argue that, like Japan, claims about the rise of China are overblown, and China's perceived threat to American hegemony will prove similarly fleeting and illusory. Analysis of the trade regime, however, refutes the notion that China is just another Japan.

Unlike Japan and other previous rising powers, China's rise has already substantially disrupted the functioning of multilateral trade governance—as well as the ability of the US hegemon to exercise power in and through the system of institutions it constructed precisely for that purpose. In the past, the American hegemon was able to successfully integrate other major economic challengers, such as the EU and Japan, into the GATT/WTO and associated aspects of the trade regime, such as the OECD Arrangement on Export Credit. But, as the failure of the Doha Round indicates, China's rise is proving more disruptive to the GATT/WTO than that of other powers. And, in contrast to the past, when the US was able to overpower resistant countries such as Japan and France and force them to participate in the OECD Arrangement, the US now lacks the leverage to compel China to participate in the export credit regime and accept such disciplines. These developments signal a weakening of the US's ability to impose its will globally. China's rise has proven profoundly disruptive to both US hegemony and global trade governance, in ways that previous emerging powers, such as Japan, were not.

As Rosemary Foot (2017) details, one of the factors that distinguishes China's rise from previous rising powers is the potential security threat it poses to the American hegemon that was not present with Japan or Europe, which were both military allies of the US and part of its sphere of influence in the context of its Cold War rivalry with the Soviet Union. But there is also another factor that distinguishes China: while China is now seen as a major economic challenger and potential rival to US hegemony, it is at a radically different level of development than the US. As I will demonstrate, in contrast to China, by the time the US grew concerned about competition from the EU and Japan, they were already developed countries with advanced-industrialized economies and therefore competing on a relatively equal footing. As such, they were in a position to engage in a reciprocal exchange of concessions in multilateral trade negotiations. Moreover, while Japan never surpassed the US as the world's largest manufacturer—a position the US held for over a century and which was seen as an important pillar of American economic supremacy—China has already done so.[6] These distinct features of China's rise, and the challenge it poses to the US, have factored heavily in the dynamics of contemporary multilateral trade negotiations.


### THE CHINA PARADOX

This book highlights the challenge of negotiating trade rules between two dominant powers at different levels of development. Paradoxically, China is now both an economic behemoth and—compared to the US and other advanced-industrialized states—a relatively poor country (Womack 2016). Although China is the world's second largest economy after the US, its per capita income is only 15 percent of that of the US (with a per capita GDP of just $8,000 compared to $57,000 in the US).[7] Compared to the US, China is thus at a significantly lower level of economic development, measured in terms of average incomes. Not surprisingly, one of China's key overarching goals is to ensure its continued economic development, in order to raise its per capita income levels and bring them closer to those in developed countries. However, this asymmetry in the levels of development of the world's two major powers creates new and unprecedented challenges for global trade governance. In the past, the most powerful states in the global political economy were all high-income, developed countries; developing countries formed the periphery of the global economy and were relegated to the margins of its governance. The rise of China, however, signals a new bifurcation of economic power and development status. China has emerged as a core country in the global economy and one of the most powerful states in the multilateral trading system, but it is still a developing country. And this contradiction between China's economic might and its level of development creates significant challenges for global rule-making.


### The Battle: What Rules Will Apply to China?

The question of how China should be treated under global trade rules has become one of the prime sources of conflict in the multilateral trading system. While China remains a developing country and continues to face significant development challenges, it is now an extremely large and immensely powerful force in the global economy and seen by many states, not just the US, as a major competitive threat. A key principle of the trading system is that developing countries should be granted special status, and allowed greater scope to continue to use tariffs, subsidies, and other trade measures to help foster development. China insists that it should be treated as a developing country, entitled to access the same exemptions and exceptions granted to other developing countries. But, in the context of its rivalry with China, for the US, making largely one-sided concessions in opening its own market without equivalent concessions from China is inconceivable. The US is unwilling to extend unilateral trade concessions to the country it sees as a major economic challenger and the chief rival to its hegemony. Instead, the US insists that China must take on greater responsibility commensurate with its role as the world's second largest economy—which, in trade, means undertaking greater commitments to open its market and accept disciplines on its use of subsidies.

The rise of China has thus heightened the tension between two core principles of the multilateral trading system: reciprocity versus special and differential treatment. For most of its history, the GATT/WTO was dominated by a relatively small number of developed countries and focused on managing trade relations among those states. When multilateral trade negotiations took place primarily among developed countries, they operated based on the principle of reciprocity—the idea that participants would enjoy roughly equivalent benefits, or, conversely, roughly equivalent costs (Brown and Stern 2012). Participants engaged in a reciprocal exchange of concessions ("I will cut my tariffs/subsidies if you cut yours") focused on negotiating broadly equal gains in global markets. Similarly, in the OECD Arrangement on Export Credit—a "rich man's club" of advanced-industrialized states—reciprocity took the form of a set of universal rules, with rights and obligations applying uniformly to all participants. Since developing countries were not—until recently—significant providers of export credit, there was no call for them to be subject to such rules.

The principle of reciprocity has coexisted with a second key principle of the trading system: special and differential treatment (SDT) for developing countries. It has long been acknowledged that developing countries should not be subject to the same reciprocal exchange of concessions, based on the view that equal treatment is not equal for states at different levels of development and that developing countries cannot be expected to assume the same obligations as developed ones. Dating back to Alexander Hamilton's (1790) argument for the US to adopt infant industry protections to enable the expansion of its manufacturing sector in the context of British industrial supremacy, there has been skepticism about free trade as a path to development and the capacity of developing countries to catch up with more advanced economies without interventionist trade policy measures such as tariffs and subsidies. Within the GATT/WTO, SDT is the product of hard-fought, coordinated political efforts by developing countries to correct the perceived inequalities of the global trading system (Gibbs 2000; Hannah and Scott 2017). According to the principle of SDT, countries at lower levels of development should not be required to open their markets at the same pace as more advanced competitors and should be given preferential and non-reciprocal access to developed countries' markets (Margulis 2017; VanGrasstek 2013). Rather than universal rules applying to all countries, developing countries should be allowed greater scope to protect their markets and promote the expansion of domestic firms and industries. While the concept of SDT, and specifically how it should be operationalized in global trade rules, has never been uncontroversial, with the rise of China as a major economic power that is also a developing country, it has now emerged as the central, overarching source of conflict within the trading system.

The key conflict between the US and China in global trade governance rests on whether the rules should be universal and concessions reciprocal, or whether China should have access to SDT and be exempted from certain rules in recognition of its status as a developing country. At the heart of this conflict are competing interests, as well as ideas of fairness. From the perspective of the US, fairness means a level playing field, based on universal rules applying equally to all, and the reciprocal exchange of concessions. But from China's perspective, what the US perceives as a level playing field is, in fact, one that serves to perpetuate its industrial and economic supremacy.

For China, maintaining the policy space needed to foster its continued economic development is an essential priority. China's development model is predicated on an active state engaged in promoting development by fostering industrial upgrading, supporting the competitiveness of national firms and industries and helping them to move up the value chain into higher value-added activities, and thereby boosting growth, incomes, and the quality of employment (Lin and Chang 2009; Stiglitz, Esteban, and Lin 2013). An interventionist state has played an important role in China's remarkable rise thus far and remains central to its strategy for continued development, as evident in its Made in China 2025 industrial policy program (Ban and Blyth 2013; Hopewell 2018; Nölke et al. 2015; Stephen 2014). China's emphasis on state intervention is backed by the experience of other successful late developers (Chang 2002; Lazonick 2008; OECD 2013: 105; Reinert 2007; Warwick 2013). As even *The Economist* (2012), normally a robust champion of free trade, acknowledges, "every rising power has relied on the state to kickstart growth or at least to protect fragile industries."

Indeed, the US and other advanced-industrialized states relied on state intervention and employed a range of protectionist policies during their own process of economic development (Kupchan 2014). This included using tariffs and subsidies to foster the growth of infant industries and sequence their integration into the global economy; aggressively adopting technology from more advanced countries; and controlling the inflow of foreign investment to direct it toward the goals of national development (Chang 2002; Gallagher 2008a; Wade 2003). Moreover, even from a position of global economic dominance, the US has continued to deviate from the principles of free trade and make use of protectionism when it serves its interests (Block and Keller 2011; Hopewell 2017b; Lazonick 2008; Schrank and Whitford 2009; Weiss 2014). From China's perspective, in seeking to preserve scope for state intervention to promote industrial development, it is simply seeking to follow in the footsteps of the US and other advanced-industrialized states, but the US is seeking to "kick away the ladder" by preventing China from using many of the same policy tools that were vital to the US's own growth and development (Chang 2002; Gallagher 2008a; Stiglitz and Greenwald 2014).

This conflict between US demands for reciprocity and China's demands for special and differential treatment as a developing country was at the center of the Doha Round breakdown. And, if anything, the issue of SDT for China has grown even more significant—and more difficult to resolve—since the Doha collapse, as evident in subsequent efforts to conclude standalone agreements on agricultural subsidies and fisheries subsidies. In addition, just as China has demanded SDT exemptions at the WTO, it has similarly refused to participate in global export credit disciplines in the OECD Arrangement or a new replacement, insisting that as a developing country it should not be bound by such restrictions.

In the context of the growing rivalry between the US and China, the issue of extending special and differential treatment to China is extraordinarily contentious. But it is also problematic for other reasons—particularly its effects on other (poorer and weaker) developing countries. Although China may still be a developing country, as the following analysis will show, its economy is now of such a magnitude that its trade policies have profound global impacts. China is now not only the world's biggest trader, but also the largest supplier of agricultural and fisheries subsidies, largest provider of export credit, and largest supplier of export credit for coal-fired power plants. The problem with exempting China from trade disciplines is thus that, given the size of its economy and the massive volume of subsidies it is now providing, its policies have major systemic consequences for the global economy and trade. Moreover, as the cases of agricultural subsidies, fisheries subsidies, and export credit for coal plants will demonstrate, exempting China from global trade disciplines threatens to jeopardize efforts to achieve crucial global development and environmental objectives.

### China's Impact on Trade and Development

For decades, the key axis of conflict over development issues in the trading system has been drawn on North–South lines. Given that it is a developing country, some might have expected that China's ascendance as a major power in the global trade regime would lead to a rebalancing of power in multilateral trade negotiations from the Global North towards the Global South, helping to make the system work better for developing countries and aiding the goal of fostering development. But, actually, just the opposite has occurred: China's rise has created new obstacles to efforts to link trade and development—as well as trade and environment—in a more equitable and resilient way.

China describes itself, in the words of one of its senior trade representatives, as a "champion" of "international fairness and justice" seeking to "uphold the basic rights of developing countries" (quoted in *Inside US Trade* 2019). China continues to frame global trade politics as a North–South struggle, but that framing is increasingly problematic. As the agriculture and fisheries cases will show, China's pursuit of its interests within the multilateral trading system often runs counter to—and comes at the expense of—other developing countries. China's trade policies now have significant implications for development in the rest of the Global South. Its agriculture and fisheries subsidies cause considerable harm to other developing countries, but China has resisted multilateral trade disciplines based on its status as a developing country. By refusing to accept disciplines on its subsidies, China is blocking reforms of the trading system that are crucial to the interests of other developing countries.

To be clear, this is far from unique to China. On the contrary, China is behaving much like any other great power—protecting what it sees as its core economic and strategic interests, largely regardless of the impact on others. In the multilateral trading system, as Dominic Kelly and Wyn

Grant (2005: 2) put it, echoing Thucydides, "the strong do what they will and the weak do what they must." Volumes have been written about the harmful effects of US and EU trade policies on developing countries and how the traditional powers have resisted changes to global trade rules that would aid development (Bukovansky 2010; Gallagher 2008b; Hannah 2015; Jones and Weinhardt 2015; McMichael 2012; Porter 2005; Sell 2006; Shadlen 2005; Singh 2017; Trommer 2014; Wade 2003). The US and other advanced-industrialized states have long been seen as obstacles to a fairer and more equitable trading order that would accommodate the needs of the Global South for development (Eagleton-Pierce 2012; Hopewell 2016; Wilkinson and Scott 2008). What this book shows, though, is that this is no longer a role reserved solely for rich countries. Now China is doing very much the same thing.

The old North–South framing of global trade politics that arose out of the era of post-war decolonization and Third World nationalism is proving increasingly inadequate amid the rise of China. Contemporary conflicts over global development in the multilateral trading system cannot simply be reduced to North versus South. The fault lines of this conflict have grown far more complex than ever before.

## China's Impact on Trade and Environment

The breakdown of global rule-making in trade has important implications not just for the governance of the liberal trading regime, but also attempts to ground and reframe that regime in terms of sustainable development. In recent years, there have been growing efforts to use global trade rules and institutions to help address climate change and achieve the UN Sustainable Development Goals, by restricting the ability of states to use trade policies that have harmful environmental effects. The goal is to achieve a "triple win"—an outcome that is positive for trade, development, and the environment. Two of the most prominent examples—negotiations on fisheries subsidies and export credit for coal power plants—are both cases analyzed in this book.

While China's role elsewhere in global environmental governance has received considerable attention—such as in the international climate change negotiations, where it is increasingly positioning itself as an emerging global environmental leader (Christoff 2016; Hochstetler and Milkoreit 2015; Pearson 2019)—there has been little analysis of China's impact on efforts to promote environmental sustainability within the trade regime. As I will show, China's trade policies are having increasingly harmful effects on the environment, but it has resisted external disciplines on the basis of its developing country status. By refusing to accept disciplines on its subsidies, China is hindering efforts to use the trading system to achieve important environmental goals, such as reducing fisheries subsidies that contribute to the depletion of global fish stocks and restricting subsidies for the export of coal power plants that contribute to climate change. Again, China is hardly alone in resisting global environmental reforms that clash with its economic interests—at various times and on various issues, other major powers like the US and EU have often been the stumbling block to progress on environmental sustainability in global governance (Falkner 2005; Hovi, Sprinz, and Bang 2012; McCright and Dunlap 2014). But, with its newfound power, China is now playing a major role in blocking environmentally oriented reforms within the multilateral trading system.

### BLAME CHINA?

Many of those who see the rise of China as a destabilizing force in the liberal international economic order are eager to point the finger of blame at China, implying that its goals must be illegitimate if they clash with the existing US-led order. Much analysis of the rise of China and other emerging powers has been shaped by a narrow framework for understanding their agendas and impact: if they do not support the status quo, existing governance regimes, or the preferences of the US and other traditionally dominant powers, rising powers are labelled "spoilers" or "shirkers" (Schweller 2011). The disruptive effects of China and other emerging powers are attributed to the fact that they are "irresponsible" (Patrick 2010) "troublemakers" (Kirshner 2012), who hold inappropriate "core values" (Castañeda 2010) and lack an adequate sense of "international civic duty" (Hampson and Heinbecker 2011).

Many of the cases presented here, however, problematize such interpretations. As an analysis of trade governance makes clear, the reality is considerably more complex. There are several problems with the "blame China" narrative. First, although they may conflict with those of the US, that does not mean that the objectives China is seeking to advance—fostering its continued national economic development, as well as essential security goals, such as ensuring food security—are illegitimate. In the case of export credit, for example, China's rise has indeed been deeply disruptive; however, this is not simply because

China is a troublemaker, but because it has important development objectives that conflict with the overarching goals of the governance regime. Second, in some cases, such as the collapse of the Doha Round, blame could just as easily be placed on the US, which could just as readily be labelled a "spoiler," "troublemaker," "shirker," or "irresponsible" for its role in preventing conclusion of the round. Third, in yet other cases, such as agriculture and fisheries subsidies, China is in fact closely emulating the longstanding behavior of the US and other Western states by resisting efforts to discipline its subsidies. The objective here is thus not simply to add to the "blame China" chorus, but to unpack the nature of the underlying conflict that is destabilizing global trade governance and to take seriously China's objectives, while nonetheless critically evaluating their effects.

### THE RISE OF TRUMP

The election of President Donald Trump, propelled in part by a surge of anti-trade sentiment that blames "unfair trade" for the current economic and social ills of the US, has raised new doubts about the future of the US-led liberal international economic order. Trump has threatened to exit the WTO or disregard its rules, impose massive tariff walls, arbitrarily restrict access to the US market, and take unilateral retaliatory trade actions against other states. With a US President hostile to free trade and international cooperation, the US appears to be abandoning its commitment to the liberal order and abdicating its leadership role. It is not clear whether Trump represents a temporary departure from historical norms or a fundamental and lasting shift in US trade policy and its approach to international economic relations—in other words, whether American foreign economic policy will "go back to normal" after Trump, or whether Trump represents the new normal. However, what this book demonstrates is that, even prior to Trump, the multilateral trading system was in considerable turmoil. The exercise of American power in global trade institutions had already been significantly curtailed by the rise of China, and growing tensions between the US and China had deeply disrupted rule-making in the trade regime, at the WTO and beyond. These fundamental challenges in global trade governance pre-dated Trump and will persist after he leaves office, even if he is replaced by a subsequent president who returns the US to its more traditional support for trade and international institutions.

## AN OUTLINE OF THE BOOK

The chapters in this book chronicle the impact of China's rise on global trade governance across a range of different areas. In Chapter 1, I show how conflict between the American hegemon and its emerging challenger led to the collapse of the Doha Round and the breakdown of the WTO's core negotiation function. At the center of the Doha standoff, I argue, is a dispute between the US and China centered on how China should be treated in the multilateral trading system. China has maintained that, as a developing country, it should be entitled to the special and differential treatment promised to developing countries in the Doha Round. The US, however, is unwilling to extend such treatment to its principal economic and political rival, and therefore refused to conclude the round without greater market opening from China. China rejected American demands that it undertake additional liberalization concessions, and, in doing so, showed that it has sufficient power to refuse to concede to US demands that it views as fundamentally against its own development interests. The US has a long track record of successfully overpowering opposition in multilateral trade negotiations and securing assent for its desired outcomes. Yet, in contrast with the past, the US has been unable to overpower China, and this deep and lasting impasse between the two powers resulted in the collapse of the Doha Round.

The next two chapters turn to examining dynamics at the WTO since the breakdown of the Doha Round. I focus on two of the prime areas of negotiations since the Doha collapse—agriculture and fisheries subsidies. Both underscore the broader implications of the tensions surrounding China's rise, as these are critical trade issues for the developing world and, in the case of fisheries subsidies, also of vital importance for the environment. As I show, the same conflict between the US and China over SDT has persisted in the post-Doha context and continues to impede global rule-making.

Chapter 2 analyzes how China's ascendance has radically altered the dynamics of one of the most prominent and controversial issues in the trading system: agricultural subsidies. Agricultural subsidies depress global prices and undermine the competitiveness and livelihoods of poor farmers and have long been seen as a symbol of the injustice of the trading system. The issue has traditionally been understood in North–South terms, with the US and other developed countries seen as the perpetrators of harm and developing countries as innocent victims. In this chapter, however, I show that this prevailing conception of the agricultural subsidies issue is no longer accurate. A momentous but underappreciated change has taken place: China has emerged as the world's largest subsidizer, upending the entrenched understanding of agricultural subsidies as a harm perpetrated by the Global North upon the Global South and profoundly transforming the global politics of agricultural subsidies. From a North–South battle, WTO negotiations on agricultural subsidies have been transformed into a conflict centered on the US and China. The US, as the world's largest agricultural exporter, is eager to restrain China's subsidies and insists that it will only agree to stricter rules on its own subsidies if they also apply to China. But China has refused, insisting that, as a developing country, it should be exempt from any new restrictions on subsidies. The US has been unable to force China to accept disciplines on its subsidies, leading to a stalemate. While reducing trade-distorting subsidies remains a pressing concern for developing countries, efforts to negotiate new and strengthened disciplines at the WTO have been paralyzed by an impasse between the two dominant powers, heavily shaped by the hegemonic rivalry between the two states. China, along with the US, is now playing a major role in blocking pro-development reform of the trading system at the WTO.

Chapter 3 explores a second major area of focus at the WTO since the collapse of the Doha Round: fisheries subsidies. This issue has been identified as a priority area of negotiations given its environmental implications and importance for many developing countries. There is widespread concern about the role of subsidies in the depletion of global fish stocks, by driving overcapacity and overfishing, and thus the need for coordinated action in the trading system to address this issue. Achieving a multilateral agreement to restrict fisheries subsidies has been seen as a key means for the WTO to contribute to addressing a pressing global environmental and development issue, and thus to resuscitate the institution and prove its continued relevance following the Doha collapse. Fisheries subsidies have therefore been the subject of intense negotiating efforts. However, like agricultural subsidies, the key issue of contention is how China and other large emerging economies should be treated under any new disciplines. The fisheries subsidies case sharply underscores the problem with extending special and differential treatment to China: since China now has the largest industrial fishing fleet in the world and provides the greatest volume of subsidies, exempting its subsidies from disciplines would severely harm the sustainability of global fisheries. Efforts to negotiate a standalone agreement on fisheries subsidies have run aground amid this central issue of dispute. The result has been a failure to arrive at new disciplines, the consequences of which are felt most keenly by poor developing countries whose populations are heavily dependent on fisheries for food security, livelihoods, and exports.

Chapter 4 analyzes China's impact on the global governance of export credit, the use of loans and other forms of financing by states to support exports. The existing system of governance for export credit—which limits the ability of states to use export credit to subsidize, and thus artificially boost, their exports—centers on the OECD Arrangement on Export Credit. For decades, the OECD Arrangement has been held up as a successful example of liberal trade governance, with its system of disciplines proving highly effective in preventing a destructive, competitive spiral of state subsidization via export credit. I show, however, that the rise of China has profoundly altered the landscape of export credit and disrupted its governance arrangements. As with agriculture and fisheries subsidies, China has emerged as the world's largest provider of export credit. Yet China has refused to join the OECD Arrangement, and while it agreed to participate in a US-driven initiative to negotiate a new set of international rules that would incorporate China and the other emerging economies, it has persistently thwarted that process. China has little incentive to agree to disciplines on its use of export credit, which plays a central role in its development strategy. Despite considerable US pressure, China has refused to capitulate and subject itself to international disciplines that it views as fundamentally against its interests. As at the WTO, China has shown that it has sufficient power to stand up to the US in defending its development interests. Yet, the result, I argue, is that China's rise is undermining the liberal regime for governing export credit by eroding the efficacy of existing disciplines and blocking efforts to construct new ones.

Chapter 5 examines the US-led effort to establish new global rules to restrict export credit for coal-fired power plants, which are highly polluting and a major contributor to climate change. Government-backed export credit for coal power plants acts as a form of export subsidy, and thus promotes the expansion of such plants abroad. Motivated by environmental concerns, the US spearheaded multilateral negotiations within the context of the OECD Arrangement to prohibit the use of export credit for coal power plants. This represented a ground-breaking effort to establish concrete global disciplines on subsidies for fossil fuel industries. However, since China is not part of the Arrangement, it was not a participant in the negotiations or bound by the new disciplines created. China's absence, I argue, weighed heavily over the negotiations and undermined US efforts to construct an ambitious agreement. China is now the world's largest exporter and financer of overseas coal power projects, accounting for nearly half of all export credit in this sector. OECD exporters were extremely resistant to agree to restrict their use of export credit when China—the dominant player in the field and their chief competitor—would face no similar restraints on supporting its exports. Moreover, without China's participation, the impact of the resulting agreement is severely limited, as it leaves out the largest supplier of export credit for overseas coal plants. This case thus highlights the difficulty of building effective global trade rules today without the participation of China.

The concluding chapter returns to the central themes raised in this introduction. Drawing on the five cases analyzed, I argue that, even though China's economic and overall power capabilities remain far smaller than those of the US, it has profoundly disrupted the exercise of US power in global trade governance. China has consistently thwarted US efforts to construct new global trade rules, producing a recurrent deadlock across a wide range of different areas of global trade governance. The rise of China, and its resulting clash with the US, is blocking global rule-making in trade and undermining the institutions designed to prevent global trade wars. The *China paradox*—the fact that China is now both a major economic power and a developing country with relatively low per capita incomes—has created significant challenges for global trade governance. The issue of whether, and how, the rules of the multilateral trading system will apply to China is proving to be a difficult and intractable source of conflict. While China demands exemptions from global trade disciplines as a developing country, the US refuses to extend special treatment to China and insists on universal rules and reciprocal concessions. As the cases analyzed in this book demonstrate, this fundamental conflict over how China should be treated in the multilateral trading system, which has paralyzed global rule-making in trade, has profound implications—not only for the governance of global trade, but also for pressing issues related to global development and environment.

# I

# The Doha Round Impasse

The WTO represents the centerpiece of the US-led liberal international economic order, providing the rules and framework for an increasingly open and integrated global economy (Ikenberry 2015b). Indeed, as one of the only international institutions that makes "hard law" that is legally binding on states and backed by a powerful enforcement mechanism, the WTO is one of the strongest and most important institutions in global economic governance (Lake 2009). Its rules have significant material consequences for states, and, as a result, it has been a critical site of contestation between China and the US.

This chapter analyzes the impact of a rising China, and its growing rivalry with the US, on the WTO. As it will show, the US actively worked to integrate China into the WTO, backing China's accession and subsequently its ascendance to the institution's core power structure. This is also a case where China is a clear system-supporter: China has been a major beneficiary of the liberal, rules-based trading system created by the WTO. China incurred significant costs to join the WTO in order to gain access to the benefits and protections of existing WTO rules and with the expectation that it would go on to reap significant gains from further liberalization in the Doha Round. Yet, I argue, China's rise has nonetheless proven profoundly disruptive to the multilateral trading system: conflict between the American hegemon and its emerging challenger led to the collapse of the Doha Round and the breakdown of the WTO's core negotiation function.

## AMERICAN HEGEMONY AND THE MULTILATERAL TRADING SYSTEM

Understanding the historical structure of power within the multilateral trading system is essential for appreciating the magnitude of the change that has taken place. Since its creation at the end of World War II, the US has been the primary force shaping the global trade regime and propelling its agenda of liberalizing trade and deepening global economic integration. The US drove the creation of the General Agreement on Tariffs and Trade (GATT) in 1948, as well as its successor, the WTO, in 1995. The creation of the GATT was motivated by a desire to foster global economic stability and prevent a recurrence of the "beggar-thy-neighbor" protectionist policies that caused a breakdown in global trade in the 1930s, exacerbating the Great Depression and contributing to the outbreak of World War II. In the ensuing decades since then, through successive rounds of negotiations to progressively expand and deepen global trade rules, the multilateral trading system has facilitated a massive and historically unprecedented expansion of global trade (WTO 2008: 15). Eight multilateral trade rounds have been concluded to date, with each progressively larger and more complex as the number of issues and states involved have grown.

Coming from a position of industrial supremacy, the creation of the liberal trade regime was driven by the US's desire to open global markets and expand opportunities for its exports, and the trading system was designed to reflect and serve the interests of its most powerful state and chief architect. Although the US has been the primary driver of liberalization in the trading system—pushing other countries to open their markets to its goods, services, and capital—its own policies have nonetheless often deviated from the principles of free trade (Baldwin 1987). The US has pursued a two-pronged strategy: in areas of vulnerability, it has used trade protections to shield sensitive import-competing sectors from foreign competition, while in areas where American firms are, or have the potential to become, world leaders, the US has actively used various forms of state support, combined with its influence in shaping international trade rules, to give its firms and industries a competitive edge and promote their global market dominance (Chorev 2008; Porter 2005; Weiss 2005; Wilkinson 2011).

## Accommodating Rising Powers

While constructed and led by the American hegemon, the multilateral trading system has previously shown itself able to adapt to and integrate rising powers. The US built the system from a position of overwhelming economic dominance: at the time of the GATT's creation, the US accounted for a third of global GDP, half of the world's industrial output, and three-quarters of its gold reserves (Anderson 2013: 22; Wilkinson 2011). Over subsequent decades, the US's share of global GDP, industrial output, and trade were steadily eroded with the rise of new economic competitors—first Europe, then Japan, and later East Asian newly industrialized countries (NICs), such as Korea and Taiwan. Yet, despite the decline in its relative economic power, the US still retained its dominance in the multilateral trading system and its ability to direct and steer global trade governance. For eight trade rounds, the US remained the chief *demandeur* at the GATT/WTO—the principal actor driving market opening and the progressive expansion of global trade rules.

Initially, the GATT was dominated exclusively by the US: the American hegemon held the reins of the institution and acted as both its primary initiator and vetoer (Curzon and Curzon 1973). Over time, power was slowly extended out to a select group of other advanced-industrialized states, with the US remaining the dominant actor. By the 1960s, as a result of the growth of European economic and political power following post-war reconstruction and unification, and the creation of the European Economic Community (EEC) in 1957 (the precursor to today's EU), Europe came to assume a leading role in the GATT alongside the US. Together, the US and Europe acted as "GATT's two rulers" (Curzon and Curzon 1973: 331). During the Kennedy Round (1964–67), for example, decision-making centered on the so-called Bridge Club consisting of the US, the EEC, and the UK. Following the rapid rise in Japan's share of world trade during the 1960s, it too was subsequently included in the inner-circle—along with Canada—as junior partners forming the "Quadrilateral Group," or "the Quad." The power structure of the GATT/WTO accordingly evolved from pure unipolarity centered on the US to progressively incorporate other Western powers, albeit as lesser players.

For many decades, the trade regime had thus been able to accommodate the rise of new powers, while continuing to successfully negotiate and conclude new multilateral trade agreements. It is therefore all the more striking that, as the analysis that follows will show, unlike previous rising powers, the current rise of China has profoundly disrupted the WTO's negotiation function. In contrast to China, however, Japan and the EU were both industrialized economies prior to WWII and—thanks to substantial US support—rapidly regained that status after the war. Following its post-war recovery, the EU was an advanced, high-income economy by 1960, and Japan was a high-income country by 1962.[1] During the early phases of the GATT, through the negotiating round concluded in 1960, the US was heavily invested in the post-war recovery of Europe and Japan, and the negotiations were oriented towards the US's longer-term political objective of strengthening its principal allies (Zeiler 2012). In this context, the US was willing to set aside its particularistic economic interests by granting non-reciprocal trade concessions to Europe and Japan and accepting discrimination against its exports in those markets (Krasner 1979). The Kennedy Round (1963–67) was the first round to reflect shifting global economic power. As the US grew increasingly concerned about growing economic competition from the rising EEC, it began to press more vigorously for expanded export opportunities. The Kennedy Round negotiations therefore focused on a reciprocal exchange of concessions between the US and Europe, although the US still continued to grant largely one-sided trade benefits to Japan (Zeiler 2012). It was not until the late 1960s that the US grew concerned about increasing competition from Japan, prompting criticism of its "unfair" trade practices and a steep rise in US trade defense measures in the 1970s, and leading the US to insist on reciprocity and the need to make gains for its exports in the Japanese market during the Tokyo Round (1973–79) (Foot 2017; Zeiler 2012). In short, by the time the US became concerned about trade competition from the EU and Japan and began to demand reciprocity, they were already developed countries and in a position to engage in a reciprocal exchange of concessions in multilateral trade negotiations. In contrast, however, China is at a much lower level of economic development, facing immense challenges that it will need to surmount before it can even come close to the levels of per capita income achieved by the US and other advanced-industrialized states. China's concern is that reciprocity is not fair among countries at different levels of development and that engaging in a reciprocal exchange of concessions could jeopardize its prospects of continued development. The issue of how to resolve this tension between China's economic power and its development status has now become a chief source of conflict within the trading system.

## Decision-Making and the Historical Marginalization of Developing Countries

For most of its history, decision-making in the multilateral trading system has been dominated by the US and other developed countries (Drache

2004; Kapoor 2006; Mortensen 2006; Raghavan 2000). The US willingly agreed to a consensus-based system of decision-making in the GATT/WTO, recognizing that this had strong normative appeal and would confer greater legitimacy, while confident that its superior economic and political might would enable it to exert sufficient influence over decision-making as to render weighted voting unnecessary (Steinberg 2002). Decision-making is therefore formally based on consensus, with each member afforded equal weight ("one member, one vote"); however, in practice, the system operates as an oligarchy, with decision-making heavily shaped by power (Trommer 2017). The most important negotiations take place among an elite inner-circle of states, and once an agreement is reached, it is then extended out to the rest of the organization's membership, thereby allowing a handful of states to set the negotiating agenda and direct the negotiations. While the composition of this inner-circle is determined informally, it encompasses those states that are recognized as key players and exert the most influence over the negotiations.

Until recently, agreements were negotiated among the US and a handful of other advanced-industrialized states and imposed upon the rest of the organization—including much of the developing world—effectively as a fait accompli (Narlikar and Tussie 2016). As one WTO official stated, "In the old days, it was a very simple game: you had the US and EU, with Canada and Japan on the sidelines. If the US and EU didn't want it to happen, it wouldn't and if they did, it would."[2] The US and, to a lesser extent, the EU, effectively enjoyed a "cartel over agenda setting and compromise brokering" (Evenett 2007). The trading order they constructed reflected their interests, focused, for instance, on liberalizing trade in industrial goods, while the areas of priority to developing countries, such as agriculture, were effectively excluded. The system did little to address the needs of developing countries, who were marginalized from decision-making and felt their interests were ignored (Muzaka and Bishop 2014). When developing country members sought to engage in the GATT, they were routinely barred from key negotiations and their proposals were blocked by the US and other dominant powers (Wilkinson and Scott 2008). Instead, many developing countries therefore attempted to pursue reform of the trading system via the UN Commission on Trade and Development (UNCTAD), though ultimately with little success (Bair 2009; McMichael 2012).

These power asymmetries were vividly evident in the last multilateral trade round to be successfully concluded, the Uruguay Round (1986–94), which resulted in the creation of the WTO. In that round, the US drove a dramatic expansion in the scope of trade rules into new issues areas—such as services, investment, and intellectual property, all areas of US competitive advantage where it was seeking to expand markets for its exports—as well as the creation of a binding dispute-settlement mechanism to enforce those rules (Chorev 2008; Hopewell 2016). The Uruguay Round was widely seen as an unfavorable deal for developing countries, resulting in a set of outcomes that privileged the interests of the US and other advanced-industrialized states at significant cost to the developing world (Gallagher 2008b; Sell 2002; Shadlen 2005). Robert Wade (2003) has likened it to "a slow-motion Great Train Robbery"—the agreement produced a significant transfer of resources from poor to rich countries, while constraining development policy space, including prohibiting many of the same industrial policy tools that advanced economies like the US had themselves used to develop. Meanwhile, the gains promised to developing countries, in areas such as agriculture, failed to materialize (Ostry 2007). Despite considerable resistance from developing countries, the round was ultimately pushed through and concluded by a raw use of power on the part of the US, including threats of unilateral trade sanctions and withdrawing access to its market (Steinberg 2002).

By creating structures of rules in new areas where none had existed before, along with a powerful enforcement mechanism, the establishment of the WTO was seen as laying the foundation for future rounds of negotiations to liberalize trade (Hoekman 1995; Sauvé and Stern 2010). The Uruguay Round agreement even included a "built-in agenda" on agriculture and services, provisions mandating countries to immediately begin new negotiations to continue liberalization in these sectors. The Doha Round of trade negotiations, which began in 2001, was thus intended to build on that foundation and continue the WTO's project of trade liberalization.

## THE DOHA "DEVELOPMENT" ROUND

In keeping with the traditional operation of the multilateral trading system, the Doha Round was decidedly a US-led project. Like previous trade rounds, the launch of the round was propelled by American power, with support from the EU and other advanced-industrialized states. Seared by their experience of the Uruguay Round and still struggling to implement many of its obligations, developing countries were strongly opposed to initiating a new round so soon, but the US and allied advanced-industrialized states used a mix of divide-and-rule tactics, threats, and inducements to compel developing countries to agree to participate (Efstathopoulos and Kelly 2014; Narlikar and Tussie 2004). Developing countries were also promised that Doha would be a "Development" Round, specifically dedicated to advancing their needs and interests. American negotiators have since acknowledged that they viewed this primarily as a branding or public relations exercise designed to sell the round—in the words of former US Trade Representative Charlene Barshefsky, "the round was launched on essentially false pretenses" (Altman 2007). Yet the development label nonetheless, as another negotiator put it, "created big expectations" on the part of developing countries.[3]

Despite its purported emphasis on development, at the start of the Doha Round, the US, along with the EU, remained firmly in the driver's seat: they played the primary role in formulating the negotiating mandate and the negotiations continued to center on the "Quad." Over the course of the round, however, a dramatic shift took place, as the traditional structure of power at the WTO "imploded," to quote one Secretariat official.[4] It was not, however, China that instigated this shift, but two other emerging powers—Brazil and India. Lacking the economic heft of China or other major powers, Brazil and India created and led major coalitions of developing countries in order to challenge the traditional dominance of the US and other advanced-industrialized states. Their mobilization and leadership of the developing world catapulted Brazil and India into the inner-circle at the WTO following the Cancun Ministerial in 2003, displacing Japan and Canada, and enabled them to play a substantial role in shaping the dynamics and agenda of the Doha Round, helping to transform the round into a confrontation between the Global North and the Global South (Hopewell 2015; Mahrenbach 2013).

In sharp contrast to Brazil and India, for most of the Doha Round, China assumed a low profile and did not play a significant agenda-setting role (Hopewell 2016; Scott and Wilkinson 2013). China is a relatively new member of the WTO, having only joined the organization in 2001, at the start of the round. Yet China invested heavily in trade-related legal capacity, which enabled it to be highly effective in identifying and defending its interests in WTO negotiations and dispute settlement (Shaffer and Gao 2018). While China was keen to benefit from the liberalization anticipated from the Doha Round, its sense of potential vulnerability discouraged it from playing an aggressive role in pursuing its offensive trade interests. As one of its negotiators stated, China did "not want to play an offensive role since many of its policies [were] already under attack from many members."[5] Its large and rapidly growing economy made China a target for states seeking greater access to its market, which was particularly a concern for China given that the deep liberalization undertaken for its WTO accession had left it with considerably lower tariff bindings than most developing countries. Many states also viewed the rapid expansion of China's industrial capacity and exports as a threat. Consequently, China potentially faced both demands that it open its market and efforts to constrain its exports.

China identified the US and other traditional powers as the principal threat. Prompted by the risk of being pushed to undertake greater liberalization commitments, China eagerly stressed its developing country status and actively sought to align itself with the developing world. China joined two major developing world bargaining coalitions: the Group of 20 (G20), led by Brazil, and the Group of 33 (G33), led by India. While its status and economic might added considerably to the weight to these coalitions, China decided, as one negotiator expressed it, to let Brazil and India "do the fighting" while providing "support from behind."[6] Another observer explained: China was "happy to leave the leadership role to India and Brazil ... there is enough China-bashing already."[7] Seeking to avoid drawing attention to itself, and with Brazil and India advancing agendas broadly in accord with its own interests, China was satisfied with letting them lead the fight against the established powers.

During the Doha Round, China actively worked to construct its "developing country" image. In their speeches and representations at the WTO, Chinese negotiators heavily emphasized China's "developing country-ness": its massive population of rural poor, its low per capita GDP, its struggles to provide sufficient employment for its population and to absorb large-scale rural–urban migration, and its vulnerability to external market forces. While this is, indeed, an important face of China, the discourse of its WTO negotiators has tended to erase the other face of China: the growing economic powerhouse whose export capacity strikes fear in its trading partners large and small. China made a strategic choice to project the former image of itself—"China-as-poor-developing-country"—in the context of the WTO, as a means to enhance China's affinity with other developing countries, while simultaneously helping to bolster its position in resisting demands that it further liberalize its market. By the latter stages of the round, when China's economic might and new centrality in the global economy had become indisputable, this self-representation provoked the ire of the US and other advanced-industrialized states; as an American diplomat in Beijing stated: "It's like the Government of China has multiple personality disorder—is China a great country or a developing country?"[8]

At the WTO, China cultivated an image of itself as a developing country like any other, struggling in solidarity against the rich countries. To quote a rival negotiator, China "will always speak out for developing countries, LDCs [least-developed countries], SVEs [small, vulnerable economies], etc., because that projects that they're supportive. But of course they're crushing these countries."[9] Since it was in China's interest that the primary line of division be drawn between developing and developed countries, it actively worked to reinforce this structure of identities and alliances at the WTO. One negotiator explained: China is "extremely careful with being close to the African countries and the most vulnerable countries, focusing on developing country solidarity against the industrial countries, avoiding it being put as emerging versus developing countries."[10] The Doha Round came to be framed in large part as a North–South conflict, a dynamic which worked to China's benefit by enabling it to piggyback on the gains secured for developing countries and helping to deflect attention from its own policies.

The developing country coalitions led by Brazil and India—and backed by the weight of China—had a significant impact on the Doha Round, transforming developing countries into a far more effective negotiating force than ever before. Developing country coalitions had unprecedented success both in blocking unfavorable proposals by the US and other advanced-industrialized states, as well as in advancing their own initiatives (Hopewell 2017a). For the first time, developing countries turned the tables and seized the offensive against the US—historically the main aggressor in GATT/WTO negotiations—and other advanced-industrialized states by targeting their most flagrantly protectionist policies: agricultural subsidies. Notably, developing countries were able to secure substantial SDT across virtually all areas of the negotiations, including weaker tariff-reduction formulas in agriculture and manufactured goods, as well as substantial flexibilities, thereby reducing the degree of liberalization that would be required of them.

## Special and Differential Treatment

The principle of providing SDT for developing countries has been a feature of the multilateral trading system for decades. It is based on the idea that, as one negotiator put it in the 1950s: "Equality of treatment is equitable only among equals. A weakling cannot carry the same load as a giant" (cited in Narlikar 2017). The classification of countries as "developed," "developing," or "least developed" is self-designated (Eagleton-Pierce 2012). SDT is intended to provide an exception to the GATT/WTO principle of reciprocity by allowing for "less-than-full reciprocity" in the case of developing countries, either by granting them greater flexibility to maintain protections in their markets or improved access for their exports to developed country markets. In effect, developing countries are not expected to fully comply with the rules of the multilateral trading system until they achieve a state of development that enables them to do so; only then are they expected to take on full obligations and bear the full costs of membership (Bukovansky 2016). The principal of SDT has not been without controversy, however, and its realization in practice has often been limited (Hannah, Ryan, and Scott 2017).

The concept has evolved gradually over many decades and reached its fullest aspiration in the Ministerial Declaration that launched the Doha Round. The Doha Declaration affirmed that "provisions for special and differential treatment are an integral part of the WTO agreements" and promised to "put the needs and interests" of developing countries at "the heart" of the Doha work program. On market access for industrial goods, for instance, it pledged that: "The negotiations shall take fully into account the special needs and interests of developing and least-developed country participants, including through less than full reciprocity in reduction commitments." Similarly, on agriculture, it stated:

We agree that special and differential treatment for developing countries shall be an integral part of all elements of the negotiations and shall be embodied in the Schedules of concessions and commitments and as appropriate in the rules and disciplines to be negotiated, so as to be operationally effective and to enable developing countries to effectively take account of their development needs.

These stated commitments to SDT could have proven little more than empty promises. However, due in large part to the activism of developing countries under the leadership of Brazil and India, by the later stages of the Doha Round, the draft texts of the proposed agreement had come to encompass substantial SDT provisions for developing countries (Hopewell 2017a).[11] As a result, under the prospective deal that emerged, relatively little liberalization would be required of developing countries. Indeed, one observer described the tariff-reduction commitments required of developing countries as so limited as to be "nearly inconsequential" (Dadush 2009: 4). Within the prospective Doha agreement, developing countries had thus been able to protect significant "policy space" to pursue their economic development objectives. At the same time, developing countries would also benefit from reductions in developed country tariffs and agricultural subsidies. Ultimately, however, it was the issue of extending such SDT to China that became a major source of conflict and came to play a central role in the breakdown of the round.

## US–CHINA RIVALRY AND THE COLLAPSE OF THE DOHA ROUND

It was not until the final stages of the Doha Round that China came to assume a decisive role alongside the US. On the eve of the WTO's Ministerial Meeting in July 2008, the round appeared to be nearing a conclusion. After seven years of contentious negotiations, the key provisions of the deal had been largely determined (such as tariff-reduction formulas for manufactured and agricultural goods and their main exemptions and flexibilities). The WTO membership had already agreed on 80–90 percent of what would constitute the final deal, and talks had shifted to focusing on finalizing remaining outstanding issues.[12] Most states were broadly satisfied with the draft texts on the table, and the WTO looked to be on the cusp of concluding the Doha Round. At that point, however, the US balked—and it did so specifically because of China. The world had changed radically since the start of the round, in ways that had significant implications for how the US came to view the prospective deal on the table.

### Enter the Dragon: A Hegemon Faces its Rising Challenger

In addition to propelling the launch of the Doha Round, the US was also a pivotal advocate and driver of China's accession to the WTO, which both occurred in 2001. It is important to recall that at that time the structure of the global economy looked very different than it does today. Then, the US remained both the world's largest exporter and manufacturer, while China's economic position was far weaker. During the 1990s, prior to its WTO accession, China's share of world trade averaged just 2.5 percent (barely more than India's today). In 1999, on the cusp of its accession, China's merchandise exports ($195 billion) were less than a third the size of the US's ($696 billion), placing it just ahead of tiny Belgium as the world's ninth largest exporter (see Figure 1.1).

The US had both economic and political motives for supporting China's WTO accession and seeking to bring it into the fold of the US-led liberal international economic order. Many expected that increasing

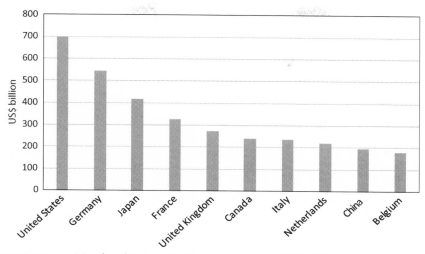

FIGURE 1.1 Merchandise exports by country, 1999 (US$ billion).
Source: World Bank data

trade and China's integration into the global economy would foster rising incomes and the growth of the middle class in China, and thereby help promote a transition to democracy. Moreover, secure in its position as the world's sole superpower in the unipolar moment following the collapse of the Soviet Union, and confident that its economic dominance would enable it to capitalize on the benefits of opening the large Chinese market to US firms and exports, the US saw integrating China into the multilateral trading system as a means to consolidate and enhance its own power in the global economic order (United States 2000a). Not only was the US incorporating China into the trading system it had created and dominated, but the nature of the WTO accession process enabled it to extract extensive one-way trade concessions from China, without having to make any new market-opening concessions of its own. The US only needed to guarantee that it would grant most-favored-nation status (MFN) to China—in other words, the same tariff levels that the US had already been offering Beijing since 1980. Summarizing the American position at the time, a senior official stated: China's WTO accession "does nothing to improve the access of Chinese companies to the United States market [but] will significantly advance opportunities for American companies to export goods and services to China. ... In trade terms, then, the case is clear: China's WTO accession overwhelmingly benefits the United States" (United States 2000b). The US anticipated major gains for its merchandise

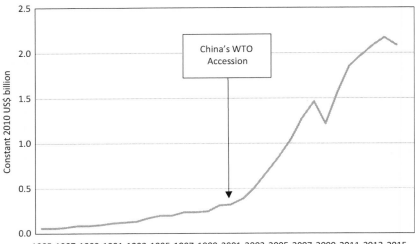

FIGURE 1.2 China's merchandise exports, 1985–2015 (constant 2010 US$ billion).
Source: World Bank

exports, including both manufactured goods and agricultural products, as well as in areas such as tradeable commercial services and intellectual property, which were high-value sectors of the global economy that the US dominated. Consequently, the US expected that China's WTO accession would significantly boost American exports and help to ameliorate its growing trade deficit with China (Lardy 2000).

Instead, however, China's exports surged following its WTO accession (see Figure 1.2). At the time of China's accession and the start of the Doha Round in 2001, the US was still the world's largest exporter—as it had been for over half a century. But, by 2007, China's soaring exports had led it to surpass the US. By 2008, China's merchandise exports stood at $1.431 trillion, compared to $1.287 trillion for the US. And in subsequent years that gap has only grown larger—in 2015, China's merchandise exports were 50 percent greater than those of the US (at $2.3 trillion versus $1.5 trillion).[13] Fueled by the growth of its manufacturing sector, China has been transformed into a trading powerhouse.

While US exports to China did grow significantly after the latter's WTO accession, they were vastly overshadowed by the increase in US imports from China (see Figure 1.3). As a result, contrary to what the US had expected, its trade deficit with China grew dramatically following China's WTO accession.

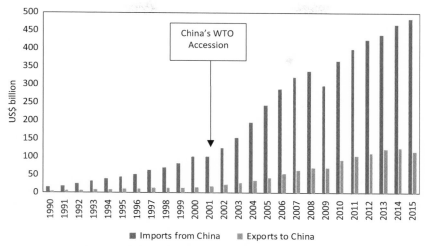

FIGURE 1.3 US trade balance with China, 1990–2015 (US$ billion).
Source: US Bureau of Census

Concurrently, the US saw a significant decline in its share of global manufacturing (see Figure 1.4). The US was still the world's largest manufacturer as late as 2000, accounting for 26 percent of global manufacturing value added, and China just 6 percent. But, over the ensuing decade, which corresponded with the Doha Round negotiations, the US was overtaken by China and its share of global manufacturing fell to 18 percent by 2010. For a country that commanded half of the world's industrial output in 1945 (Anderson 2013: 22), this represented a startling shift. And, since then, China's share has only continued to increase—it now constitutes 24 percent of global manufacturing value added, while the US's share has fallen further to 17 percent.[14]

At the time of its WTO accession, China was seen chiefly as a potential economic threat to countries at comparable levels of development, with similar export structures, based on similar resource and labor endowments. These were countries exporting lower-value-added, labor-intensive manufactured goods, such as Mexico, India, and other Asian exporters, which were China's direct competitors in its areas of specialization at the time, primarily textiles and apparel, footwear, and electronics (Lardy 2004). However, not only has China's export expansion turned out to be far greater and more successful than anyone ever envisioned, but it has also moved up the value chain with extraordinary speed, with the result that it is now rapidly moving into the more

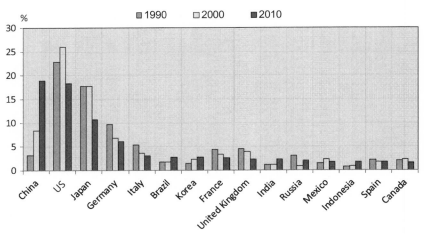

FIGURE 1.4 Percentage share of global manufacturing value added, 1990, 2000, 2010.
Source: OECD

advanced industries previously dominated by the US and other advanced-industrialized states.

In the US, there is thus growing anxiety about its declining share of global manufacturing amid increasing competition from China. While the share of manufacturing in US GDP and employment fell steadily with the growth of its services sector over the latter part of the twentieth century, manufacturing still plays a vital role in its economy. There are also important interdependencies between manufacturing and other sectors in high-income economies like the US—with backward and forward linkages to R&D, product design, and engineering—such that the distinction between manufacturing and services is increasingly blurred. Although the US and other advanced economies maintain a lead in higher-value-added, medium-high, and high-tech manufacturing, these are areas where China and other emerging economies are rapidly gaining ground (OECD 2013). As one OECD report states, "competition from emerging economies is growing, even in activities and markets that were, until recently, considered the core strengths of OECD countries" (Warwick 2013: 7). In the US, as well as other high-income countries, there are therefore concerns that the loss of core manufacturing activities may erode adjacent activities in the value chain, leaving these countries struggling to retain high-value activities such as innovation, R&D, and design (Block and Keller 2014; Pisano and Shih 2012; Warwick 2013).

From the US's perspective, incorporating China into the multilateral trade regime has thus unleashed significant unintended consequences, or at least consequences that were not sufficiently anticipated at the time. While the US viewed China's WTO accession as a means to enhance American economic and political power, instead, it has fueled contemporary power shifts by spurring the ascendance of China as a leading global manufacturer and exporter, a major center of global economic power, and a growing threat to US economic dominance. As a Western trade official who negotiated China's WTO accession stated,

At the time, we may not have measured the consequences [of China's accession] properly—as we have now come to see since then. If you look at China's share in world trade pre-accession, it was fairly small—now, it has become the top trader. Nobody had anticipated how quickly China would rise and how successfully it would upgrade.[15]

From the perspective of the US and other advanced-industrialized states, as one negotiator stated, "China has been hands down the biggest beneficiary from membership in the WTO."[16] Meanwhile, as the US's industrial and economic supremacy has eroded, it has increasingly attributed its relative decline to China's "unfair" trading practices and seen itself as insufficiently protected by the rules of the trading system.

## The 2008 Doha Breakdown

In this politically charged context, the draft Doha agreement on the table at the WTO in 2008 had, by that point, become untenable in the US. The core elements of the proposed agreement incorporated substantial preferential treatment for developing countries, including China and other large emerging economies, in the form of reduced liberalization commitments, greater flexibilities and exemptions, and longer implementation periods. The draft text on trade in manufactured goods (known as "Rev3"), for example, would apply a "Swiss" formula for tariff reductions (applying the deepest cuts to the highest tariffs), with different coefficients for developed and developing countries, with a smaller coefficient representing deeper cuts.[17] While the coefficient for developed countries would be 8, developing countries would be able to apply a coefficient of 20, 22, or 25, with greater flexibilities provided if they selected the lower coefficients. The tariff reductions would be implemented gradually over a period of five years for developed countries and ten years for developing countries. China would also be given another three years to phase in its commitments, in recognition of its status as a "recently acceded member" (RAM) that had made recent tariff cuts in its accession.

On agriculture, the draft text (known as "Rev4") would apply a "tiered" formula for reducing tariffs, with the largest cuts for goods with the highest tariffs.[18] Developed countries would be required to undertake tariff reductions of between 50 percent and 70 percent, with a minimum average cut of at least 54 percent to their tariffs. Developing countries would be required to cut their tariffs by between 33.3 percent and 46.7 percent, with a minimum average tariff cut of at least 36 percent. Cuts would be phased in over a five-year period for developed countries and ten years for developing countries. Rev4 included a sensitive products exemption allowing countries to deviate from the formula by one-third, one-half, or two-thirds of the cut on up to 4 percent of tariff lines for developed countries and 5.3 percent of tariff lines for developing countries. In addition, the draft text provided a special products exemption for developing countries alone, on up to 12 percent of tariff lines; with up to 5 percent of tariff lines being exempt from cuts altogether. It also created a new special safeguard mechanism (SSM) exclusively for developing countries, which would allow them to raise tariffs in response to an import surge.

On subsidies (or "domestic support"), the draft agriculture text would apply a tiered formula for cutting levels of Overall Trade-Distorting Support (OTDS), ensuring that countries providing the most support (such as the US and the EU) would be required to make the biggest reductions. The EU would be required to cut its OTDS by 80 percent and the US by 70 percent, representing a substantial reduction in domestic support compared to historical bound levels. In addition, within these cuts, states would see the cap on their most trade-distorting support (their "Aggregate Measure of Support," or AMS) reduced significantly—by 60 percent in the case of the US. Rev4 would also put in place product-specific caps on highly trade-distorting ("Amber Box") forms of support. Levels of allowable *de minimis* support for developed countries would be cut in half from 5 percent to 2.5 percent of production immediately and for developing countries would be cut by one-third over three years from 10 percent to 6.7 percent of production. "Blue Box" support (capturing direct payments to farmers made under production-limiting programs) would be limited to 2.5 percent of production for developed and 5 percent for developing countries, with product-specific caps.

In 2008, just as the WTO appeared poised to conclude the Doha Round on the basis of these terms, which had been negotiated over the preceding seven years, the prospective agreement provoked protest from powerful members of US Congress and its business and farm lobby groups (Hopewell 2016). These actors viewed the deal taking shape— with what they saw as weak tariff-reduction formulas and extensive flexibilities for China and other large emerging economies—as unfair and unbalanced against the US. The US National Association of Manu- facturers, for example, criticized the draft agreement on manufactured goods (non-agricultural market access, or "NAMA") as follows:

The "Swiss Formula" that advanced developing countries are entitled to use is so full of holes it is more properly called "The Swiss Cheese Formula." It severely imbalances the NAMA negotiations for the United States, requiring major cuts in US tariffs but only minor cuts in the applied rates of the advanced developing countries.

(NAM 2008)

Similarly, the American Farm Bureau objected that, while the US would be made to reduce its subsidies, its hopes for market access in agriculture had been "continually whittled away," particularly by the exemptions granted to the advanced developing countries (Blustein 2009). Leaders from both parties in the House and Senate committees responsible for trade complained that "the negotiating texts currently on the table would provide little or no access for US goods" (United States 2008).

These actors expressed deep dissatisfaction with the prospective Doha agreement. They argued that the US would be required to significantly cut its tariffs, as well as its agricultural subsidies, while making insufficient gains in expanding access for its exports, particularly in China (United States 2008). Their core complaint was that the deal did not go far enough in demanding new market opening from Beijing. Under the terms of the proposed agreement, China would be entitled to the substantial SDT that developing countries had been able to secure in the round. From the US's perspective, it would be making substantial, meaningful conces- sions in opening its market but see little from China in return (United States 2008). As one US negotiator put it, "we'd be giving everything and getting nothing."[19] The US had become unwilling to extend that kind of less-than-full-reciprocity to a country that it now saw as a major com- petitor and threat to its hegemony.

American negotiators determined that the best way to improve the package and sell it to their domestic constituencies would be to secure additional liberalization commitments from China in manufacturing and agriculture (Hopewell 2016). The US pressed China to participate in "sectorals" (aggressive tariff reduction in specific industrial sectors) in two key areas of US competitiveness—chemicals and industrial machinery. Sectorals were effectively an add-on to the core agreement, pushed by the US as a means to extract additional market opening from China and other large emerging economies. The US also pressed China to informally agree not to use its special product exemptions in agriculture against specific products of export interest to the US—namely, cotton, wheat, and corn—in order to guarantee the US market access gains in those areas. To this end, the US also sought a restrictive operationalization of the SSM in agriculture in order to ensure that its market access gains were not eroded. In short, by 2008, as one negotiator stated, "the main demands" of the US "couldn't be addressed without getting a 'yes' from China."[20] The US therefore invited China to join the inner-circle of WTO negotiations—the core power structure of the institution—at the 2008 Ministerial, where it has remained ever since, specifically because the US wanted to extract these concessions from China.

China proved far less malleable, however, than the US anticipated. From China's perspective, the US's growing demands were a violation of the implicit bargain struck during its accession, where in exchange for the deep concessions China was forced to make in opening its market it was promised that relatively little new liberalization would be required of it during the Doha Round. From China's point of view, the US was now trying to renege on its earlier promises. China also saw the US's new demands as a violation of the development mandate of the Doha "Development" Round, which had promised to deliver real benefits to the Global South. A core aspect of the Doha mandate was the principle that developing countries, including China and other large emerging economies, would not be required to engage in an equal exchange of concessions with the advanced-industrialized states, but instead that the final agreement would be reached on the basis of "less than full reciprocity" in favor of developing countries. China argued that the US was now trying to change the terms of the deal and its new demands were unfair and unjustified: the US was seeking less than full reciprocity in its *own* favor, in clear violation of the development mandate of the round.

As a result, China refused to concede the additional concessions the US was demanding on agricultural and manufactured goods, which it saw as unjustified relative to the concessions the US was willing to make and beyond the scope of the terms already agreed to. From Beijing's perspective, the US's demands were in direct conflict with China's development objectives. Chinese officials believe it is vital for China to maintain the policy space needed to engage effectively in industrial policy and foster industrial upgrading, in order to continue its process of economic development and avoid becoming stuck in the middle-income trap. China therefore refused to agree to the sectoral agreements sought by the US in chemicals and industrial machinery, which are key sectors China is trying to foster as part of its industrial upgrading strategy. If it opened those sectors, relinquishing its infant industry protections, Chinese policymakers fear they would be wiped out by foreign competition, arresting its continued economic development. Similarly, on agriculture, China is eager to ensure that it retains its ability to use trade policy tools to protect vulnerable (and potentially politically volatile) parts of its population—such as poor, peasant farmers—which is why China refused to concede the market access concessions the US demanded on agriculture and instead insisted on a maximal definition of the SSM and that it retain full use of its special product exemptions.

The Doha negotiations broke down in 2008, ostensibly due to conflict over the design of the SSM. Although the SSM had not previously been a high-profile topic, it came to be closely associated with the proposed tariff cuts on agricultural products and erupted into a major issue of contention at the 2008 Ministerial (Margulis 2019). The US was concerned that this mechanism would provide a means for developing countries to undo whatever liberalization was achieved through the tariff-reduction formula. While states had previously agreed to an SSM in principle, the dispute centered on the specific rules governing how the mechanism could be used, including the trigger (that is, under what conditions the SSM could be invoked) and remedy (such as what cap would apply to the size of the safeguard duties imposed), and particularly whether and when states could breach their pre-Doha Round commitments. Most coverage of the SSM dispute has focused on India, which took a highly vocal and public stand in confronting the US. In reality, however, even on the SSM, the US's chief concern is China (Hopewell 2016; VanGrasstek 2013). India has a considerable amount of "water" in its tariffs (the gap between its WTO tariff bindings and its actual applied tariff rates)—meaning that it has plenty of room to raise its tariffs in response to import pressure. In contrast, China has almost no water in its tariffs and, consequently, the SSM might be its only recourse in any effort to restrict imports (VanGrasstek 2013). China is thus most likely to actually use the mechanism, and it is also the most important market for US agricultural exports. Due to the SSM, American exporters worried that the Chinese market could be even more restricted *after* the Doha Round negotiations than it had been before.

Conflict over the SSM—with the US on one side and China, along with India and other import-sensitive developing countries, on the other—thus became the proximate cause of the breakdown of the Doha negotiations at the 2008 Ministerial. However, the deeper reason for the Doha breakdown was the fundamental conflict between the US and China over the US's desire to "rebalance" the deal by securing greater access for its agriculture and manufactured goods to the Chinese market. China stood firm, refused to give in to the US, and rebuffed its demands for additional market opening. In doing so, China showed that it had sufficient power to refuse to concede to US demands that it viewed as fundamentally against its own interests. As a result, the 2008 Ministerial intended to conclude the Doha Round ended in collapse.

## THE NEW "G2"

The dynamics of WTO negotiations and their underlying power relations have evolved rapidly. Historically, negotiations were dominated by a "G2" consisting of the US and the EU, with Japan and Canada on its periphery. Until the 2003 Cancun Ministerial, the negotiations continued to center on these traditional powers. Then, following a developing world revolt at the Cancun Ministerial, for much of the Doha Round—including the most active phase of negotiations between 2003 and 2008, which led to and produced the final version of the draft texts proffered at the 2008 Ministerial—the primary axis of conflict was drawn on North–South lines: with the developing world, led by Brazil and India, backed by China, on the one hand, faced off against the advanced-industrialized states, led by the US and the EU, on the other (Hopewell 2016). Since 2008, however, there has been another profound change: the core negotiating dynamic has come to center squarely on the US and China.

China has clearly emerged as one of two supreme powers within the WTO. As a WTO Secretariat official stated:

When I joined the WTO Secretariat many years ago, there was a sense that the US was the big pushy power, pushing other states around to get what it wanted. Now it's China. If you can't get America to agree, they have the power to stop anything—and that is clearly now China too.[21]

Even major powers like the EU, India, and Brazil, who were previously central actors in the Doha negotiations, have become ancillary players in a conflict centered on the US and China. While these countries still have the power to influence WTO negotiations, they are now secondary to the new "G2" consisting of the US and China. As a Chinese negotiator summarized:

Wherever China and the US can't agree, nothing is going to happen. It's the simple, ugly fact. Of course, even when China and the US want to do something, if other countries—like India or the EU—refuse, it will be an obstacle. But in the first instance, it is the US–China relationship that really matters. Without them, nothing is going forward.[22]

A Secretariat official echoed this: "Other players can come up with all the great ideas in the world, but as long as the US and China are at logger-heads, nothing is going to happen."[23]

Fundamentally, what happens at the WTO now comes down to the US and China, and relations between these two dominant powers. In the words of one negotiator, "the US–China relationship now colors every-thing in this organization."[24]

## THE ROOT OF THE US–CHINA IMPASSE

There has been no further substantive progress in the Doha negotiations since the breakdown in 2008. Conflict between the US and China has led to a lasting stalemate, which has only grown deeper and more entrenched in subsequent years. In short, the SDT extended to China in the draft texts of the proposed Doha agreement made the agreement intolerable to the US. The US has refused to commit to liberalization in the Doha Round unless greater liberalization is required of China and the other large emerging powers (United States 2011). Yet China staunchly maintains that, as a developing country, it is entitled to SDT, and it has refused to make further concessions to appease the US. With the US and China at loggerheads, the negotiations became deadlocked. All efforts to break the standoff have failed. The Doha Round negotiations were officially declared at an impasse at the 2011 Geneva Ministerial, and the 2015 Nairobi Ministerial Declaration openly acknowledged that many members now consider the round dead.

The core cause of the WTO breakdown is thus a dispute between the US and China, centered on how China should be treated in global trade governance. The issue of differentiation—whether China and other major emerging economies should be entitled to SDT or forced to engage in a more equal exchange of concessions with the US—lies at the heart of the Doha Round collapse. As one participant summed up, "the issue of differentiation became the central stumbling block in the Doha Round, across virtually all areas of the negotiations."[25] A vast gulf separates the two sides in this conflict, with no sign of any resolution.

## Washington's Perspective

The development aspect of the Doha "Development" Agenda—with its provisions for SDT enabling developing countries to benefit from global trade liberalization while shielding them from the requirement to liberalize their own markets—is perceived in the Global North as "an agenda for charity" (Narlikar and Tussie 2016: 212). But, by 2008, when the round collapsed, the US was much less willing to extend "charity" to China—the country it had now come to see as its main economic and political rival. As one US negotiator put it, "the Doha Round was a development round, but the world had changed since [the round began in] 2001."[26] From the US perspective, it no longer made sense to treat China and other emerging economies as developing countries. As a former US Trade Representative argued, "the size and growth trajectories of the emerging economies combined with the fact that some are now leading producers and exporters in key sectors, such as chemicals, information technology, car parts, pharmaceuticals, and environmental goods, set them apart" (Schwab 2011).

According to the President's Trade Agenda (United States 2011):

> The remarkable growth of emerging economies like China, India, and Brazil has fundamentally changed the landscape—and their growth is expected to continue in the coming years. In a negotiation in which the United States is being asked to significantly cut tariffs on all industrial and agricultural goods, we are asking these emerging economies to accept responsibility commensurate with their expanded roles in the global economy.

Explicitly singling out the need for greater market opening from China, it continued: "For these talks to remain relevant, they must address the world as it is and as it will be in the coming decades ... countries with rapidly expanding degrees of global competitiveness and exporting success should be prepared to contribute meaningfully towards trade liberalization."[27] The US has thus sought to restrict China's access to SDT, arguing that it and other large emerging economies have "graduated" from developing country status and need to take on "greater responsibility" proportionate to their increased economic might.

In its official statements, the US often refers to "large emerging economies" or "advanced developing countries." But, privately, officials, policymakers, and industry representatives make it clear that their primary concern is China. China's economic might vastly overshadows that of other advanced developing countries: India and Brazil are the two next largest emerging economies after China, but China's GDP ($11.2 trillion) is five times larger than India's ($2.3 trillion) and six times larger than Brazil's ($1.8 trillion), and the latter countries play a much smaller role in world trade (while China's exports represent 11 percent of world trade, India's and Brazil's constitute only 2 percent and 1 percent, respectively).[28] Moreover, not only is China far more significant to the US in economic terms, but it is also more politically significant due to the geopolitical rivalry that is not present with other emerging powers. As one American negotiator stated, "Our problem is very much one-country focused—China."[29]

For the US, the draft Doha agreement no longer adequately accounted for the profound shift in global economic power towards China. In the words of one negotiator: "In 2008, part of the reason the negotiation failed was that the world had changed and there was already a sense then that what was on the table no longer fit."[30] From the US perspective, the draft texts of the proposed Doha agreement that had been arrived at by 2008 (Rev3 for industrials and Rev4 for agriculture) were profoundly unsatisfactory. While requiring significant market opening from the US, the SDT provisions they contained severely reduced the amount of liberalization that the US would see in the Chinese market. As a US negotiator stated, "we were the ones under pressure to accept them. But we really had major problems with Rev3 and Rev4."[31] US attempts to improve the terms of the deal in its favor by applying pressure to China and other emerging economies proved fruitless. As another American negotiator stated: "In 2008, we felt we would never get the ambition we wanted from Doha. For a few years afterwards, we kept continuing to try, but then realized we were never going to get anything we could sell [to our domestic constituencies back home]."[32] Without greater liberalization from China, the prospective Doha agreement was simply unacceptable to the US.

## Beijing's Perspective

Efforts by the US to restrict China's access to SDT and force it to undertake greater liberalization commitments have been fiercely—and successfully—resisted by China. The current tension between the US and China at the WTO has deeper origins, dating back to China's accession, which profoundly shaped how China sees the relative responsibilities of the two countries in the Doha Round. The US views China's WTO accession as a boon to China, given the explosive growth of its merchandise exports post-accession, but in China its accession is seen very differently. Its process of joining the WTO took an arduous fifteen years of negotiations—the longest for any state at that time. China was motivated to join the WTO as a means to secure and improve its access to foreign markets, especially the US, as well as to lock in domestic economic reforms (Breslin 2003). But, for China, the process of negotiating the terms of its WTO accession with the US was, to quote one negotiator, a "bitter experience."[33] As even a Western official who negotiated China's accession acknowledged, "WTO accession negotiations are very unfair towards those countries wanting to join."[34] The US used its superior bargaining leverage to extract significant unilateral concessions, requiring China to undertake major reforms of virtually all aspects of its economic and trade policy, including substantially reducing its trade barriers in manufacturing, agriculture, and services. Indeed, to join the WTO, China was required to make concessions that far exceeded those of existing WTO members (Lardy 2004; Scott and Wilkinson 2013). As one negotiator summarized, "China thinks they did way too much in their accession—they think they went overboard in their accession and so do their industry."[35] The requirements of China's WTO accession generated considerable internal resentment: there is a strong sense that the country was bullied by the US and forced to surrender too much during its accession. Moreover, China was led to believe that it would "get paid" for its accession during the Doha Round, when other major economies, like the US, would undertake greater concessions of their own. This has contributed to Beijing's intense resistance to the US's growing demands that it undertake further liberalization in the Doha Round.

Furthermore, China argues that it is entitled to the SDT promised to developing countries. China considers itself a developing country and views its access to SDT as a core part of the development commitment of the Doha Round. Importantly, for China, as one of its former negotiators stressed, "a condition we laid down as part of our accession to the WTO was that we would join as a developing country."[36] Thus, in the words of negotiators, China "strictly opposes any talk of differentiation" and "[its] line is clear: SDT should apply equally to all developing countries."[37] China fiercely guards the remaining policy space it retains under global trade rules. Continuing its path of economic development requires fostering the ongoing development and upgrading of its industries. Thus, from China's perspective, it needs to be able to shield strategic industries from foreign competition and provide them with the support to become viable competitors in global markets.

China maintains that it has a legitimate claim to the SDT granted to other developing countries. While the US views China primarily as a leading economic power and potential rival to its hegemony, from China's perspective its situation looks very different. Despite impressive gains, the country's level of development and per capita income still lag far behind the US and other advanced-industrialized states. As one developed country negotiator stated, "China is still very poor, but less extremely poor than before."[38] At the time of the Doha breakdown in 2008, poverty remained a problem on an enormous scale: China had over 350 million people living in poverty (27 percent of the population) and over 150 million in extreme poverty (12 percent), ranking 91st (of 187 countries) on the UN Human Development Index.[39] China housed 13 percent of the world's poor, making it the country with the second largest number of poor people (World Bank 2013). While China has continued to make significant gains in poverty reduction since 2008, its development challenges remain significant. As a senior Chinese trade negotiator put it, "China is indeed a large country and a major economic power," but, "no, China is not yet a developed country."[40]

China insists that it remains a developing country and therefore cannot be expected to assume the responsibilities demanded of a high-income, developed country. It needs flexibilities to protect its market to continue its development process. When the US insists that China assume "greater responsibility" within the trading system, as one Chinese negotiator stated, "it just means they want us to give up more concessions to them."[41] China considers its status as a developing country at the WTO, and corresponding access to SDT, inviolable. In the words of a former senior Chinese trade official, given its developmental challenges, China, along with other large emerging economies, "would not, at least not in the foreseeable future, agree to be put into a different group and undertake obligations that they believe go beyond their developmental stage" (Lu 2015). China firmly insists that the WTO's distinction between developed and developing countries is sacrosanct and a core principal that cannot be undermined.

## The Collision of Two Titans

At the center of US–China conflict at the WTO and the collapse of the Doha negotiations is tension between China's position as a developing country and its status as one of the world's most powerful economies. As a senior Chinese trade negotiator encapsulated the situation, "China is not yet a developed country. But it remains much more powerful than a normal developing country."[42] It is this new bifurcation of economic power and development that is creating unprecedented challenges for the governance of the multilateral trading system.

In the context of its growing rivalry with China, for the US, making unilateral concessions without similar concessions from China is inconceivable. As one negotiator stated: "A big part of this is political—how heavily China weighs in the US. The political optics of a situation where the US gives up something and China doesn't is unfeasible. Regardless of the commercial considerations, this is the underlying political reality."[43] For China, however, being treated as a developing country and therefore granted access to SDT is, in the words of one of its negotiators, a "red line."[44] As one Chinese official openly acknowledged, this is an issue of "high political sensitivity"—simply put, for China "to accept that its obligations are the same as developed countries would be political suicide"[45] Consequently, on maintaining its right to SDT as a developing country, as another negotiator put it, "China is completely inflexible at the WTO. It won't budge."[46] And, as a WTO Secretariat official stated, "China will do whatever they need to vigorously defend their position."[47]

To continue to develop, China firmly believes that it needs to maintain scope for state intervention to protect and promote key sectors, and thus to shield them from WTO-mandated liberalization. But American officials are intensely skeptical of China's demands for development policy space, which, they argue, "at the end of the day just means 'we should be able to do whatever we want'."[48] Allowing a blanket carve-out from WTO liberalization for the world's second largest economy and its chief rival is a non-starter for the US. However, from China's perspective, the US's stance and its behavior in the later stages of the Doha Round are a signal that it is not willing to allow China the space it needs to develop.

One US congressional official thus characterized the situation as follows: "Obviously it comes to a stalemate when I [the US] am coming from the perspective of market access and opening and the other side is coming from the perspective of reducing poverty and building up their industries."[49] From the perspective of the US and other traditional powers, as one Western negotiator summarized:

What's on the table is it's the big players that have to pay and what do they get in return? They don't get anything? ... GATT was about integrating the EU into the world trading system after the war; then it became a mechanism to integrate Japan into the multilateral trading system; and now the goal is to integrate China into the multilateral framework, and if it doesn't rein China into the system, there's nothing in it for the US, or the EU—only to pay. If you continue to have an exemption for the country you are interested in having in the system, it's illogical.[50]

The problem, in the words of one former negotiator, is that "there hasn't been any serious discussion of what it means to integrate China into the trading system, or what its status should be."[51] It is conflict over precisely this—how China should be treated in the multilateral trading system— that has so severely disrupted global trade rule-making at the WTO.

The US has been unable to overpower China or force it to accept greater liberalization. The Doha Round ultimately ran aground on the US's inability to extract the additional concessions it wanted from China. When it became clear that China would not budge, the US started publicly to say the round was doomed and should be abandoned. Unable to get its way in the face of China, the US, which had forcefully initiated the Doha Round, became the actor that wanted to put "the nail in its coffin."[52] The contrast with previous rounds is striking: the US has a long track record of successfully overpowering opposition in multilateral trade negotiations and securing assent for its desired outcomes. Now, however, the US has been unable to overpower China, and conflict between the two powers has led to the collapse of the Doha Round.

Since the breakdown of the round, there has been an effort to salvage the negotiating function of the WTO by attempting to hive off smaller, more specific and seemingly less controversial issues where it may be easier for states to reach agreement. At the 2013 Bali Ministerial, states reached agreement on trade facilitation, food stockholding, and select issues related to SDT for LDCs (Wilkinson, Hannah, and Scott 2014). Similarly, the 2015 Nairobi Ministerial produced agreement on agricultural export subsidies, certain LDC issues, and expansion of the plurilateral Information Technology Agreement involving a subset of WTO members (Wilkinson, Hannah and Scott 2016). However, this shift to narrowly focused, piecemeal deals is a far cry from the comprehensive trade round originally envisioned for the Doha Round and the WTO's intended function of continuing to craft broad-based universal deals through a single undertaking. And even with a piecemeal approach there have been few areas where states have been able to reach agreement, primarily due to persistent conflict between the US, on the one hand, and China and other emerging powers, on the other, over differentiation and SDT. At the 2017 Buenos Aires Ministerial, which was the first to take place during the administration of President Trump, not a single multilateral agreement was reached—not even a Ministerial Declaration affirming the multilateral trading system.

As evident in the collapse of the Doha Round, US–China conflict is having a profound impact on the global trading system. The collapse of the round represents a breakdown in the core negotiating function of the WTO. Until now, the multilateral trading system worked through successive rounds of negotiations to progressively and steadily push forward the liberalization of international trade and the integration of global markets. Yet, after eight successful trade rounds since the 1940s, each increasingly comprehensive and inclusive in nature, the failure of Doha brought this process to a halt. While the WTO's existing rules remain in force and subject to its dispute-settlement mechanism, the continued expansion of global trade rules through the negotiation of comprehensive multilateral trade agreements has been brought to a standstill. Conflict between the American hegemon and its emerging rival has thus significantly disrupted the functioning of a central institution of the US-led liberal international economic order.


## CONCLUSION

While the multilateral trading system was able to adapt to previous rising powers, the rise of China is proving far more disruptive—both to the exercise of US power and to the system itself. The WTO represents a case in which China has been willingly incorporated into a central institution of global economic governance and given a seat in its inner circle of decision-making. Yet China's rise has nonetheless created serious problems for cooperation in the multilateral trading system: US–China conflict has led to an institutional stalemate, blocking global rule-making in the realm of trade. As evident in the collapse of the Doha Round, under the weight of growing rivalry between the US and China, the core negotiating function of the WTO—the negotiation of successive multilateral trade agreements to drive forward the opening and liberalization of global markets—has broken down.

The US's influence and authority in global trade governance has been substantially diminished by China's emergence as a countervailing power.

The launch of the Doha Round was a product of US power, and it is a sign of the diminished power of the American hegemon that it was unable to conclude the round. Instead, thwarted by China and unable to over-power its new challenger, the US was forced to abandon the Doha Round when it could not achieve its desired outcomes. For half a century, and eight trade rounds, the US was able to successfully bring multilateral trade agreements to conclusion, using various forms of leverage where neces-sary to secure the participation of other states. Now, however, the power of the US to steer multilateral trade negotiations and secure its preferred outcomes has been curtailed by an assertive China that is willing and able to counter US dominance. The Doha Round impasse is an important signal of the weakening of the US's ability to impose its will globally.

US–China rivalry was at the heart of the Doha Round breakdown: the US was willing to extend special and differential treatment to much of the developing world, but not to China—the country it sees as its major economic competitor and geopolitical rival. It was this clash between the two dominant powers that ultimately caused the collapse of the round. And, as the following two chapters will show, the same fundamental conflict between the US and China over whether the latter should be entitled to SDT has persisted in the post-Doha context and remains a major barrier to reaching multilateral agreement on critical trade issues.

# 2

# The New Politics of Agricultural Subsidies:
# A US–China Battle

This chapter turns to analyzing contemporary dynamics at the WTO since the collapse of the Doha Round. It focuses on how the rise of China has radically altered the dynamics of one of the most high-profile and contentious issues in the multilateral trading system: agricultural subsidies. Agricultural subsidies have long been seen as a symbol of the hypocrisy of the US and other rich countries and the injustice of the trading system (Bukovansky 2010; Porter 2005; Singh 2017). Subsidies provided by rich countries distort global markets and depress prices, undermining the competitiveness and incomes of poor farmers in the developing world. There is widespread consensus that reducing agricultural subsidies would increase the welfare of developing countries and the world's poorest and most vulnerable agricultural producers. Agricultural subsidies emerged as a central issue in the Doha Round, where reducing rich country subsidies became the key unifying demand of developing countries and helped to transform the WTO into a North–South battleground (Clapp 2007). The primary axis of conflict in WTO negotiations on agricultural subsidies has thus been understood as lying between North and South: developed countries have been seen as the perpetrators of harm and developing countries as innocent victims.

In this chapter, however, I show how this conventional understanding of the international politics of agricultural subsidies has been complicated by the rise of China. In recent years, China has emerged as the world's largest subsidizer of agriculture, with substantial implications for global markets and trade. China's emergence as a major subsidizer, I contend, upends the entrenched conception of agricultural subsidies as a harm perpetrated by the Global North upon the Global South. Moreover, as

I show, agricultural subsidies are once again at the center of the agenda at the WTO: since the collapse of the Doha Round, states have identified agricultural subsidies as a priority area of negotiations, seeking to achieve a standalone agreement to reduce global agricultural subsidies. The axis of conflict, however, has shifted profoundly.

From a North–South battle, multilateral negotiations on agricultural subsidies have been transformed into a conflict centered on the two dominant powers, the US and China. Given its major agricultural export interests, the US is eager to rein in China's subsidies and insists that it will only agree to new disciplines on its own subsidies if they also apply to China. But China has refused, insisting that, as a developing country, it should be exempt from any new disciplines, caps, or reductions in subsidies. The US has been unable to force China to accept disciplines on its subsidies, leading to a stalemate. While reducing trade-distorting subsidies remains a pressing concern for much of the developing world, this fundamental conflict between the American hegemon and its emerging rival has paralyzed the negotiations and barred any progress on constructing stricter disciplines on agricultural subsidies at the WTO. China—along with the US—is now a major barrier to establishing stricter global trade rules on agricultural subsidies.

## THE OLD POLITICS OF AGRICULTURAL SUBSIDIES AT THE WTO

Agricultural subsidies have been one of the most prominent issues in the international trading system (Margulis 2016; Scott 2017; Sneyd 2016). A multitude of actors—including developing countries, NGOs, the World Bank, IMF, UN, and the international media—have denounced the subsidies provided by the US and other rich countries, decrying their impact on the welfare of poor countries (Aaronson and Zimmerman 2006; Bukovansky 2010; Ilcan and Lacey 2006; Margulis 2010). Arguably, no other issue in the multilateral trading system has generated as much public attention and outrage around the world. As Matthew Eagleton-Pierce (2012: 85) argues, agricultural subsidies have "served as a touchstone for deeper concerns about economic and political justice within North–South relations."

Agricultural subsidies and other forms of protection are widely seen as tools that have been used to "tilt the global trade field in favor of developed nations" (Singh 2014). Identifying the US and EU as the worst offenders, Oxfam (2002: 96, 112) argues that their agricultural subsidies "have devastating effects on poor farmers in developing countries," who

are "losing global markets and facing ruinous competition from subsidized exports." As Oxfam notes, "these subsidies have a major bearing on
the structure of competition in international markets," such that "farmers
in the poorest nations" are forced to compete "against the financial power
of the world's richest countries." Focusing on cotton, Alan Beattie (2014),
a columnist for the *Financial Times* writes:

> It is no exaggeration to say that the lower prices created by US subsidies almost
> certainly cost thousands of lives a year as desperately poor people who grow
> cotton as their main cash crop are unable to pay for food, clean water and
> healthcare. ... [B]etraying millions of the poorest people in the world because of
> a small cabal of rich, well-organized, welfare-scrounging farmers ... the US in this
> matter has proven to be a selfish, craven malefactor.

The prevailing understanding of agricultural subsidies thus identifies rich
countries as the clear "villains" (Oxfam 2005: 19) and developing countries as their victims.

For many, agricultural subsidies epitomize the "rigged rules and
double standards" of the trading system, as Oxfam puts it—the unfair-
ness of global trade rules and how they are structured against the world's
poorest countries. With the majority of the population in the developing
world employed in agriculture, agriculture is vital to livelihoods, employment, and food security in developing countries (Eagleton-Pierce 2012).
However, while agriculture is one of the most important areas of international trade for many developing countries, free trade has been only
partially and unevenly applied to agriculture, which remains one of the
least liberalized sectors of global trade (Clapp 2015). The rules of the
trading system have been heavily shaped by power asymmetries: historically dominated by the US, EU, and other advanced-industrialized states,
liberalization was concentrated in their areas of export competitiveness,
while areas of greatest importance to developing countries—such as
agriculture—remained heavily protected (Muzaka and Bishop 2014).
Agriculture was only brought into the trading system with the Uruguay
Round in 1995, and the gains promised to developing countries failed to
materialize: developed countries continued to provide high levels of subsidies, with harmful consequences for poor farmers throughout the
developing world. Since reducing agricultural subsidies is recognized as
one of the key ways that global trade rules can help promote international
development and alleviate poverty, the issue has been identified as a
"litmus test" of whether the WTO can work for the poor (Hopewell
2016) and indeed "a test of the legitimacy of the WTO system as a whole"
(Quark 2013: 129).

During the Doha Round, the emerging powers formed a coalition of developing countries—the Group of 20 (G20), representing over half of the world's population and two-thirds of its farmers, with broad-based support from the rest of the developing world—to counter the US and other advanced-industrialized states and press those countries for agricultural reforms, particularly on subsidies (Clapp 2007; Narlikar and Tussie 2004; Narlikar and Wilkinson 2004). By challenging rich country agricultural subsidies, the G20—under the leadership of Brazil and India, and backed by China—enabled developing countries to seize the offensive against the US and other advanced-industrialized states and make their protectionist policies a key target at the WTO (Hopewell 2016; Muzaka and Bishop 2014). For the first time, the US—historically the key aggressor in the GATT/WTO—found itself increasingly isolated and on the defensive, while developing countries assumed the role of *demandeurs*. In addition, Brazil—with China, India, and numerous developing countries as third parties—launched and won landmark WTO disputes against US cotton and EU sugar subsidies. The activism of the emerging powers on agricultural subsidies profoundly altered the dynamics and agenda of the Doha Round and helped to catalyze broader power shifts at the WTO, challenging the unfettered dominance of the US and other advanced-industrialized states (Hopewell 2016). The Doha Round came to be defined by a conflict between developed and developing countries, focused heavily on agricultural subsidies (Singh 2017).

As the following analysis will show, however, amid the rise of China, the international politics of agricultural subsidies have changed dramatically, such that they are virtually unrecognizable from just a decade ago. The agricultural subsidies issue was previously conceived in North–South terms, with a clear set of villains (developed countries) and victims (developing countries). If rich countries have been seen as the villains on the agricultural subsidies issue, it is because, as Oxfam (2005: 20) could accurately state until recently: "WTO figures show that developed countries are almost exclusively responsible for the problems of trade distortion caused by farm subsidies. Agricultural support in developing countries is marginal in comparison." Today, however, this no longer holds true. China—a developing country—is now the world's largest subsidizer. The contemporary politics of agricultural subsidies cannot be understood by focusing solely on the policies of the US and other developed countries. New fault lines are emerging, which are far more complex than the North–South struggle that characterized the Doha Round.

This chapter draws attention to a lesser-known aspect of China's economic transformation and its changing role in the global political economy. China is primarily seen as a manufacturing powerhouse and a rising financial power. But what is often missed amid the focus on the extraordinary growth of its manufacturing sector is that, thanks to a dramatic expansion in agricultural production, China is now the world's largest agricultural producer. Given its large domestic market, most of its agricultural output is consumed internally, but China has still become the world's fourth largest agricultural exporter (WTO 2017b). Like the US and Europe, China is now *both* a major industrial economy and a leading agricultural producer and exporter. Indeed, China's rise is part of a larger reconfiguration of global agricultural production and trade flows from the traditionally dominant grain-producing nations of the US, EU, Canada, and Australia to emerging "agro-powers" in the Global South (Margulis 2014). Moreover, China enjoys tremendous power in global agriculture due to the size of its market and its importance as an importer (Quark 2013). While frequently overlooked, this side of China—its role as a major agricultural power—has significant consequences for global trade politics.

## THE WORLD TURNED UPSIDE DOWN: CHINA'S AGRICULTURAL SUBSIDIES BOOM

There has been a profound change in the global landscape of agricultural subsidies and the politics surrounding this issue at the WTO. As China and other emerging economies have grown richer, they have become major subsidizers of agriculture. Over the past two decades, since China's accession to the WTO, there has been a significant increase in China's agricultural support, as it has transitioned from taxing its rural sector to providing subsidies, in an attempt to support farmers' incomes and incentivize domestic production. This is not unique to China—other emerging economies, such as India, Indonesia, the Philippines, and Turkey, have been similarly increasing their agricultural support. Consequently, as one former negotiator summarized, "the real problem with agricultural subsidies is increasingly in developing countries, not developed countries anymore."[1]

In developed countries, agricultural support has been falling steadily over the past two decades. During this time, however, China's support has risen dramatically. As a result, China surpassed the OECD average in 2013, with its support to producers reaching more than 20 percent of

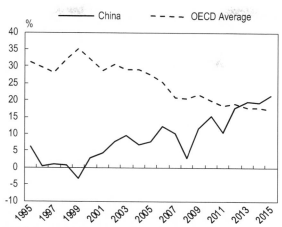

FIGURE 2.1 Producer support estimate as percentage of gross farm receipts, 1995–2015, China and OECD average.
Source: OECD

farm receipts in 2015 (see Figure 2.1). China's total support to agriculture, at 2.4 percent of GDP, is now four times higher than the OECD average (OECD 2017a: 92). China provided an estimated $212 billion in farm support in 2016, significantly more than the EU ($100 billion), US ($33 billion), or any other country (OECD 2017a).

In China, state support to producers now makes up a significant portion of their revenue from many commodities. During the period from 2014 to 2016, for example, state support constituted 38 percent of gross farm receipts for wheat, 29 percent for corn, 32 percent for rice, 49 percent for sugar, and 44 percent for cotton (see Figure 2.2). By comparison, in the US, state support constituted 8 percent of gross farm receipts for wheat, 4 percent for corn, 2 percent for rice, 34 percent for sugar, and 15 percent for cotton.

It is not just the volume of support that a country provides that matters but the form in which that support is provided. Certain types of subsidies distort trade far more than others. The most heavily trade-distorting subsidies are those that incentivize increased production (such as price supports or subsidies linked to inputs or output levels), whereas income support payments decoupled from production are among the least trade-distorting. While developed countries have been moving towards less trade-distorting forms of support, China's subsidies are concentrated in the most trade-distorting forms of support. Many of its subsidy mechanisms are tied to production incentives and lead to increased production of

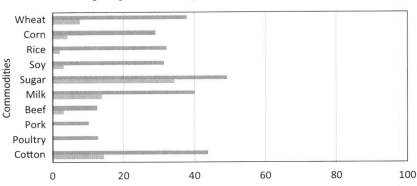

FIGURE 2.2 Transfers to specific commodities, 2014–2016, China and US.
Source: OECD

Chinese agricultural products. China is now providing more trade-distorting subsidies than the US or the EU. In China, support to agricultural producers represented 15 percent of gross farm receipts in 2014–16, and of that 74 percent was provided via the most trade-distorting forms of support. By comparison, support to farmers in the US constituted 9 percent of gross farm receipts, with only 33 percent provided in the most trade-distorting forms of support (see Figure 2.3).

China's support to agriculture is dominated by market price support, direct payments based on production, and input subsidies, which are the most trade-distorting means of providing agricultural assistance. Market price support, through the purchase of commodities by state agencies at a minimum guaranteed price, represents an important pillar of China's agricultural support. China's intervention in agriculture markets has intensified since the Global Food Crisis of 2007–8, which shook global agriculture markets with rising farm commodity prices and input costs (Margulis 2014). China responded by increasing market price support as well as sharply raising input subsidies and other support measures. Between 2008 and 2015, support prices were raised for wheat by 58 percent, corn by 50 percent, and rice by 80 percent (USDA 2015a). As a result, China alone now accounts for more than half of the world's support for rice and more than three-quarters of support for corn (Greenville 2017).

China's policy of supporting producers through the purchase of agricultural commodities at above-market prices has led to the accumulation

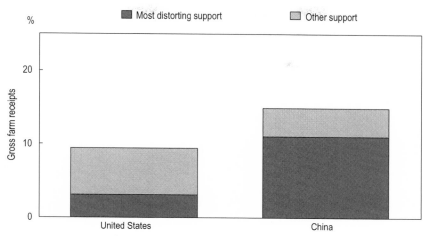

FIGURE 2.3 Composition of producer support estimate, 2014–2016, China and US (percentage of gross farm receipts).
Source: OECD

of massive stocks of wheat, rice, corn, cotton, and other products in state reserves. China has amassed 60 percent of the world's cotton supplies, over 50 percent of its corn, 40 percent of wheat, and 21 percent of soybeans (Rabobank 2016). To dispose of these large stocks, the government auctions them off at below acquisition cost, while using various measures to discourage imports (USDA 2016a). Given the size of its state reserves, China's policies exert "a colossal influence" on world prices (Rabobank 2016). China's mass sell-off of sugar from its reserves in 2016, for example, helped to push the global price of sugar down by almost a quarter (Mera 2017).

The impact of China's policies is magnified by its increasing centrality in global agriculture. China's agricultural production has grown dramatically: its share of global production has more than doubled, from 18 percent in 1995–97 to over 43 percent in 2014–16 (see Figure 2.4). Since China is now the world's largest producer and consumer of agricultural products, its policies have a profound impact on global markets and trade. Although the commodities it subsidizes are primarily sold in the domestic market rather than exported, as one WTO official stated, China "is just such an enormous import market that its impact on global trade patterns is extremely significant."[2] China's subsidies artificially boost its agricultural production, resulting in reduced demand for imports and lower global prices, to the detriment of agricultural producers and exporters around the world (Gale 2013; Mera 2017; Rabobank 2016).

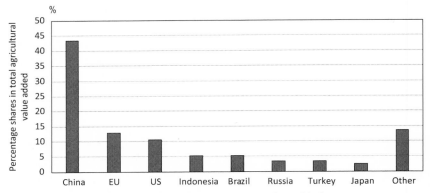

FIGURE 2.4 Country shares in total agricultural value added, 2014–2016.
Source: OECD

### FROM VILLAIN TO VICTIM? THE US POSITION

The US and other advanced-industrialized states, as the world's biggest subsidizers at that time, were the primary targets of subsidy reduction efforts in the Doha Round. But, since the collapse of the Doha Round, prompted by the boom in China's agricultural subsidies, the US has turned the tables and gone on the offensive against China's subsidies in both WTO negotiations and dispute settlement. Of course, the US has defensive motives for targeting China's subsidies: it is happy to deflect attention from its own subsidies and shift the blame elsewhere. But the US also has significant commercial interests at stake: as the world's biggest agricultural exporter, the US has a major interest in securing a reduction in Chinese subsidies. Moreover, the issue is also linked to broader issues of economic competition and geopolitical rivalry between the US and China.

Ironically, the US—long seen as the villain in this area—has increasingly come to view itself as a victim of China's agricultural subsidies. The level of support the US provides to its agricultural producers has been consistently below the OECD average and falling over time (OECD 2017a: 166). Since the Uruguay Round, and the Brazil cotton dispute, the US has undertaken reforms of its farm programs, moving towards less trade-distorting forms of support. The US's producer support declined from 21 percent of gross farm receipts in 1986–88 to 9 percent in 2014–16, with the proportion provided in the most trade-distorting forms of support falling from 51 percent to 33 percent. Yet, now, the US finds its chief market and competitor, China, moving in the opposite direction. Today, as one negotiator stated, China is "comprehensively outspending them in a way the US can't respond to because of its fiscal limitations and its WTO limits on production-linked spending."[3] From the US's perspective, to quote one of its former negotiators, not only are China's subsidies "distorting world markets but they have become significantly more trade-distorting than subsidies in developed countries" and "the US, as the biggest agricultural exporter, suffers most from these distortions."[4]

Agriculture is important to the US economy as a major source of exports. Accounting for 10 percent of total US exports, agriculture is one of the few sectors of the US economy that runs a trade surplus, helping to reduce the size of the country's overall trade deficit (USDA 2015c). American agriculture depends heavily on foreign markets, with more than a third of farm revenues generated from exports (USDA 2015c). For some commodities, such as wheat, rice, and cotton, export markets absorb half or more of US output (CRS 2017; ITC 2015). While the US remains the world's leading agricultural exporter, its dominance has been substantially eroded. Its share of global grain exports has fallen from 65 percent in the mid-1970s to 30 percent today (Newman and McGroarty 2017). The US agriculture industry identifies two key factors behind its declining market share: the rise of new competitors and the use of protectionist trade policies by other states.[5] According to the House Agriculture Committee Chair: "One of the biggest impacts to the health of the US agriculture industry is competition from foreign governments—in particular foreign subsidies and tariffs."[6]

As the largest market for US exports, China is a key focus. US agricultural exports to China peaked in 2012 at $26 billion, but in subsequent years fell by over 25 percent (USDA 2016a). This precipitous decline was caused primarily by China's subsidy programs and its bulging government reserves (USDA 2016a). The US believes its exports would be considerably higher if not for Chinese subsidies and trade barriers: in the words of the Secretary of Agriculture, "we could be doing much better if our exports could compete in China on a level playing field" (United States 2016c). The US wheat industry, for instance, maintains that China's subsidies cost world wheat exporters $3 billion in lost farm revenue annually, with American farmers specifically losing over $650 million.[7] It estimates that removal of China's price-support program for wheat would boost the country's imports by nearly 10 million metric tons annually and raise world prices by 3 percent; US exports alone would rise by 6 percent or 1.5 million tons (*Inside US–China Trade* 2016a).

In addition to the market distortions caused by China's subsidies, significant tariff and non-tariff barriers also restrict access to the Chinese market. The US Chamber of Commerce (2016) estimates that US agricultural exports to China could increase by $12 billion if the latter's agricultural trade barriers were eliminated.

The US launched two WTO disputes in 2016 challenging China's subsidies and administration of its tariff rate quotas (TRQs) for grains (wheat, rice, and corn).[8] In the first case, the US argues that China's price-support programs encourage domestic grain production, displacing imports and distorting prices. Washington alleges that China's grain subsidies have exceeded its WTO commitments for every year since 2012 and were nearly $100 billion in excess of its WTO obligations in 2015. While the case only challenges China's market price support, US producers maintain that other subsidies—including direct subsidies to grain producers as well as input subsidies to cover fuel and fertilizer costs—would increase China's violation of its WTO domestic support commitments even further (*Inside US–China Trade* 2016c). The US maintains that it is challenging these subsidies to ensure that American farmers are treated fairly and able to "compete on a more level playing field" (United States 2016c). Although the case focuses exclusively on grains, there are allegations of similar dynamics in other commodities, such as cotton, where US producers maintain China has been exceeding its WTO subsidy limits since at least 2011 (*Inside US–China Trade* 2016a).

The second case challenges China's administration of its TRQs for wheat, rice, and corn. TRQs allow for quantities of a product imported within a given quota to be charged a lower tariff than those outside the quota. Under WTO rules, while countries are not necessarily required to fill their TRQs, they are required to administer them in "a transparent, predictable, uniform, fair and non-discriminatory basis using clearly specified timeframes, administrative procedures and requirements." The US maintains that China is not meeting these requirements, but instead has been restricting its TRQ to block imports (United States 2016b). In the case of wheat, for instance, China's WTO commitments require it to implement an annual 9.64 million metric ton TRQ. Based on market conditions, since world prices have been lower than Chinese prices for many years, China should be importing large quantities of wheat, putting its TRQ utilization at or near 100 percent. In most years, however, China has filled only about one-third of its TRQ, and in some years even less (*Inside US–China Trade* 2016c). Industry sources allege that China rarely fills its wheat TRQ because 90 percent is administered by state-owned enterprises, which have been ordered by the government not to import wheat (*Inside US–China Trade* 2016b). The US maintains that, if China's TRQs had been fully utilized, China would have imported an additional $3.5 billion worth of grains in 2015 alone (United States 2016b). Nearly thirty other countries have joined the two cases as third parties, including other major grain exporters such as the EU, Russia, Canada, Australia, India, and Thailand.

In addition, the US argues that efforts to address Chinese agricultural subsidies, either through WTO negotiations or dispute settlement, have been complicated by the fact that many of China's policies are highly opaque. Countries are required to notify their subsidies to the WTO, and this transparency is seen as essential to the institution's monitoring and enforcement function. China's notifications, however, have been significantly delayed: as of 2017, for instance, it had reported its farm subsidy spending only until 2010. Critics, such as the US, maintain that China's notifications have contained serious omissions and they also contest the methodology used by China to calculate its subsidy levels, particularly for its price support policies and direct payments, which they argue results in China systematically under-reporting its subsidies (USTR 2017).

## CHINA'S STANCE: DEVELOPING COUNTRY MEANS DEVELOPING COUNTRY

Despite growing pressure, China has intensely opposed efforts to discipline its subsidies at the WTO. China objects even to being called a "large subsidizer," or classified with countries like the US, emphasizing the vast socio-economic differences that separate emerging and developed countries. China, along with other emerging subsidizers, argues that "the support provided by countries with different levels of development [is] not directly comparable" (WTO 2015). Its negotiators stress that China remains a developing country—albeit an upper-middle-income one—with a GDP per capita of just $8,000, compared to $57,000 for the US.[9] Chinese officials emphasize that average farm size is far smaller in China and, on a per capita basis, the levels of support it provides are considerably lower than those of the US or other advanced-industrialized states. China contains 40 percent of the world's farmers, and its agriculture sector is dominated by small-scale, household farming (USDA 2016a; Zha and Zhang 2013). Its average farm size is just 0.5 hectares in size (equivalent to half a sports field), while average farm size in the US is nearly 400 times larger, with many US farms over 1,000 hectares

(USDA 2015b; USDA 2018). China therefore insists, as one of its negotiators stated, that "you cannot just ask China, because it is a big economy, to make the same cuts [to its subsidies] as others."[10] As a rival negotiator put it, when pressed at the WTO to reduce its subsidies, China "does a lot of banging its fists on the table—'you're ignoring our development situation'"—although, as his comment signals, this stance is met with skepticism by other states.[11]

China justifies its subsidies on the grounds of its own national development goals, including promoting food security and rural development. Beijing stresses that agriculture "is a sector of vital importance" affecting the livelihoods of millions of producers (*Bridges Weekly* 2017d). Despite China's manufacturing boom and the rapid growth of its cities, nearly half of China's population remains rural, with a third of the population employed in agriculture.[12] Poverty is concentrated in rural areas, and the income gap between urban and rural households in China is one of the largest in the world, with average incomes three times higher in urban than rural areas (Frazier 2013). As one of its senior officials stated, "China confronts a lot of challenges. Some provinces or regions are similar to African countries [in terms of their level of development]. So China can never be looked at as just one picture; it has lots of different faces."[13]

The Communist Party views urban–rural inequality as potentially destabilizing and a threat to maintaining its grip on power. Consequently, as one former Chinese negotiator indicated, "Agriculture is a very difficult and very political issue for China. To simply ask China to stop providing domestic support [to agriculture] is political suicide. In China, the priority of agriculture is indisputable, no one can challenge it. Every year, the first State Council decree for the last 15 years has been on agriculture."[14] Furthermore, he continued: "And if the state stops buying from Chinese farmers, where would they go? China is facing significant challenges with urbanization, and we are already struggling to absorb [rural-to-urban] migrants. Urbanization is a long slow process."[15]

In addition to supporting its rural population, China's interventionist agriculture policies are also driven by the desire to secure domestic supply, amid concerns that it cannot necessarily rely on global markets to feed its population (ICTSD 2015). Managing grain production and supplies has long been a central priority of China's agricultural policy, with China seeking to improve food security through a push for self-sufficiency in grains (USDA 2015b). Beijing has set the policy goal of achieving 95 percent self-sufficiency in wheat and rice, which are seen as strategic commodities. China's emphasis on ensuring food security is shaped by the country's recent historical experience of hunger and famine (Zha and Zhang 2013). Furthermore, China is "not just another major developing country" (Chin 2010), and its self-sufficiency policies are also informed by its status as an emerging power in an international system dominated by the US. As a former Chinese negotiator explained:

Some say China's food supply issue can be easily resolved through international markets. OK in normal times, yes, because China has the resources [to import]. But the top agricultural exporters—where are they from? The US and EU—they control a big part of world production and exports. Imagine if we have a change in the political situation, like a new cold war, or a real war, where could China buy its food? Food security is not just about whether there is an international market but where your food is coming from and whether you will always be able to buy the food you need.[16]

The US used economic sanctions, including embargos on food exports, in its conflicts with China and the Soviet Union during the Cold War (Margulis 2016). Strikingly, in the late-1950s, amid the worst famine in history, China was prevented from purchasing grain on international markets to feed its population by the US's food embargo (Zha and Zhang 2013). This experience is seared in the minds of Chinese policymakers, who fear that access to food could once again become a weapon in a geopolitical conflict with the US (Morton 2017; Zha and Zhang 2013).

As Gregory Chin (2010) details, China's food reserves are part of a larger "grand reserve system" directed at crisis prevention through self-insuring, which encompasses foreign exchange, energy, and material supplies. Although the Chinese authorities recognize the need for some reform of the grand reserve system, "they remain steadfast in believing that a substantial level of national reserves is still needed to ensure national defense, economic security and social stability are protected" (Chin 2010: 700). In this broader sense, China's efforts to maintain national reserves are far from unique: the US, EU countries, Japan, India, and Russia also keep national reserves for a range of strategic items, including oil and gas. China's support for its agriculture sector thus takes place amid the backdrop of larger strategic considerations, particularly related to its relationship with the American hegemon.

For China, the Global Food Crisis in 2007–8, and subsequent food price spikes, which disrupted global food trade flows and prompted many countries to impose food export restrictions, further underscored the danger of relying on unpredictable and unstable global agriculture markets (Margulis 2014). China was relatively fortunate: thanks to its food self-sufficiency targets that had bolstered domestic production, low levels of import-dependence helped to insulate the country from the global food crisis. In the words of a National Development and Reform Commission report on enhancing food security, "the world food market caught a cold, but China did not even sneeze" (cited in Morton 2017). As food riots helped to spark the Arab Spring and a wave of political upheaval across the Middle East and North Africa, the crisis reinforced China's distrust of international food markets, including concerns that exposure to price volatility in international markets could lead to social unrest and political instability (Morton 2017). In the years following the crisis, China doubled the value of its support for agriculture (Gale 2013).

Price support and general input subsidies have been the main instruments used in China, because these policies yield quick returns and are relatively easy to operate, as opposed to less-trade-distorting direct support, which is often seen as less effective in stabilizing food production (ICTSD 2015). Critics argue, however, that if its objective is to support its farmers, China has other, more efficient and more effective policy options at its disposal, which would have less harmful effects on global markets and producers in other countries. There are also better ways to address rural poverty and support rural development, including through providing improved rural pensions, healthcare, education, and infrastructure (OECD 2017a). But China has vigorously defended its agricultural subsidies at the WTO, maintaining that it is providing "necessary and essential support" to its rural sector (*Inside US–China Trade* 2017a). Indeed, China argues that it is simply claiming the right to support its agricultural sector, as the US and other advanced-industrialized states have long done (MOFCOM 2016).

The soaring costs of its ballooning stockpiles have prompted China to take some steps to reform the design of its agricultural support programs (Yu 2017). For certain commodities—soybeans, cotton, and corn—China has recently moved from government procurement and stockpiling to new pilot target price programs, where farmers receive a direct compensation payment from the government if the market price is lower than the target price (Hejazi and Marchant 2017). While less trade-distorting than government purchases at intervention prices, these new subsidy programs remain closely linked to prices and still distort production and trade.[17] Indeed, in the case of soybeans, for example, the target price has been set at a high level specifically to boost production. Although China is experimenting with changes to its policies for non-food commodities (soybeans and corn are used primarily for animal feed rather than human food), it is far less open to reforms for rice and wheat, which are food staples and therefore considered of strategic importance. Rather than continuously increasing the minimum prices for wheat and rice, the government has stabilized or lowered these prices, but they still remain far above international market prices (Hejazi and Marchant 2017). For these crops, no move away from government purchases and stockpiling is anticipated in the foreseeable future.

Importantly, China's reforms have been driven by pragmatic, domestic considerations, rather than external forces or concerns about the effects of its policies on global markets or foreign producers. And they have not in any way altered China's negotiating stance or willingness to accept disciplines from the WTO. As one negotiator stated, "China is going to reform when they are ready, regardless of what is going on at the WTO."[18] China wants to maximize its policy flexibility, including maintaining the option to increase its subsidies in the future—which is why China has fiercely resisted *any* new disciplines on its agricultural support at the WTO.

### China's Critique of US Subsidies and Existing WTO Rules

China, like many developing countries, views the WTO's existing subsidy rules—established in the Uruguay Round Agreement on Agriculture (AoA) and heavily influenced by the interests of the US and EU—as unbalanced. As one negotiator put it, "the AoA was shaped around and to cater to the policies" of the world's two major powers at that time—the US and EU.[19] Subsidies ("domestic support") are classified into different "boxes" based on the degree to which they distort production and trade: the "Amber Box" is for trade-distorting subsidies, such as measures related to production level or selling price; the "Blue Box" encompasses direct payments to farmers made under production-limiting programs; "Green Box" support is that with no, or minimal, distortive effects on trade; and Article 6.2 (the "Development Box") provides an exemption allowing developing countries to provide certain forms of investment and input subsidies for the purposes of fostering agricultural and rural development.[20]

The AoA established limits solely on the trade-distorting, or Amber Box, support that states can provide. For countries with high levels of support at that time, their Amber Box support was capped and subject to reductions (20 percent reduction over six years for developed countries);

the resulting new limit is referred to as a country's bound "Aggregate Measure of Support" (AMS). *De minimis* provisions allow minimal levels of Amber Box support (5 percent of the value of production for developed countries and 10 percent for developing countries) to be exempt from the calculation of their current AMS. The US, for example, was given a bound AMS (of $19.1 billion) and allowed to exempt *de minimis* levels of support from the calculation of its current AMS. In contrast, most developing countries, which had little or no domestic support at that time, were not given a bound AMS. Consequently, for those countries, including China, its *de minimis* threshold acts as an effective limit on domestic support. In sum, while developed countries were given AMS entitlements plus *de minimis* exemptions, most developing countries were limited to *de minimis*. Developing countries have long criticized these rules as unfair, allowing developed countries that historically provided large amounts of trade-distorting support the flexibility to continue doing so (Clapp 2015; Hopewell 2016). The overall reduction in developed-country subsidies occasioned by the Uruguay Round was minimal, with much of their support transferred to the Green Box.

From China's perspective, these iniquities were compounded by the terms of its WTO accession. China has no AMS entitlement, its *de minimis* commitments (8.5 percent) are lower than other developing countries (10 percent), and it is not entitled to the Article 6.2 exemptions afforded to other developing countries. As one negotiator noted, "China paid heavily in its accession and doesn't want to again."[21] Another elaborated: "Even if you look at agriculture alone, they gave up too much to enter the organization—AMS, Article 6.2, *de minimis*. From their perspective, other members should come to their level before they make further reforms."[22] In short, for China:

Its position is that "we were promised in our accession negotiations that the Doha Round would be concluded with the US taking major cuts to AMS." That was the implicit deal and how it was sold to stakeholders and even some in the Chinese bureaucracy. Their lack of flexibility is a function of this. They feel cheated. For them, it's a question of fairness.[23]

China thus maintains that it should not have to accept any further disciplines on its subsidies because its existing commitments already exceed those of other developing country members. Instead, it argues, the responsibility lies on the US and other developed countries to do more in reducing their subsidies, to live up to the promises made to China during its accession and developing countries more broadly in the Doha Round.

## POST-DOHA NEGOTIATIONS ON AGRICULTURAL SUBSIDIES

Agricultural subsidies have re-emerged as a central and highly contentious issue in WTO negotiations, but, as one negotiator stated, "the terms of the debate have shifted significantly."[24] Since the collapse of the Doha Round, the WTO has focused on negotiating targeted agreements on specific trade issues, leading to the successful conclusion of agreements on trade facilitation and agricultural export competition, for example, in 2013 and 2015 (Wilkinson, Hannah, and Scott 2014; Margulis 2018). Since 2015, there has been a push to negotiate a standalone agreement on domestic support for agriculture. However, these efforts have run aground due to a US–China standoff. The US has refused to cut its subsidies unless China does the same; but China has refused, insisting that as a developing country it should not be forced to cut its subsidies. China maintains that any negotiations on domestic support should be based on the final draft agriculture text that emerged from the Doha Round in 2008 (known as "Rev4"), immediately prior to the round's collapse. China is unwilling to accept more onerous commitments than those outlined in Rev4, which did not require any cuts to its domestic support—and the US refuses to accept Rev4 as the basis for negotiations for precisely that reason.

Rev4 introduced a new measure of support—Overall Trade Distorting Support (OTDS), which includes AMS, *de minimis*, and blue box support—and used tiered cuts to OTDS and AMS, with the countries that provided the largest amounts of support in the past undertaking the greatest reductions. The US and EU would cut OTDS by 70 percent and 80 percent, respectively.[25] Under Rev4, the US's bound OTDS would decline from $48.5 billion to $14.5 billion and its bound AMS of $19.1 billion would drop to $7.6 billion (Orden 2013). While for the EU, bound OTDS would fall from €79 billion to €23.8 billion and its bound AMS would be reduced from €72.2 billion to €21.7 billion (Orden 2013). Rev4 also introduced product-specific caps on Amber and Blue Box support.

For most developed countries, their current WTO subsidy limits are so high that the new disciplines introduced in Rev4 would just be cutting "water" (the gap between their actual and bound subsidy levels). At the time of negotiating those terms in 2008, the US's actual OTDS was less than $7 billion and thus far below its proposed cap. Since then, however, its OTDS has been rising, due to a combination of lower global prices and new domestic support policies introduced in the 2014 farm bill (Anderson 2017). Now, the US is distinctly vulnerable to the proposed caps under

Rev 4, which would likely bite into its actual levels of domestic support. Under the terms of Rev4, as a US negotiator summed up: "everyone else is OK, but it's the US that got trapped."[26]

In contrast, Rev4 represented a highly favorable deal for China. Since 2005, in the Hong Kong Ministerial Declaration, it had been agreed that "developing country members with no AMS commitments will be exempt from reductions in *de minimis* and the overall cut in trade-distorting domestic support."[27] This was reaffirmed in Rev4, which stated that developing countries without AMS entitlements (like China) would not be required to undertake reduction commitments in their OTDS.[28] China maintains that any negotiations on domestic support must be based on these previously agreed principles. They reflect a key promise of the Doha Round: that developing countries would be granted "special and differential treatment" (SDT), including reduced liberalization commitments and greater flexibilities and exemptions. China considers itself a developing country and staunchly maintains that it is entitled to the SDT promised to developing countries. Its negotiators insist that the principles of SDT "should be fully preserved and for all members" and identifies this as a "redline" on which it is unwilling to budge (WTO 2015). China argues that, as a developing country, it is entitled to SDT and should not be required to make further concessions. From China's perspective, the US is trying to renege on the terms of the deal that had been broadly agreed in 2008. For China, it has become a matter of principle that it is not doing more than Rev4, which, as one WTO Secretariat official put it, "for China basically means nothing."[29]

The US, however, argues that China needs to agree to undertake cuts as part of any multilateral deal on domestic support. The US has urged the WTO to "step away from rigid notions of who is a developing country and what are their responsibilities" based on "an antiquated snapshot of the past."[30] According to the US Trade Representative, "when major emerging economies are providing trade-distortive agricultural subsidies at a greater volume than all of the developed countries put together, we can no longer turn a blind eye."[31] Referencing the grain subsidy dispute, in which the US asserts that China is providing nearly $100 billion per year in trade-distorting subsidies above its WTO limits, he argued: "Think about that for a minute. $100 billion is more than the GDP of 130 countries. How can we have a serious conversation about distortions to global agricultural trade if we pretend that trade-distortive subsidies at this level don't exist?"[32] The US argues that since China has become one of the world's leading economies, it needs to assume greater responsibilities commensurate with that role. In this case, that means being willing to undertake commitments to limit its agricultural subsidies. As a WTO Secretariat official summarized, the conflict over agricultural subsidies "all comes down to the old question of differentiation and who pays what."[33]

The US agriculture industry is intensely frustrated that China, as one representative put it, "still wants to claim developing country status for agriculture and get the benefits."[34] Another explained their resistance to Rev4 as follows: "We were being sacrificed. The US was giving everything and getting nothing in return—that's just not going to fly."[35] According to a US congressional official, with Rev4: "our industry gets thrown under the bus, while China gets a completely free pass. It's pretty hard to swallow. ... Especially since China impacts the market more than us."[36] The US argues that the world has changed significantly and any agreement on domestic support needs to reflect that new reality: as one negotiator put it, "we need to look at this in the context of today's data and negotiate from there."[37] For the US, any agreement on domestic support where it is forced to make significant cuts without concessions from China is a non-starter.

Driven by its export-oriented producer groups, the US has led the charge against the agricultural subsidies provided by China and other advanced developing countries. But it has been joined by other developed countries and agricultural exporters, including the EU, Australia, Canada, Brazil, and other competitive Latin American exporters, and members of the Cairns Group of agricultural exporters.[38] As one exporter stated:

This is more than just US rhetoric. There's a serious issue here with the amount of money that China is spending and its impact on trade. It is having significant effects in distorting trade, including through import-substitution policies. The US is not alone in this; others share their concerns. Everyone's feeling it—some are just saying more than others.[39]

Although many of these countries were once satisfied with the domestic support disciplines in Rev4, particularly for gains it offered in reducing US subsidies, they now no longer see Rev4 as a viable starting point—both because of the depth of US opposition and because they too now want to see disciplines on the agricultural subsidies provided by China and other emerging economies. According to one negotiator:

Most developed countries don't think Rev4 is an acceptable starting point now. Our analysis shows that it would mean real cuts into US domestic support while China would be doing nothing. As much as we'd love to see the US reduce its subsidies, that's just not realistic. And Rev4 doesn't meet our needs anymore because China wouldn't be doing anything.

To reach an agreement on domestic support, he continued:

Politicians will have to feel the agreement is relevant to their stakeholders today, and it's not the same world that is was in 2001. The carve-out of China is problematic in that sense. Rev4 really reflects an outdated way of thinking about domestic support. To us, all trade-distorting forms of support are problematic, regardless of which country is providing them.[40]

The problem with Rev4, in the words of a Secretariat official, is that it "targets those who have been reducing their support and leaves off the hook those who are increasing their subsidies."[41] As a negotiator stated:

There's no way that's going to happen. It's just the political reality in the US. They can't be made to undergo reforms and tell their Congress and constituencies that China is carved out. And it's also systemically problematic if, just as the WTO is starting to discipline US and EU subsidies, they are simply replaced by other big subsidizers.[42]

Yet, despite their frustrations, these states have been powerless to move the agenda forward amid the entrenched stalemate between the US and China.

Other WTO members have sought to break the US–China deadlock, advancing proposals targeting subsidies provided by both developed and emerging economies. New Zealand, a low-support country, led a group of exporters in putting forward a proposal to move beyond the developed/developing country distinction by targeting a new category of "major members."[43] Various exporters, such as the EU, Brazil, other Latin American states, and certain members of the Cairns Group, have pushed for an overall limit on trade-distorting domestic support, either as a fixed monetary cap or a floating ceiling linked to the value of production.[44] There have also been calls for product-specific caps, including for cotton. For China, however, any proposal that erodes the distinction between developed and developing countries, or threatens the privileges afforded to it as a developing country, is untenable. Thus, as one of its negotiators stated regarding any proposal for reductions by both developed and emerging economies, "China will never agree to that."[45] China has refused to budge, insisting that it will not accept any disciplines on its domestic support.

China's position is supported by other emerging subsidizers. In July 2017, China put forward a joint submission with India calling for the total elimination of existing AMS allowances for developed countries as a prerequisite for any further reforms (such that their *de minimis* limit would become a de facto ceiling, as is currently the case for most developing countries), while allowing developing countries to maintain their current *de minimis* flexibilities, without any new ceilings or cuts (*Bridges Weekly* 2017a). The proposal was supported by several emerging economies, including Indonesia, the Philippines, and Turkey (*Inside US–China Trade* 2017b). In effect, China has now moved beyond its insistence on Rev4 as the only acceptable starting point for negotiations, but to an even more extreme position—where the US and other developed countries would be required to do substantially more than Rev4, while China and other emerging economies would still do nothing to reduce their subsidies. Furthermore, the problem is that because agricultural production has grown dramatically in China, so too has its *de minimis* limit (since it is calculated as a percentage of the total value of production). With its current total value of agricultural production at $1.4 trillion (OECD 2017a), China's current aggregate *de minimis* limit would permit it to spend up to an enormous $119 billion on trade-distorting subsidies—and China's cap will continue to grow with the value of agricultural production.

Negotiators report that China has assumed an "extremely defensive" stance, "digging in its heels" and refusing to discuss any reductions or disciplines on its domestic support: China is "unwilling to accept *any* caps or make *any* commitments at the WTO."[46] There is little to induce China to participate in a new WTO subsidies agreement. Not only does China want to maintain its own subsidies, but it has no offensive interest on the issue. With rapid economic growth and rising incomes, booming consumer demand for more and better food has far outpaced China's ability to fill that demand with its domestic supply: "They are a major food-importing country; if prices are lower because of foreign subsidies, that's not necessarily bad for them."[47] As a result, as one negotiator observed:

China has no incentive to agree to a cap on domestic support. They don't care about reducing other countries' domestic support, so there's no trade off in it for them. They rail about US domestic support, but I don't think they really mind. They import US food and feed, and the fact those products are subsidized means they are cheaper. Ultimately, China has nothing to gain from an agreement on domestic support.[48]

To quote a WTO Secretariat official:

What would they be getting out of the deal? In agriculture, China is totally defensive. They have no offensive interests in agriculture; they don't want anything out of agriculture. So they are perfectly fine leaving things as they are. Why would you go for a deal where you get absolutely nothing out of it? You may love the system and multilateralism but at the end of the day, you still need to sell the deal back home. So you can't just be expected to pay [and not get anything in return]. Why on earth would they pay? The Chinese are good negotiators. If they were just a small country, it would be different, but they're a big country.[49]

And, for its part, the US is equally obstinate—refusing to consider any solution that does not include a contribution from China.

While China is not the only emerging economy that is increasing its agricultural subsidies, it has been the chief target of the US and the US–China conflict has dominated the negotiations. In the words of one Secretariat official: "the dynamic is primarily between the US and China. The US is overwhelmingly focused on attacking China, and frankly it's not talking much about India or the others."[50] Another seconded this: "The real political friction is between the US and China. Clearly, the US–China relationship is absolutely crucial. We have a standoff where the Chinese say we're not going to reduce our domestic support, or even talk about it, unless you reduce your subsidies—US, you go first."[51] Although India has played a prominent role on the issue of food stock-holding (Margulis 2018; Narlikar and Tussie 2016; Singh and Gupta 2016; Wilkinson, Hannah, and Scott 2014), which involves securing an exemption from existing subsidy rules, the conflict over creating new domestic support disciplines has been primarily a fight between the US and China. This is partly for economic reasons. For the US, China is a far more important agricultural export market than India: US agricultural exports to China are nearly twenty times the size of its exports to India.[52] The Indian market also remains protected primarily via high tariffs and other non-tariff barriers rather than subsidies (USDA 2016b). But the US focus on China is also a product of their larger economic and geopolitical rivalry. As one negotiator summarized, the impasse between the US and China on subsidies is:

partly related to the role of their defensive positions in agriculture but it is also about China–US competition in a broader sense. The US looks at things through the prism of what China would do [under any potential new rules] and China looks at it in exactly the same way with regards to the US. The politics goes beyond their pure interests in agriculture.[53]

This fundamental conflict between the US and China has barred any progress on disciplining agricultural domestic support.

Addressing domestic support is "a priority for virtually all delegations" (WTO 2017a), but the negotiations have become blocked by the standoff between the US and China. To quote one negotiator, "these are not small countries that you can just roll over."[54] With the renewal of negotiations on domestic support, many states hoped for an outcome at the 2015 Nairobi Ministerial, but the stalemate between the US and China resulted in the issue being taken off the agenda for the Ministerial. According to the agriculture negotiations chair, there was "near universal" consensus on the importance of reaching an agreement on subsidies at the 2017 Buenos Aires Ministerial, yet nothing was achieved (*Bridges Weekly* 2017c). Despite the best efforts of many states, negotiators describe the prospects of agreement on domestic support as "if not zero, then very close to zero" and report that "there has been no movement and there are no signs that there will be movement any time soon."[55] Indeed, with the two most powerful states at the WTO dug in, as a Secretariat official put it, "we don't have anything even remotely resembling a negotiation."[56]

The dynamics of the domestic support negotiations highlight the exceptional degree of power wielded by the US and China compared to other states at the WTO. With a conflict between the US and China barring any potential for movement in negotiations, other states have been rendered largely peripheral players and relegated to the sidelines— this includes even traditional powers like the EU, emerging powers like India, Brazil, and Russia, and historically important players in WTO agriculture negotiations like Japan, Canada, and the Cairns Group. Multilateral negotiations on agriculture once centered on the old "G2" of the US and EU, with Canada and Japan acting as their junior partners: the Uruguay Round Agreement on Agriculture, for instance, was constructed on the basis of a bilateral deal between the US and the EU (Margulis 2018). But the EU has now been displaced from its dominant role in the agriculture negotiations by China. The new "G2" centers on Washington and Beijing and dynamics between these two pivotal powers are proving far more fractious.

Since the breakdown of the Doha Round and the collapse of efforts to negotiate broad-based, comprehensive multilateral trade agreements at the WTO, there has been a proliferation of bilateral and regional free trade agreements (FTAs). While these agreements provide an alternative avenue for reducing tariffs and other trade barriers, that is not the case for subsidies. Most believe subsidies—because the benefits of liberalization are non-excludable—can only be dealt with multilaterally. As one developing country exporter stated, "For reducing agricultural subsidies, the WTO is the only way. This is the only place where you have any hope of getting anything on domestic support. There is no other option."[57] Thus, agricultural subsidies represent a crucial area of global trade distortion that risks being left behind in a turn away from multilateralism and towards liberalization via bilateral and regional FTAs.

## THE PERSPECTIVE OF DEVELOPING COUNTRIES

For developing countries, in particular, disciplining and reducing agricultural subsidies remains a crucial priority. Yet with the post-Doha negotiations on agricultural subsidies dominated by conflict between the US and China, the interests of developing countries have been largely sidelined. At the WTO, China continues to present itself as a victim of rich country subsidies but elides the role of its own massive subsidies in victimizing other developing countries. China justifies its subsidies as necessary for its development, while ignoring the impact of its policies on poorer, weaker countries. China's argument, as one negotiator put it, is that its subsidies are "morally different" because it is a developing country.[58] As a WTO official summarized, "the debate has become my subsidies are better than your subsidies."[59] China maintains that its subsidies support rural development and poverty alleviation, while the US argues that its subsidies are more responsible because they are less trade-distorting. Yet, while China and the US argue back and forth about "whose support is more virtuous," another added, "the reality is that the impact on other developing countries is the same regardless of where the money is coming from."[60]

While China's agriculture policies are informed by important domestic considerations, they have major spillover effects for producers in other countries. China's subsidies distort production and trade, displacing imports from the Chinese market and depressing world prices. China may still be a developing country, but, given the aggregate volume of subsidies it is providing, its impact on global markets and other developing countries is significant. As a developing country negotiator stated,

China doesn't consider itself to be a large subsidizer—because of their number of farmers and they say it's about domestic welfare. That's all true, but from the perspective of international markets or poor farmers in Africa, it doesn't matter where it's coming from—China or the US or another developed country—the impact is the same. You have to appreciate the fact that you are so big and so powerful that your policies have a huge impact on everyone else everywhere in the world.[61]

For smaller developing countries and LDCs—as a former African negotiator stated—"We don't care who is doing the subsidizing. All countries—regardless of whether they are developed or not—if they are providing subsidies that are impacting us they should be disciplined."[62]

As a Secretariat official bluntly stated, many states "detest what both sides—China and the US—are doing."[63] Reducing trade-distorting subsidies would have a significant impact on the livelihoods and welfare of poor farmers around the world. It is estimated that removing agricultural subsidies would generate nearly $16 billion in added annual global welfare (Greenville 2017) and removing all agricultural trade distortions could reduce the number of extreme poor by 3 percent (World Bank and WTO 2015). Yet, despite its importance to developing countries, the US–China impasse has blocked efforts at the WTO to reform global agricultural subsidies. Caught in a battle between these two major powers, as one developing country negotiator summed up, "ultimately it's the little guys that get hurt the most."[64]

## Don't Poke the Dragon

While developing countries are harmed by agricultural subsidies and the US–China impasse, many are hesitant to challenge China. As a Secretariat official stated: "African countries, LDCs, even though these are small countries, they have this moral weight because they are poorer than China. So, if they start to say, 'Your subsidies are bad for us,' that would be very damaging and dangerous for China."[65] China, however, is "extremely defensive. They often don't even like the facts available being discussed."[66] An advisor to several developing countries summarized the situation as follows:

They're not stupid—of course they realize these subsidies could be harmful to them. But it's very political. They are very careful, very circumspect about directly criticizing China and the other larger developing countries for political reasons. They don't want to be seen as criticizing the emerging powers.[67]

Many developing countries report that it is more difficult to criticize China and other emerging powers than it is to criticize the US or EU.[68]

As an African negotiator noted, "a lot of sensitivities remain around showing solidarity."[69] After years of maltreatment in the trading system, the level of distrust and animosity of many developing countries towards the US and other advanced-industrialized states is extremely high. During the Doha Round, developing world coalitions centered on China and other emerging powers such as Brazil and India helped to significantly strengthen the bargaining position of developing countries vis-à-vis the US and other advanced-industrial states (Clapp 2007; Hopewell 2017a; Narlikar and Tussie 2004; Narlikar and Wilkinson 2004). Developing world solidarity remains a powerful force at the WTO, and developing countries worry that criticizing China's trade policies could alienate their most powerful ally against the US and other advanced-industrialized states.

Many developing countries are also hampered by a lack of the technical expertise required to analyze the impact of China's trade policies on their exporters. As a former African negotiator stated: "Small developing countries and LDCs lack the technical capacity to do studies to isolate and assess the effects of Chinese subsidies on their producers, markets, and exports. The simple fact is they lack the technical capacity to do those kinds of studies."[70] Such capacity is overwhelmingly concentrated in the large, well-resourced exporters like the US, EU, and Cairns Group members. And, for many developing countries, communication channels between their agriculture producers at home and their negotiators in Geneva are weak.[71]

Furthermore, many developing countries now rely on China as their largest export market and fear that antagonizing China by criticizing its trade policies could provoke retaliation and jeopardize their access to its market. As one major emerging economy agricultural exporter indicated, "Internally, we increasingly see our agriculture sector concerned about China's subsidies, but China is our biggest agriculture market now, so we have to be very careful."[72] These fears are not unfounded—China has cut off access to its market in retaliation against states in the past (Hopewell 2017b)—and nor are they limited to weaker states—even the US agriculture industry shares the same concerns.[73] In addition to their dependence on its market, China also exerts influence over weaker developing countries through foreign aid and investment. As one negotiator reported, during China's 2016 Trade Policy Review, the forum established specifically for criticizing a country's protectionist trade policies, "the whole afternoon, just about every African country took the floor one after another to thank China for the thing it had built for them—roads, stadiums, airports. In all my time here, I have never seen anything like that before."[74]

At the WTO, China appears to exert greater and more effective influence over developing countries than the US. As a former negotiator put it: "The Americans are no good in their relations with LDCs. The Africans don't trust the Americans, they don't like them, but they accept that they behave like gorillas." In contrast to the more overt, chest-thumping displays of dominance weaker countries are accustomed to from the US, he continued, China's exercise of power is more subtle: "China does things quietly. If they want you to do something, they'll say quietly and subtly that you better do it or it will affect our relationship. And you would know there would be consequences if you didn't."[75]

Consequently, in the words of one developing country negotiator, given China's "big political influence" across much of the Global South, "developing countries are not going to point the finger and say, 'you China—you're a bad guy, don't do that anymore'."[76] While developing countries will not openly or directly criticize China, according to negotiators, "they are starting to voice more oblique complaints—like 'we're suffering from subsidized competition *in general*', without specifying where those subsidies are coming from. If you read between the lines, it's not difficult to see who they are really talking about."[77] Similarly, developing countries "won't single out China but instead will now talk about 'big subsidizers' or 'big producers'," and recently they "have started saying 'we want to look at trade-distorting support that has the greatest impact on the products we produce and trade'—without distinguishing between developed and developing country subsidies."[78] Despite their economic interests at stake, developing countries thus face significant constraints in their ability to challenge China's agricultural subsidies or criticize its role in blocking new disciplines.

### SQUEEZED BETWEEN TWO GIANTS: THE COTTON EXAMPLE

Cotton subsidies provide a striking illustration of the new politics of agricultural subsidies at the WTO, and how developing country interests have become caught in the middle of the US–China standoff. Cotton is among the most heavily supported agricultural commodities and was singled out as a priority area within the agriculture negotiations because of its importance to the Cotton-4 (C-4) group of West African cotton producers (Mali, Chad, Benin, Burkina Faso), as well as many other developing and least-developed countries in Africa and throughout the world. Cotton is one of the most important crops in sub-Saharan Africa, with some 15 million people in the region directly dependent on it (Meyer and Terazono 2014). Some of the poorest countries on the continent rely on it for as much as 40 percent of their export revenues (Singh 2014). For these countries, cotton is their lifeblood, vital to generating employment and reducing poverty (Sneyd 2016).

As J. P. Singh (2017: 135) argues, "cotton is symbolic of the developing world's efforts to pry open developed world agricultural markets" and reap greater benefits from trade. African cotton producers are among the most competitive in the world, but the subsidies provided by more affluent countries leave them struggling to compete in global markets. Increasingly, however, the source of the problem lies not just with developed countries but with China. China and the US are among the world's least efficient cotton producers, with their average costs of production four times higher than some African countries—but thanks to state subsidies and other distortionary trade policies, China and the US are the second and third largest cotton producers, respectively (ICAC 2016a).[79] There is a pressing need for trade disciplines to ensure a fair international market for poor cotton-producing countries, with reducing global cotton subsidies "crucial for millions of farmers who live on the poverty threshold" (IDEAS Centre 2013).

The world cotton market now revolves around China, as the world's largest consumer, importer (until recent import restrictions), and stock-holder of cotton by sizable margins, and the second largest producer (after India) (Quark 2013). As the location of over half the world's textile production (USDA 2015b), China is by far the most important market for cotton producers in Africa and around the world. In a sign of how quickly this reorientation of global trade has occurred, in 1999, Benin, a member of the C-4, had almost no trade with China on cotton, but by 2010 China was the destination for nearly half of Benin's exports (ICTSD 2013). China's cotton policies therefore have profound global consequences. These effects are felt most keenly in the countries of West Africa, which are collectively the world's second largest cotton exporter (ICAC 2016a).

Like its broader support for agriculture, China's cotton subsidies have expanded dramatically, and China became the world's largest cotton subsidizer in 2009. During 2011–13, government purchases at above-market prices led to a massive accumulation of reserves, doubling the size of world cotton stocks. To draw down its stocks, China suspended government purchases of cotton in 2014–15, replacing this with direct payments to producers (ICAC 2016b). But even after these reforms Chinese cotton subsidies were estimated at $5.3 billion in 2015–16 (compared to $1.1 billion for the US) (ICAC 2016b). China accounts for nearly three-quarters of the $7.2 billion in cotton subsidies provided worldwide (see Figure 2.5). In China, cotton subsidies constitute more than 40 percent of gross farm receipts, compared to less than 20 percent in the US (Greenville 2017).

In addition to heavy subsidies, China supports cotton production by controlling imports, imposing tariffs of up to 40 percent on cotton imported outside its WTO-mandated TRQ commitment. Given the importance of the Chinese market and the high tariffs China imposes on

(US$ million)

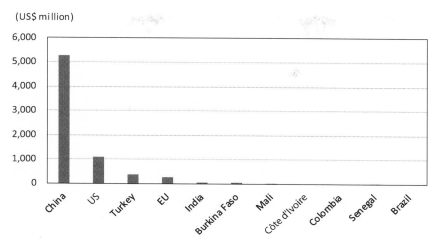

FIGURE 2.5 Global cotton subsidizers.
Note: Subsidies provided by some countries are too small to be visible on the graph.
Source: ICAC 2016

cotton, if China were to allow cotton from LDCs to enter duty free, it would provide a significant boost to African cotton producers. However, while China has offered Duty-Free Quota-Free (DFQF) access to LDCs, it excluded many of their most important exports, including cotton (ICTSD 2013). When LDCs requested at the WTO that China expand DFQF access to cover cotton, China refused. In fact, since 2014, with the objective of reducing government stocks, China has sharply restricted imports—to at or near the level of its WTO TRQ obligation of about 1 million tons (compared to import levels as much as six times higher in the past) (ICAC 2016a; ICAC 2016b).

With its extraordinary market power and massive cotton stocks, China effectively dictates the market for global cotton prices, leaving farmers in rich and poor countries alike at the mercy of Chinese government policy (Imboden 2014; Meyer and Terazono 2014). This is evident in the effects of China's cotton reserves, which, as one exporter summarized, led to "a meteoric rise and subsequent crash in global cotton prices."[80] China's growing cotton stockpile initially contributed to increasing world prices, but then when China started selling off its reserves its imports were drastically curtailed and global prices plummeted (Anderson 2017). The global fallout from this drop in prices has hit poor countries the hardest (Sneyd 2016). In Zambia, for instance, the national farmers union leader reports that there has been a steep fall in incomes, causing serious pain in a sector that employs 21 percent of the population and making life "increasingly difficult" for farmers (Meyer and Terazono 2014). Lower prices are expected to continue until China runs down its enormous stockpile. As one negotiator stated, China's cotton stocks are "the cloud hanging over the market keeping prices down—and everyone's fear is that they will actually export."[81]

China's strategy of using heavy subsidization and import barriers to support its cotton farmers causes significant harm to farmers elsewhere. As Adam Sneyd (2016: 41) puts it, China has "exported pain" by transferring hardship to poorer and weaker countries. Although China's per capita GDP ($8,000) is indeed small compared to that of the US, it vastly exceeds that of the C-4 countries (between $650 and $800).[82] China has considerable resources available to address poverty and rural development, as well as a broad array of alternative policy mechanisms it could use to achieve these objectives without the harmful spillover effects of trade-distorting agricultural subsidies.

The importance of the US in global cotton markets—and hence its subsidies—has diminished; today, world cotton prices are set more by China's trade policies than those of the US (IDEAS Centre 2013). This is not to let the US off the hook. To be clear, US cotton policies remain part of the problem, but as the volume of its subsidies and its market share have declined, the impact of its subsidies on global markets is now dwarfed by that of China. On cotton, to quote one negotiator: "It's no longer the US that's most important. Now it's China. Cotton production is declining in the US, but in China it's been growing—along with their subsidies."[83] Consequently, according to Nicolas Imboden (2014), of the IDEAS Center, an NGO that has been the principal advisor to the C-4 at the WTO: "any solution to the cotton issue will have to include China." As a long-term advocate for developing countries on the cotton issue argued: "At this point, it's no longer possible to just go after the US— you have to put China into the same basket because there is no question they have a major impact on global cotton prices and the exports of the C-4. Clearly, both China *and* the US have to do something."[84]

However, WTO negotiations on cotton have become blocked by the standoff between the US and China. US cotton subsidies, production, and market share have all fallen since the late-1990s, particularly since its reforms following the Brazil cotton dispute (UNCTAD 2016). Yet, from the US's perspective, having reformed its own cotton programs, it now finds itself the victim of China's subsidies. As a US congressional official stated:

Our producers are incredibly frustrated and upset. On cotton, our biggest competitor is China, and look at what they're doing—their subsidies are huge and they've wreaked havoc on the market with their policies. We went through this tortured process to reform our cotton programs ... and now China is giving support we haven't since the '80s. We eliminated our programs and now the consequences of what China is doing are bearing down on markets, with prices collapsing, and our guys don't have the programs to support them. It makes folks furious. Anything that demands more of us in isolation, that puts our producers at a disadvantage, it's just not fair. With all that China's doing, we'd just be handing over the market to them.[85]

The US thus refuses to reduce its cotton subsidies further if China's are not similarly disciplined.

For China, however, its cotton subsidies are considered untouchable, a matter of national security as well as agricultural policy. The autonomous region of Xinjiang—a restive area in the far northwest of the country along the Central Asian border that is home to China's Muslim Uighur minority, whose separatist movement has been violently repressed by the government—accounts for more than half of China's cotton production. There most cotton is grown by the Xinjiang Production and Construction Corps, a quasi-military agricultural conglomerate consisting of Han Chinese settlers (Hornby 2015). As one former Chinese official stated:

Cotton in China is extremely political. Most cotton is produced in Xinjiang, where there is lots of regional and political instability—like Tibet. And that is where China is devoting lots of resources to supporting producers. Otherwise they will want to separate. So when others try to say you can't support your cotton producers, no way. It's like asking the US to stop supporting the rust belt—or its cotton producers, for that matter.[86]

China's subsidies and other protections for its cotton sector are closely tied to an internal process of colonization, suppression of the Muslim minority, and maintaining internal control over its territory. China has therefore thwarted efforts to discipline its cotton subsidies at the WTO.

China is now a significant part of the cotton problem, but it has sought to evade any responsibility in WTO cotton negotiations. One negotiator characterized its strategy as, "we're the elephant, but we just have to make our self as little and as invisible as possible."[87] China continues to insist that all blame for the cotton problem lies solely with the US and maintain that as a developing country it is on the same side as the African countries and LDCs in fighting the US. As another negotiator stated, "China keeps insisting 'cotton is not our issue'. They are trying to keep out of it—and they manage to because others are not putting them on the spot."[88] As in the domestic support negotiations more broadly, the C-4 and other cotton-producing developing countries are extremely reluctant to complain about China's policies: as one of their advisors explained, "They're afraid of China. They hate the Americans and Europeans but they're not afraid of them. They feel dependent on China [as the biggest cotton market]. And of course China is also giving lots of money to these countries."[89] China is providing substantial sums of aid, investment, and credit across the developing world. Plus, following in the footsteps of the US, China is now attempting to evade pressures to reform its cotton policies by providing aid to cotton-producing countries in Africa—as one negotiator bluntly summarized, "that's what happens—give them money to make them shut up."[90] The value of this aid, however, is only a small fraction of the potential gains that could be reaped by poor countries from the elimination of cotton subsidies.

Given their cost-competitiveness, the removal of global cotton subsidies would lead to a significant shift in production to African countries and increased trade volumes sourced from the region (Greenville 2017). But, as with the broader negotiations on domestic support, efforts to negotiate new disciplines on cotton have become mired in finger-pointing between the US and China. As one negotiator from an African cotton-producing LDC summarized:

The US says "China, you tell us you only subsidize poor farmers, but if you look in aggregate, you see how important they are in distorting the market." Then the argument from China is "we're not exporting, you the US are exporting, so you are more dangerous for the C-4 and LDCs than me." China points at the US like it is guilty and the US in return points to China as guilty. It's like ping pong. "You're responsible." "No, not me, you're responsible." But, in the end, both have the same impact on us [the C-4 and LDCs] and nothing is being done.[91]

Another participant similarly observed:

Cotton acreage in the US is declining. Increasingly the US has said we can negotiate this issue if China's policies are on the table as well. But that's politically impossible for China. So the poor C-4 countries are just getting squeezed between the two giants. China has dug in its heels, the US has dug in its heels, and there's been virtually no progress on cotton.[92]

Meanwhile, however, he continued, "the real market dynamics, beyond the games people play at WTO, really matter for the lives of people on the ground—they have real consequences." Weaker developing countries thus find themselves caught in a struggle between the system's two dominant powers—the US and China. While both the US and China present themselves as victims of the other's agricultural subsidies, arguably the chief victims in this battle are the world's poorest and most vulnerable developing countries. With the US and China at loggerheads, each blaming the other for the cotton problem, efforts to discipline cotton subsidies via the WTO have come to a standstill.

## CONCLUSION

As this analysis has shown, while agricultural subsidies remain a highly contentious issue at the WTO, the dynamics of the negotiations have changed dramatically as a result of contemporary power shifts. The traditional conception of the agricultural subsidies issue—articulated through a North–South lens with the US and other developed countries as perpetrators and developing countries as victims—has been turned on its head by China's emergence as the world's largest subsidizer. From a North–South struggle, the primary axis of conflict at the WTO has shifted to a battle between the US and China, heavily shaped by the hegemonic rivalry between the two states. An intractable conflict between the US and China has thwarted any progress on the establishment of a new and strengthened set of disciplines on agricultural subsidies, with negative consequences for much of the developing world. This case underscores the centrality of US–China conflict in contemporary multilateral trade negotiations, and how it is blocking rule-making in an area of critical importance to global development.

The shifting landscape of agricultural subsidies also highlights the problem with continuing to treat China as a developing country in multilateral trade negotiations and allowing it to be shielded from subsidy reductions, given the massive aggregate volume of subsidies it is providing and their damaging effects on other developing countries. China is now so big, as a market and a subsidizer, that its policies have systemic implications—not only for global markets but also for development in the rest of the Global South. As this case demonstrates, developing countries remain at the mercy of the dominant powers. The US and other advanced-industrialized states were once seen as the chief barrier to making the trading system work for developing countries. However, what the case of agricultural subsidies shows is that it is no longer just the US or other rich countries that are barring important changes to global trade rules that would benefit developing countries, but also China. China has become a major part of the problem: along with the US, it is now blocking pro-development reform of the trading system at the WTO.

# 3

## The Dragon in the World's Oceans: Fisheries Subsidies

Like agriculture, fisheries have also been delinked from the Doha Round and identified as a priority target for a standalone agreement at the WTO. The goal is to create an international regime for the regulation of fisheries subsidies. Not only are fisheries subsidies seen as a critical development issue, like agriculture, but they are also identified as a pressing environmental problem. Subsidies are contributing to a global fisheries crisis by fueling overcapacity and overfishing, leading to the decimation of global fish stocks and plummeting fish harvests. For many developing and least-developed countries dependent on fisheries for food security and livelihoods, overfishing has profound economic implications. Within the trading system, US leadership has been the crucial driver behind this issue from the start: it was the US who first put fisheries subsidies on the agenda at the WTO, and the US has been the primary actor pushing for ambitious disciplines. While the fisheries negotiations were halted with the collapse of the Doha Round, they have since gained new life.

The impetus behind reviving the WTO negotiations on fisheries subsidies has come from the UN Sustainable Development Goals, which identified eliminating harmful fisheries subsidies as a major objective of the international community. Since 2015, there has been substantial momentum and high-level political will behind renewed efforts to secure a WTO fisheries subsidies agreement (Tipping 2018). Indeed, since the 2017 Buenos Aires Ministerial, fisheries subsidies has been one of the only active areas of multilateral negotiations at the WTO. Achieving an agreement on fisheries subsidies is thus seen as essential to demonstrating the continued relevance of the WTO as a negotiating forum and rule-making authority in international trade.

As this chapter will show, however, China's rise has created severe difficulties for constructing global disciplines on fisheries subsidies. China has become a pivotal actor in the fisheries negotiations, alongside the US, and the issue of how China should be treated within any new disciplines has become a central point of contention. The 2005 Hong Kong Ministerial Declaration enshrined the principle of SDT for developing countries as an integral part of the fisheries negotiations. Given the importance of fisheries to many developing countries, and the relatively less developed nature of their industries, the principle of extending SDT to developing countries was then widely supported and relatively uncontroversial. At that time, developed countries—such as the EU, Japan, and South Korea—were identified as the key source of the problem and the focus was on reducing their subsidies. China was not even on the radar: while China was already a major fish producer, its central government did not then provide fisheries subsidies. It was only in 2006—the year after Hong Kong—that the Chinese central government began subsidizing its fishing sector. Since then, the rapid growth of its subsidies has made China the world's largest subsidizer. Heavy subsidies have fueled the aggressive outward expansion of China's industrial fishing fleet across the world's oceans, with the result that China now has the largest fishing industry in the world.

The question of whether China should have access to SDT has become a fundamental issue of dispute in the negotiations, and the chief stumbling block to an agreement to discipline fisheries subsidies. China has demanded, as a developing country, access to SDT that would exempt its fisheries subsidies from proposed new disciplines. Yet this is a case where China is clearly not like other developing countries. Given the massive size of China's industrial fishing fleet and the large scale of its subsidies, China's subsidies have serious systemic consequences. As a result, exempting China from WTO fisheries subsidy disciplines would severely undermine the objective of disciplines and have negative implications for both the environment and other developing countries. The case of fisheries subsidies thus provides a striking illustration of the problem with treating China like any other developing country.

Analysis of the fisheries subsidies negotiations underscores how the bifurcation of economic power and development status embodied by a rising China—in this case, the divergence between the might of China's massive industrial fishing sector and its continued status as a developing country characterized by relatively low incomes nationally and particularly in its fisheries sector—is creating a vexing problem for global trade governance. As this case demonstrates, the issue of how China should be treated in global trade rules has become a central source of conflict in WTO negotiations.

## ENVIRONMENTAL AND DEVELOPMENT RATIONALE
## FOR DISCIPLINING FISHERIES SUBSIDIES

Fisheries subsidies have been identified as a critical environmental and development issue. An estimated $35 billion in fisheries subsidies are provided worldwide (UNCTAD-FAO 2016). Fisheries subsidies take a variety of forms, including support for capital costs, operating costs, port infrastructure, processing facilities, income support, price support, and subsidies for acquisition of fishing access rights. From an environmental perspective, not all subsidies are harmful: some subsidies have beneficial impacts in supporting fisheries resources, such as those to fisheries management programs, R&D, and investments in fisheries resources (Sumaila, Bellmann, and Tipping 2014). The problem, however, is with subsidies—such as for vessel construction and fuel—that reduce the cost of fishing and related activities, which contribute to the build-up of excess capacity, create incentives to overfish and lead to the overexploitation of fish stocks (Sumaila et al. 2013). Overcapacity and overfishing—"too many vessels chasing too few fish"—has a debilitating impact on fragile marine ecosystems and undermines the sustainability of costal and off-shore fisheries. Nearly two-thirds of all subsidies provided to the global fishing industry—or approximately $20 billion annually—are capacity-enhancing (UNCTAD-FAO-UNEP 2016).

As a result, the global fishing fleet is severely over-capitalized (CUTS 2017). With a massive increase in fishing capacity and the rapid depletion of fish stocks, the productivity of fishing harvests has plummeted (World Bank 2009). According to the UN, 90 percent of global fish stocks are already fully exploited and almost a third are overfished (fished at a biologically unsustainable level) (FAO 2016). Subsidies allow fleets to intensify and broaden the scope of their fishing and have played a major role in the expansion of distant water fishing in particular. Backed by heavy subsidies, major industrial fishing nations are able to build and operate larger boats that can travel greater distances and remain at sea for longer periods, in order to fish in the high seas or in the national exclusive economic zones (EEZs)[1] of other states (McCauley et al. 2018). According to fisheries experts, "without subsidies, high-seas fishing at the global scale that we are currently witnessing would be unlikely"

(Sala et al. 2018). Indeed, without subsidies, it is estimated that more than half of current global fishing activity in the high seas would not exist (Sala et al. 2018).

Fisheries subsidies have significant distributional consequences. Worldwide, 86 percent of people employed in fishing are small-scale, artisanal fishers (*Bridges Weekly* 2017b). Yet the vast majority of global fisheries subsidies—approximately 85 percent—go to large-scale fishing activities (Schuhbauer et al. 2017). Subsidies thus affect the dynamics by which global fisheries resources are divided, "shap[ing] competition between large-scale, capital-intense industrial fisheries and small-scale fisheries, with cascading effects upon the health, prosperity, and well-being of the communities that depend on small-scale fisheries" (McCauley et al. 2018).

Consequently, fisheries subsidies are not just an environmental issue but also an economic one, with particularly significant implications for the Global South. Fisheries subsidies create an un-level playing field between richer countries that can afford to provide subsidies and poorer countries that cannot, leaving the latter at a significant disadvantage. Moreover, developing and least-developed countries are especially vulnerable to the impact of stock depletion, due to their disproportionate reliance on fisheries.

The heaviest economic and social dependence on fisheries is in the developing world, where fisheries play a crucial role in livelihoods and nutrition security (Tipping 2017). Fisheries are an important source of nutrition: over 3 billion people rely on fish for over one-fifth of their protein, and in some LDCs and small island developing states, fish contributes more than 50 percent of total animal protein intake (FAO 2016). Fish production is also a vital source of employment, directly or indirectly supporting the livelihoods of an estimated 10 percent to 12 percent of the world's population, who are involved in fishing, processing, and related activities (CUTS 2017; Tipping 2017).

For many coastal and island developing countries, fisheries are an important contributor to economic growth and development. Fish is one of the most traded sectors of the world food economy, and this trade has expanded considerably in recent decades, fueled by growing production and high demand (FAO 2016). Since 2010, developing countries have been the main exporters of fish. Fish exports are essential to many developing economies, accounting for more than 40 percent of the total value of traded commodities for some island states (FAO 2016). Fisheries trade thus represents a significant source of foreign exchange for many developing countries, in addition to its importance in income generation, employment, food security, and nutrition (FAO 2016). As one Ambassador for a small island state summarized: "We are dependent on fish—for our livelihoods, our economies, and a significant food source. It is our only resource."[2]

Subsidies have enabled countries with large industrial fishing fleets to exploit resources beyond their own waters, in the high seas close to or in the EEZs of poor countries, at the expense of local fishing communities in those countries (Tipping 2017). Fish is an important source of food for over 400 million Africans, for example, mostly supplied by small-scale, artisanal production (Fevrier and Dugal 2016). Yet, as in many developing countries, the technology used for fishing is often very basic: in Africa, nearly 65 percent of vessels used for fishing are not motorized (FAO 2016). As a result, most of the fish caught on Africa's coasts are caught by heavily subsidized foreign fleets (Fevrier and Dugal 2016). In addition, overcapacity fueled by subsidies has resulted in high rates of illegal, unreported, and unregulated (IUU) fishing, which, due to a lack of enforcement capacity, affects developing countries most heavily (Tipping 2017).

For fishery-dependent economies, prohibiting subsidies that contribute to overfishing is critical to their economic welfare. A WTO agreement on fisheries subsidies is therefore identified as a major priority for developing countries. As a negotiator for an African LDC stated:

We are a coastal country but a net importer of fish. The fish we import is fish these other countries catch in our seas, take back to their country to process and then sell back to us. When you look at the operators fishing in our seas, how many are from [our country] or other African countries? All these operators from around the world come into our waters, catching the fish and making our waters poorer. Then when our fisherman go to fish they are not able to catch [enough] and the consequence is they can't feed their families. We have more than one million fishers and their families living on our coast. So you can imagine how significant disciplines would be for [our country].[3]

In short, to quote the Peruvian Ambassador to the WTO and Chair of the UN Oceans Forum, the "cost of not acting to address harmful fishing subsidies is extremely high" (*Bridges Weekly* 2017b).

The urgency of the need for WTO disciplines to address global fisheries subsidies is firmly established. According to the Chair of the fisheries negotiations, there is a "strong consensus" within the WTO "that the state of global fisheries resources is alarming and getting worse."[4] All WTO members, he continued, "recognize that this is a crisis of exceptionally serious implications for all humankind, and particularly for the poor in many countries who are heavily dependent on fisheries as a source of nutrition and employment." And there is widespread recognition "that subsidies play a major role in contributing to these problems," thus necessitating WTO action. As the Chair indicated, fisheries represents a classic tragedy of the commons problem: pursuit of individual payoffs leads to overfishing, which in turn imposes economic loss—as well as severely negative environmental effects—on all parties involved.[5] It is clear that the economic costs of overfishing are significant: the World Bank (2017) estimates that allowing global fish stocks to recover from over-exploitation could substantially increase annual harvests, yielding $83 billion in economic benefits and significant improvements in the incomes and food security of communities that depend on fisheries. But this is a problem that requires collective action: it is widely believed that fisheries subsidies, like other forms of subsidies, can only be effectively addressed through multilateral cooperation at the WTO. The prospect of a WTO agreement on fisheries subsidies is therefore seen as a "triple win," in which trade liberalization could bring substantial benefits to the environ-ment and development (Campling and Havice 2013). As a former African negotiator stated: "Here is a clear opportunity for members to do some-thing to significantly improve the well-being of the world."[6]

## US HEGEMON SETS THE AGENDA

The impetus behind the WTO fisheries negotiations came from the US, who initiated and drove the negotiations, despite opposition from certain other major powers. Led by the US, the WTO set out to create an entirely new set of sector-specific disciplines for fisheries subsidies, and the US has been the key *demandeur* leading efforts to secure far-reaching disciplines. As one former developed country negotiator stated, "fisheries subsidies has always been a priority for the US and the US has always been the heavyweight in the corner for having ambitious disciplines from the begin-ning."[7] Environmental groups heavily advocated for US leadership on the issue. As one negotiator stated: "the US has a very strong environmental lobby that pushed very hard on this, and it had support from high-level members of Congress on both sides." Advancing disciplines on fisheries subsidies at the WTO also served broader strategic objectives for the US. In the late 1990s and early 2000s, the WTO came under intense criticism and protest from civil society actors concerned about the harmful environ-mental impacts of its trade rules. Seeking to launch a new round of WTO negotiations, the US was eager to blunt such criticism and overcome opposition from environmental groups by demonstrating that the WTO could be harnessed to achieve environmentally desirable outcomes.

In addition, the US has domestic fishing interests, with relatively high operating costs (Campling and Havice 2016). The US has traditionally ranked far behind other major powers—the EU and Japan, historically, and now China—in the level of subsidies it provides to its fishing industry, leaving US fleets at a competitive disadvantage (UNEP 2011). Although the US provides nearly $2 billion in subsidies annually, the vast majority (85 percent) are for fisheries management, enforcement, and research rather than capacity-enhancing subsidies (EU 2016). The US fishing industry would therefore benefit from restricting the subsidies provided to its competitors and joined US environmental groups in supporting disciplines (Campling and Havice 2016; UNEP 2011). While US efforts to secure disciplines on fisheries subsidies were driven primarily by environmental objectives, rival negotiators are quick to point out that its motives were not entirely pure—this was an issue where the US could potentially score a significant environmental win, at no commercial cost to itself, and where new subsidy disciplines could in fact moderately improve its position vis-à-vis its commercial competitors.[8] Fisheries subsidies was thus an issue where environmental objectives and US commercial interests aligned, enabling the US to play a leading role in advocating for disciplines.

In the lead-up to the 1999 Seattle Ministerial, the US announced its intention to seek a negotiating mandate on fisheries subsidies as part of the anticipated new round (Crutsinger 1999; Williams 1999). The US mobilized support from a number of countries, including both developed countries with strong and largely unsubsidized fishing industries—such as Iceland, Australia, New Zealand, and Norway—and developing countries concerned about the negative impacts of foreign subsidies on their own fishing sectors—such as Peru, Argentina, Chile, and the Philippines. However, US efforts to bring fisheries subsidies into the WTO faced opposition from what were then the WTO's other two major powers, the EU and Japan. Both significant subsidizers, the EU and Japan were strongly resistant to international action to reform fisheries subsidies, questioning the link between subsidies and resource depletion and arguing that such issues were beyond the remit of the WTO and better left to bodies such as the UN Food and Agriculture Organization (UNEP 2011). Despite their opposition, driven by the "vigorous diplomatic leadership" of the US and aided by an aggressive media campaign by the World Wildlife Fund (WWF) that specifically targeted the EU, the fisheries subsidies issue gained substantial momentum in advance of the Seattle Ministerial (UNEP 2011). By the time the Ministerial began, fisheries subsidies had become a prominent issue on the agenda and preliminary drafts of the ministerial declaration contained language launching work on fisheries subsidies within the anticipated new round (UNEP 2011). The Seattle Ministerial ultimately collapsed, however, due to conflict over other negotiating items, delaying the launch of the round to the Doha Ministerial two years later.

Fisheries subsidies was on the "short list" of American demands for the new round, and, driven by the US, became part of the Doha Round. Although the EU remained resistant to disciplines, its stance was muted by the fact it had sought to position itself as a leading proponent of addressing "trade and environment" issues, making outright opposition to including fisheries subsidies in the Doha mandate impossible (UNEP 2011). Instead, as a fallback, the EU attempted to downgrade the issue by placing it under the remit of the WTO's Committee on Trade and Environment, which would effectively relegate it to the periphery of the Doha Round. The US prevailed, however, and fisheries subsidies emerged from the Doha Ministerial as a key item in the mainstream negotiations over WTO rules. Fisheries subsidies were placed in the Negotiating Group on Rules, to be negotiated alongside other issues (such as anti-dumping duties) whose commercial importance gave them high political priority within the round. This reinforced the seriousness of the fisheries subsidies negotiations and increased the likelihood of arriving at meaningful disciplines by creating possibilities for bargaining trade-offs with other core negotiating areas (UNEP 2011).

Propelled by the US, at the 2005 Ministerial in Hong Kong, which represented an important milestone in elaborating the Doha mandate, members agreed to negotiate "to strengthen disciplines on subsidies in the fisheries sector, including through the prohibition of certain forms of fisheries subsidies that contribute to overcapacity and over-fishing" (WTO 2005). States also established that the final agreement would include SDT:

Appropriate and effective special and differential treatment for developing and least-developed Members should be an integral part of the fisheries subsidies negotiations, taking into account the importance of this sector to development priorities, poverty reduction, and livelihood and food security concerns.

Affirming this commitment to SDT for developing countries was relatively non-controversial at the time. Importantly, the Chinese central government was not then even providing fisheries subsidies, and most contemporaneous accounts of the negotiations made little or no mention of China. Instead, the conflict over fisheries subsidies continued to center primarily on the US and others seeking stringent disciplines, on the one side, and their principal opponents, the EU and Japan, on the other.

### SUBSIDIES AND THE GLOBAL EXPANSION OF CHINA'S FISHING INDUSTRY

Although China was a peripheral player in the initial phase of the fisheries negotiations, the dynamics of the negotiations changed dramatically in subsequent years. China became an increasingly central player, as large subsidies fueled the explosive growth of its fishing industry over the next decade. China, as a developing country, has sought SDT exemptions to allow it to continue subsidizing its fishing sector. Yet, while China remains a developing country, it has not only joined but now leads the ranks of the large industrial fishing nations. Disciplining Chinese subsidies has therefore become a key objective of many states, and its demands for SDT a prime issue of contestation.

As the *New York Times* put it, "when it comes to global fishing operations," China has emerged as "the indisputable king of the sea" (Jacobs 2017). China now dominates the global fishing industry: it has developed the world's largest fishing fleet and is the largest fisheries producer, consumer, importer, and exporter (FAO 2016; see Figures 3.1 and 3.2). China alone accounts for over a third of global fish catch and over 60 percent of global aquaculture production (EU 2016; FAO 2016). Fueled by rising incomes, China now accounts for 38 percent of global fish consumption (FAO 2018: 62). The value of China's fisheries exports increased nearly five-fold, from $4.5 billion to $21 billion, between 2002 and 2014 (EU 2016).

The dramatic growth of China's fishing industry has been driven by outward expansion—moving from fishing in local waters to offshore waters, other countries' EEZs, and the high seas (Zhang and Wu 2017). Backed by heavy subsidies, China's long-distance fishing fleet has expanded at an extremely rapid rate: the annual catch of its distant water fishery grew by 80 percent between 2010 and 2016 (Godfrey 2018a). China now has the world's largest and furthest-ranging fishing operation, accounting for 42 percent of global fishing activity and outstripping the next ten biggest countries combined: Chinese vessels spent 17 million hours fishing in 2016; the next biggest was Taiwan, with 2.2 million

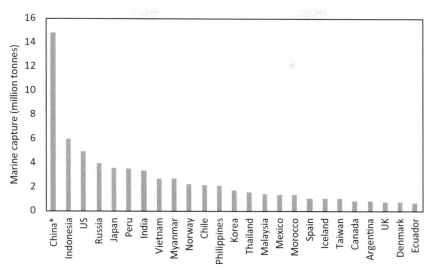

FIGURE 3.1 Marine capture production: top 25 producers.
* Evidence that China chronically under-reports its distant water fishery capture
by a factor of ten or more (Potts et al. 2017; Zhang and Wu 2017) suggests the
above figure profoundly underestimates China's actual capture.
Source: FAO 2016

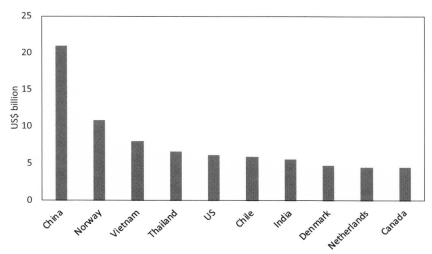

FIGURE 3.2 Top fish exporters (US$ billion).
Source: FAO 2016

hours of fishing (Kroodsma et al. 2018). In just two years, from 2012 to 2014, the number of Chinese vessels involved in distant water fishing—fishing in the high seas or in other countries' territorial waters—grew from 1,830 to 2,460 (Greenpeace 2016). In comparison, the US has only 225 large-scale vessels with tonnage and capacity equivalent to China's vessels for distant water fishing (Greenpeace 2016); China's long-distance fleet is thus now more than ten times larger than that of the US. And China accounts for nearly 40 percent of fishing activity in the EEZs of other developing countries (McCauley et al. 2018).

Until the late 1990s, the growth of China's fishing industry was driven primarily by fishing in its territorial waters (Zhang and Wu 2017). Subnational governments provided substantial support to fishing communities and companies to expand and intensify their activities. Yet subsidies led to overfishing: fish stocks plummeted, and most of China's own fisheries resources, particularly commercial stocks, are now heavily depleted (Mallory 2013). The Chinese government has acknowledged, for instance, that there are practically "no fish" left in the East China Sea (Hancock 2018b). In its domestic waters, Chinese policy shifted towards efforts to conserve and restore its fishery resources, including strictly restricting fishing and paying fishers to scrap small near-sea boats (Hancock 2018b). But both the central and sub-national levels of government are eager to maintain jobs on fishing boats and in processing plants (Hornby 2017). Having severely damaged its own stocks and with excess capacity in its fisheries sector (FAO 2018), China has responded by providing subsidies—for diesel, shipbuilding, and processing—to enable its fleet to expand into international waters (Hancock 2018a).

The Chinese government identified fisheries as a strategic industry and made expanding the country's long-distance fishing fleet an explicit policy goal (Sala et al. 2018). Subsidies have played a major role in the explosive growth of China's fishing industry, helping to propel a structural transformation from small-scale to industrial fishing, and from local to distant water fishing. China's fleet has expanded far beyond its own local and regional waters and now fishes heavily, for example, off the coasts of West Africa, Central and South America, and Antarctica. Chinese boats can range such vast distances due to a tenfold increase in diesel subsidies between 2006 and 2011, after which Beijing stopped releasing statistics (Hornby 2017). Fuel subsidies have played a major role in the explosive growth of China's distant water fishing industry (Greenpeace 2016), as fuel costs account for the largest share of operating costs (approximately 60 percent), especially for high seas fishing.[9] According to the head of

China's largest private fishing company, Ningtai Ocean: "If it weren't for the diesel subsidy under these conditions most fishermen would fold. Before, conditions were better and we were profitable without the subsidies. Now, we need them" (quoted in Hornby 2017).

The same dynamics of overcapacity present in other Chinese industrial sectors—such as steel, aluminum, cement, construction, and coal power— are thus also evident in its fishing industry. Subsidies have led to "massive overcapacity" in China's fishing industry (Sala et al. 2018), and China is now effectively seeking to "export" its overcapacity by providing subsidies to support fishing far from its own shores. In the case of fisheries, though, China's response to overcapacity and the depletion of fish stocks in its own waters—encouraging its fleet to fish in international waters—has put added pressure on global resources.

Historically, developed countries were the main source of fisheries subsidies, but China has now become the world's largest subsidizer (OECD 2017b). While local governments had been supporting fishing for several decades, the Chinese central government only began providing subsidies in 2006, as part of its effort to bolster rural incomes. These subsidies grew extremely rapidly. The central government now provides an estimated \$6.5 billion in annual subsidies to the fishing sector, the largest portion of which (over 90 percent) is for fuel (EU 2016; Mallory 2013). It also provides a significant volume of subsidies for the construction, upgrading, and renovation of fishing vessels, though the full extent of these subsidies has not been disclosed (Greenpeace 2016; Mallory 2016). The above figure also does not include subsidies provided at the sub-national level—by provincial, municipal, and county governments— which, while highly opaque and non-transparent, are believed to be substantial (EU 2016). It is estimated that the vast majority of China's subsidies—approximately 95 percent—are environmentally harmful (Mallory 2013).

China's subsidies are an important driver of fishing activities that would otherwise be unable to generate sufficient revenue and thus not be economically viable. Analysis has shown that most of China's high seas fishing activity would not be profitable without subsidies (Sala et al. 2018). It takes a month for Chinese fishing vessels to travel to West Africa, for example (Jacobs 2017). Fuel subsidies—providing half-price or even fully subsidized diesel (Greenpeace 2016)—enable China's fishing fleet to cheaply travel vast distances and with refueling at sea remain at sea for long periods of time (some boats for as much as two years). According to an industry analyst, "subsidies from central government are often the difference between profit and loss at big players like Shanghai Kaichuang and CNFC" (Godfrey 2017).

## Economic and Geopolitical Motives behind China's Subsidies

Many fisheries experts now classify China as a "developed country," due to the size and level of sophistication of its fishing industry (Sumaila et al. 2013). However, despite the extraordinary expansion of China's industrial fishery, incomes for those employed in the sector remain far lower than in developed countries: an average fisher in China earns just $2,320 annually (Zhang and Wu 2017). To put this in perspective, the World Bank's poverty line for upper-middle-income countries like China is approximately $2,000 annually ($5.50 per day). While the per capita GDP of the country as a whole now places China in the ranks of an upper-middle-income country, the incomes of China's fishing sector are comparable to the average incomes of a lower-middle-income country. And even these low incomes are higher than incomes available in agriculture, attracting peasant workers from China's inland provinces to join the fishing industry along its coast (Zhang and Wu 2017). Fishing thus represents a source of higher-paid employment that has helped to absorb surplus agricultural labor migrating from the countryside. Although China is now an industrial fishing behemoth, the low incomes in its fishing sector are a sign that it remains very much a developing country. For China, supporting its fishing sector is part of its developmental strategy and effort to support rural incomes.

In defending its subsidies at the WTO, China maintains that they are needed to cushion low-income fishers from poverty. Critics, however, argue that China is providing subsidies in forms that have the worst effects on the environment and on other developing countries, and that it has alternative and better means at its disposal to boost the incomes of its fishers. Support for operating costs—like fuel subsidies—plays a major role in contributing to overfishing but is least likely to benefit fishers' incomes, as much of the benefit is captured by providers of these inputs (Tipping 2018). Direct income support would instead be a far more effective way for China to support its fishers and would have less harmful environmental effects. However, China's goal is not just to support incomes: its fisheries subsidies are driven by a much larger and more complex set of factors.

The objective of China's fisheries subsidies is not simply to boost incomes, but specifically to increase the output and global dominance of its industrial fishery, in order to advance a combination of interlinked development, food security, and geopolitical and security objectives. China's fishing industry is of considerable economic importance: generating nearly $300 billion annually; it directly employs over 14 million people and supports over 10,000 fish processing companies (Mallory 2013; Zhang and Wu 2017). The continued expansion of China's fishing industry into offshore and distant waters is part of its larger "going global" strategy, encouraging the international expansion of Chinese firms and industries. In its 12th National Five-Year Plan released in 2010, the central government identified fisheries as a strategic industry and made the continued expansion of China's distant water fishery a key national policy goal (Zhang and Wu 2017). Backed by heavy state subsidies, the government's specific policy objectives include continuing to "vigorously develop" high seas fishing, supported by the construction of overseas fishing "bases," providing port, processing, and logistics facilities for China's fishing fleet, as well as subsidies for building, modernizing, and upgrading distant water vessels to further increase the overall capacity of its fleet, and increasing exploration and exploitation of previously untapped fisheries resources, such as in Antarctica (EU 2016; Mallory 2013). China's subsidies have been critical to driving the process of industrial transformation and upgrading in China's fishing industry to date, and China has made it clear that this is a process it intends to continue.

The continued expansion of its international fishing operations is part of China's aim of becoming a "Great Ocean Power" (Godfrey 2018a). For Chinese policymakers, growth of its distant water fishery and associated infrastructure is not only important for economic development, but contributes to advancing the country's maritime interests (Zhang 2016: 67). China is using subsidies to help consolidate its dominant position in regional and international waters. The Chinese leadership has increasingly emphasized the strategic importance of its international fishing operations, amid China's growing assertiveness in international affairs (Zhang and Wu 2017). Their objective is to build China into a global maritime power, in order to enhance its comprehensive national power, increase its international competitiveness, and minimize its vulnerability to risk (Mallory 2015). At the 18th National Party Congress in 2012, then President Hu Jintao pledged that China would become a major sea power by "enhancing its capacity for exploiting marine resources, developing marine economy, protecting the marine ecological environment, and resolutely safeguarding China's maritime rights and interests"

(Zhang and Wu 2017). Analysts report that China's emphasis on maritime power has continued under President Xi Jinping and, if anything, grown even more assertive (Mallory 2015). Fisheries subsidies are thus part of a broader geopolitical strategy.

The fishing industry has been identified, for instance, as one of the priority areas for the Belt and Road Initiative (BRI), with support from both the central government and China's major fishing provinces (Zhang and Wu 2017). As part of its plans to construct the 21st Century Maritime Silk Road, the maritime component of the Belt and Road Initiative, China is engaged in the construction of overseas fishing bases across Africa and the Pacific (Godfrey 2018b). This infrastructure is intended to support the continued development and increased efficiency and competitiveness of the Chinese fleet, as well as expanding China's overseas presence.

Similarly, China is using its heavily subsidized fishing fleet to bolster its maritime claims in the East and South China Seas (Erickson and Kennedy 2016; Zhang and Bateman 2017). China's adjacent regional seas are rich in fisheries resources: the South China Sea, for instance, accounts for a tenth of the global fish catch (*The Economist* 2017). Subsidies enable China's "fishing militia" to purchase larger boats and travel further into disputed territory. The central and provincial governments encourage boat owners to fish in and around the Spratly Islands (claimed by the Philippines), Paracel Islands (claimed by Vietnam), and Senkaku/Diaoyu Islands (claimed by Japan). The central government even provides dedicated subsidies for fishing in disputed territories: offshore fishing in waters near the Spratly Islands is not covered by China's South China Sea seasonal fishing ban, for instance, and those who fish there receive additional fuel subsidies under the Spratly Islands Special Fuel Subsidy program (Zhang and Wu 2017). Backed by the firepower of Chinese naval frigates, China's fishing militia has driven away thousands of Filipino fishers from the rich waters around the Spratly Islands (Jacobs 2017). In 1985, only thirteen small vessels from China regularly fished near the Spratly Islands, but in 2013, over 700 large Chinese fishing boats with over 14,000 fishers were engaged in fishing activities around the islands (Zhang and Wu 2017). By using civilian fishing craft and personnel to assert its territorial claims, China is able to avoid direct military-to-military conflict, while attempting to establish greater control over disputed waters. According to US officials, "China's strategy is to secure its objectives without jeopardizing the regional peace that has enabled its military and economic development" (United States 2016a). While maritime militias have a long history in China, they have gained new momentum since 2013, when President

Xi Jinping urged that their development be accelerated, leading to an increase in financial resources directed towards the fishing militia (Erickson and Kennedy 2016). China's fisheries subsidies are thus driven by a combination of economic and political motives that make it highly resistant to disciplines at the WTO.

## Implications for Other Developing Countries

The explosive growth of China's industrial fishery is having significant global impacts. China's fleet has expanded into forty countries' EEZs and most of the high seas (Zhang and Wu 2017). In the words of one industry analyst, China's large fishing companies:

> operate at an unfair advantage to international peer companies that don't get similar-sized checks from government. And they operate with complete dominance in the waters of West Africa and Pacific Island nations, where there's no significant local fleet to compete and where artisanal fishermen are being squeezed out of livelihoods just to help supposedly hard-up Chinese fishermen, who happen to be sailing on cheap fuel.
>
> (Godfrey 2017)

As a Greenpeace representative stated, "Chinese fleets are all over the world now, and without these subsidies, the industry just wouldn't be sustainable" (Jacobs 2017). Yet, he continued, for many coastal and island developing countries, "the impact has been devastating."

West Africa, for example, has some of the world's richest fishing grounds, but its fish stocks are rapidly being depleted as industrial trawlers comb the oceans (Doumbouya et al. 2017). Foreign fleets are "nearly pick[ing] clean the oceans off Senegal and other northwest African countries, ruining coastal economies," and whereas other industrial fishing countries (including the EU and Russia) were also once major culprits, increasingly, with China overtaking these competitors, it "stands alone as the major predator" (*New York Times* 2017). In West Africa, locals fishing from hand-hewn canoes have found themselves competing against "mega-trawlers" with mile-long nets that can sweep up everything from seabed to surface: indeed, "most Chinese ships are so large that they scoop up as many fish in a week as Senegalese boats catch in a year" (Jacobs 2017). Diminishing fish stocks have resulted in falling incomes for local fisherfolk and those employed in associated activities, along with reduced domestic food supply and higher prices. Senegal and other coastal countries, according to the former director of the country's oceanic research institute, now face "an unprecedented crisis" (Jacobs 2017).

For Senegal, "the ocean is the economic lifeblood": fishing supplies 85 percent of the country's protein consumption, seafood is its main export, and fishing-related industries employ nearly 20 percent of the work force (Jacobs 2017). As the president of a local fishing association stated: "We always thought that sea life was boundless. [But now] we are facing a catastrophe" (Jacobs 2017).

This situation is not limited to Africa. Chinese overfishing has been similarly documented in the South Pacific, Northwest Pacific, and South Atlantic (Mallory 2013). Even CNFC has acknowledged the link between the expansion of China's distant water fishing activities and the depletion of fish stocks, stating in its annual report that: "in recent years, the number of Chinese fishing vessels in South America has increased rapidly, and there has been a clear dilution of resources" (Harkell 2017).

Many countries, particularly in the developing world, are also concerned about the illegal fishing practices of China's fleet. Due to their limited enforcement capacity, the losses to many developing countries and LDCs from IUU fishing are considerable: West African countries alone are estimated to have lost nearly $25 billion to IUU fishing between 2010 and 2015 (Doumbouya et al. 2017). Analysis of illegal fishing suggests that Chinese vessels are among the worst offenders: along the West African coast, Chinese fishing boats report just 8 percent of their catch and an estimated two-thirds of Chinese vessels are engaged in illegal fishing and never caught (Jacobs 2017). According to Greenpeace, Chinese distant water fishing companies often ignore regional and international fisheries regulations (Greenpeace 2015). The IUU fishing practices employed by Chinese companies reputedly include: bottom trawling, illegal mesh size, under-reporting vessel tonnage and catch, transshipment at sea, harvesting prohibited species, automatic identification system inconsistencies, bycatch, and fishing in marine protected areas (Zhang and Wu 2017). In 2014, China Tuna Industry Group, the biggest company in China's tuna industry, publicly acknowledged that it had exceeded international fishing quotas for years and yet never been punished by Chinese authorities (Zhang and Wu 2017).

The massive global expansion of China's fishery and the practices of its fleet have raised tensions with other countries. Numerous countries around the world—including Ecuador, Argentina, Indonesia, South Korea, the Philippines, Senegal, Guinea, Sierra Leone, Guinea-Bissau, and South Africa—have all had confrontations with Chinese fishing fleets for illegally fishing in their waters (*The Guardian* 2016; Hancock 2018b; Reuters 2017b; Reuters 2017c). In 2016, for instance, Argentina shot at two Chinese fishing vessels illegally fishing in its EEZ in separate incidents. In a dramatic confrontation that garnered worldwide media attention, one of the Chinese vessels was captured, its crew evacuated, and the boat sunk by the Argentine navy (Schvartzman 2016).

As Joris Larik and Abhijit Singh (2017: 214) have written, "the immensity of the Chinese fishing industry and the significance of its policies for sustainable oceans governance is only starting to be fully appreciated." With the world's largest fishing fleet, China's fishing activities undoubtedly have a major impact on global fish stocks (Mallory 2013). The rapid expansion of China's fishery sector threatens the sustainability of ocean fisheries and biodiversity, and it also poses a significant challenge for efforts to construct effective subsidy disciplines at the WTO. Although China remains a developing country, given the size and reach of its industrial fishing fleet, providing China with an SDT exemption would severely undermine the efficacy of any new rules intended to discipline harmful fish subsidies and conserve global fish stocks.

## IMPACT OF A RISING CHINA ON THE FISHERIES SUBSIDY NEGOTIATIONS

The 2005 Hong Kong Ministerial had confirmed that SDT for developing countries would be part of any final WTO fisheries agreement, but the precise nature and extent of those flexibilities remained to be negotiated. The dispute over China's subsidies began to emerge two years later, when a concrete set of potential rules was first proposed, which included a narrow conception of SDT that would significantly restrict China's subsidies. China responded by demanding a far more expansive conception of SDT that would exempt its subsidies from disciplines, sparking an intense debate that persists today. The issue of SDT—particularly for China—became a major source of conflict, and one of the most controversial issues in the negotiations (*Bridges Weekly* 2010). Indeed, if anything it has only become more contentious over time as the size of China's subsidies and industrial fleet have continued to grow.

In 2007, the Chair of the negotiating group put forward a draft text of proposed new rules on fisheries subsidies.[10] The proposed rules were structured as a broad prohibition on capacity-enhancing subsidies (banning, for example, subsidies for vessel construction and operating costs), accompanied by a list of narrowly tailored exceptions (such as for beneficial subsidies), as well as specific SDT provisions for developing countries. LDCs would be exempt from the new disciplines, and other developing countries would have certain exemptions, particularly for subsidies to subsistence-type fishing in their territorial waters. The proposed rules would also prohibit subsidies to any vessels engaged in IUU fishing and subsidies affecting overfished stocks. For proponents of restrictions on fisheries subsidies, this was seen as a highly effective set of disciplines. These proposed rules were well-received by the US[11] and the so-called Friends of Fish, a group of countries supporting strong disciplines on fisheries subsidies (*Bridges Weekly* 2007). The proposed rules were also strongly endorsed by environmental organizations, such as WWF, which described them as containing "the necessary elements of success" to address harmful subsidies (WWF 2007).

The Chair's draft text prompted intense opposition from China, however, who objected to its proposed restrictions on SDT as "too rigid and overly burdensome" (*Bridges Weekly* 2007). For many, the motivation for providing SDT to developing countries is to ensure poor countries can provide support to vulnerable populations dependent on small-scale, subsistence-based fisheries, which have minimal environmental impact. But China has pushed for a much broader version of SDT that would allow it to continue to subsidize its industrial fishing fleet.

In the fisheries negotiations, China has generally sought to avoid tabling proposals on its own—as a US negotiator put it, "they know they are the target"[12]—and has instead chosen to make most of its proposals in conjunction with various other large emerging economies, such as India, Brazil, Indonesia, and Mexico, though the others have much smaller and less developed fisheries than China. In a series of proposals made with shifting configurations of other emerging economies, China expressed "strong concerns" with the Chair's draft text.[13] China argued that: "the provisions on special and differential treatment must provide effective, substantive flexibilities to developing countries" and "must allow developing countries to develop their fishing sector in a sustainable manner."[14] Furthermore, "in no case should conditionalities be inserted which would hamper our countries' developmental aspirations by means of rendering the S&DT provisions actually devoid of meaning."[15] China has firmly insisted that any "applicable controls should allow developing countries to achieve development priorities, poverty reduction, and address their livelihood and food security concerns."[16]

The Chair's text proposed a differentiated SDT for different types of fisheries activities (a multi-tiered or "sliding-scale" approach). Subsidies to the smallest-scale, least-commercial, near-shore activities would be subject to the fewest restrictions and conditionalities, with increasing

TABLE 3.1 *Conflict over SDT provisions*

| Chair's Draft Text—Proposed Rules[a] | China's Demands[b] |
|---|---|
| Governments would be allowed to provide: | |
| All forms of subsidies to subsistence-type activity. | All forms of subsidies for *any* fishing within own territorial waters (not just subsistence). |
| Capital and operating subsidies for small-scale fisheries, defined as vessels under 10 meters. | Capital and operating subsidies for vessels up to 24 meters. |
| For all other vessels (i.e., larger vessels), capital subsidies (not operating subsidies) for fishing within their own EEZ. | For larger vessels, capital *and* operating subsidies for fishing within own EEZ *and* on high seas and in other countries' EEZs where have access arrangements. |
| Subsidies for port infrastructure and processing facilities; income support; and price support. | [No change to proposed rule.] |
| Access to latter three SDT exceptions would be conditional upon adhering to specific fisheries management obligations. | No requirements for fisheries management. |

[a] Draft Consolidated Chair Texts of the AD and SCM Agreements, Negotiating Group on Rules, TN/RL/W/213, Annex VIII, Fisheries Subsidies, November 30, 2007.
[b] Submission by India, Indonesia, and China. TN/RL/GEN/155/Rev.1, May 19, 2008.

levels of discipline as the scale, degree of commercialization, and area of operation of the subsidized activity expanded, and no subsidization would be permitted for any fisheries activities on the high seas.[17] While the Chair's draft proposed a relatively narrow and specific set of SDT exemptions, China rejected this restricted construction of SDT and, in a submission with India and Indonesia, insisted that each SDT provision be dramatically expanded (see Table 3.1).[18]

Under the rules proposed in the Chair's draft text, developing countries would be allowed to provide all forms of subsidies to subsistence fishing. Yet China proposed that this be expanded to allow developing countries to provide subsidies for *any* fishing activity within their territorial waters, not just subsistence. Similarly, under the proposed rules, developing countries would be allowed to provide capital and operating subsidies for small-scale fisheries, defined as vessels under ten meters in length. China, however, sought to increase this to twenty-four meters, which environmentalists indicate would include many industrial fishing boats.

According to the WWF, supposedly "small-scale" fleets that were once confined to inshore or near-shore operations are now increasingly venturing long distances in search of new fishing grounds and markets. Facilitated by at-sea transfers or distant water in-port processing, smaller boats can play an important role in what is in fact large-scale industrial fishing (WWF 2007).

According to the Chair's draft, for all other vessels (i.e., larger vessels), developing countries would be allowed to provide capital subsidies (but not operating subsidies) for fishing within their own EEZ. This exception would allow developing countries to subsidize the construction and modification of vessels, including for commercial or industrial-scale activities, up to a level of capacity consistent with the sustainable exploitation of their own fisheries resources, on the basis that vessel capital costs can present an insurmountable hurdle for operators in developing countries. However, China responded by demanding that capital *and* operating subsidies (such as fuel subsidies) be allowed for fishing not just within the limits of a country's own EEZ but also on the high seas and in other countries' EEZs where access arrangements are in place. The Chair's text would allow developing countries to provide subsidies for port infrastructure and processing facilities; income support; and price support. Access to all of the above SDT exceptions would be conditional on adhering to specific fisheries management obligations, designed to ensure the conservation of fish stocks and prevent overfishing. China, in contrast, insisted that there be no requirements for developing countries providing subsidies to engage in fisheries management. Critics thus expressed concern that China was arguing for what would effectively amount to unconditional SDT for developing countries (*Bridges Weekly* 2008b).

Accommodating China's demands would explode efforts to construct a narrow and carefully defined set of SDT exemptions for developing countries. Instead, China's proposed rules would leave developing countries with virtually no obligations, other than not subsidizing illegal fishing. China's proposal met with considerable criticism from a wide range of states, as well as environmental NGOs (*Bridges Weekly* 2008a). The US, for example, argued that it would amount to a total carve-out for developing countries without conditionalities (*Bridges Weekly* 2008a). Under the terms of the proposal, developing countries, including China, would be allowed nearly unlimited and unconditional flexibility to subsidize their fisheries. Even other developing countries took issue with China's expansive approach to SDT, arguing that "such flexibility cannot be used as a blank check."[19]

Driven primarily by China, the issue of whether developing countries should be allowed to provide subsidies for high seas fishing became one of the most contentious issues in the negotiations.[20] China's principal objection to the Chair's draft text is that no subsidization would be permitted for any fishing activities on the high seas, and SDT would be restricted to fisheries operating solely within a country's own EEZ. China, along with several other major developing countries, contends that high seas fishing "is an important means to address livelihood and employment issues."[21] And therefore "it does not make sense... to preclude developing countries from being able to provide support to fishing activities in the high seas."[22] China and other large emerging economies maintain that this is an issue of equity, arguing that developing countries are latecomers to high seas fisheries and should be able to use whatever means they deem necessary in order to catch up to the developed world.[23] China contends that it is "unfair to restrict the very subsidies that developed countries have historically given to their fishermen," explicitly singling out the US as one such country.[24] Moreover, China argues, it is developed countries and their subsidies that are responsible for the overfishing of high seas stocks: "developed countries have already provided these very subsidies historically to develop their fisheries sector, which in turn has landed us in the current situation of overfished waters."[25] From China's perspective, it is hypocritical for those countries to now seek to deny developing countries the use of such subsidies.[26] China therefore maintains that it should be allowed to subsidize both capital and operating costs for high seas fishing.[27]

Many other countries, however, have significant concerns about the prospect of any country being allowed to subsidize high seas fishing.[28] Given the absence of strong jurisdiction and enforcement power on the high seas—where a significant portion of fish stocks are already fully or over exploited—many consider a universal prohibition on subsidies to high seas fisheries to be critical. In light of the enormous overcapacity that already exists, subsidies that fuel the creation of any additional capacity will have severely detrimental effects on sustainability. Opponents of an SDT exception argue that there is no development rationale for subsidizing high seas fishing comparable to that for subsidizing poor countries' subsistence or small-scale fisheries. They argue that fishing activities in the high seas are by definition highly industrialized operations and all countries engaged in high seas fishing, regardless of their development status, should face the same subsidy rules.[29]

The Chair's draft text produced deep divisions. China was far from alone in seeking an exemption for its subsidies; many other countries also sought to carve out scope for their own subsidies within the new rules. The ambitious set of rules proposed by the Chair provoked objections from many different corners and revealed multiple areas of dispute among states, yet by far the most contentious issue to emerge, and what has become the principal conflict in the fisheries negotiations, is the issue of extending SDT to China. In 2011, after four years of heated debate, the subsequent Chair of the rules negotiations was asked to prepare a new draft text, in an effort to move the negotiations closer to a conclusion; however, he determined that states were too far apart to even present a revised set of proposed rules.[30] Instead, the Chair was merely able to produce a report summarizing the state of the negotiations, indicating that they "remain in more or less the same impasse... with positions if anything hardening."[31] On SDT, in particular, the Chair noted, there had been "no convergence."[32] The fisheries negotiations thus came to a standstill in 2011, and with the Doha Round collapse were effectively on hiatus until external events in 2015 prompted a resurgence of the negotiations. The fundamental impasse over SDT that erupted in response to the rules proposed in the 2007 Chair's draft text has persisted and, even amid the post-Doha rekindling of the fisheries negotiations, remains the principal impediment to achieving an agreement to discipline fisheries subsidies.

## THE CONFLICT OVER SPECIAL AND DIFFERENTIAL TREATMENT FOR CHINA

China has thus emerged as a key player in the WTO fisheries negotiations, with its demands for SDT becoming one of the most controversial issues in the negotiations and a major impediment to achieving a meaningful agreement to discipline harmful fisheries subsidies. As one developed country negotiator with offensive interests stated:

This is a negotiation about China, because it's the biggest catching nation, the biggest subsidizer and the biggest trading nation. It's all about China. I mean in the end it was all about China in the DDA [the Doha Round], but now in the fisheries negotiations it really is nothing but China.[33]

Specifically, it is the issue of SDT for China that, to quote another negotiator, is "hobbling the negotiations on fisheries subsidies."[34] While China is not the only large emerging economy seeking exemptions for its fishery through SDT, it is by far the greatest concern given the size of its fishing industry and the impact of its subsidies. For many, disciplining China's subsidies is essential: as one negotiator summarized, "If you look at what and where they are catching, they're everywhere. The facts are clear—China's subsidies keep growing, they keep catching the fish, and people are suffering."[35]

Many states—both developed and developing—are concerned that China is effectively seeking a blanket exemption for its subsidies under the rubric of SDT, and argue, as one put it, that SDT "can't just be a free for all."[36] As an LDC representative stated:

China doesn't need SDT in fields where it's already the major exporter. It is absolutely unacceptable to say I need special treatment when you are the major player in the market. Of course, for some things, China should be treated like a developing country, that's fair, but for some things, like fisheries, it just doesn't make any sense.[37]

Similarly, in the words of a former African negotiator:

China, even if it's a developing country, is a major fishing nation. It's principally subsidies for industrial fishing that need to be addressed, and the scale of China's industrial fishing sector is huge. But the problem is that China wants access to the same SDT as all other developing countries. The big question is can we make a distinction between developing countries at different levels of development.[38]

Yet this question of treating major players like China differently than other developing countries, as a developed country negotiator explained, "is just too explosive. You can't even have this conversation, especially in the fisheries context."[39]

At various points, countries have floated proposals for distinguishing between developing countries, based, for example, on GDP or share of global fish catch, where SDT would only be available if a country fell below a certain threshold.[40] But these proposals have provoked intense resistance from China, as they are seen as effectively creating new subcategories of developing countries. China—backed by other large emerging economies such as India, Indonesia, Brazil, and South Africa—argues that the only acceptable subdivision of developing countries is between LDCs and all others. As another negotiator indicated, "China's line is clear: any SDT should apply equally to all developing countries, regardless of capacity, size, or FAO ranking [for fish capture]."

China insists that SDT must be equal for developing countries and is firmly opposed to differentiating among developing countries. Its position is that "the principles of S&D treatment and LTFR [less than full reciprocity] should be fully preserved and for all Members."[41] China's opposition is such that, as even one of its former negotiators acknowledged, "at a political level, trying to differentiate between developing

countries is mission impossible" and any effort to introduce differentiation in the fisheries negotiations "will undo anything you're trying to
do."[42] The stakes go beyond the fisheries negotiations, as another negotiator explained:

> If China agreed to accept differentiation here, it would create a precedent. . . . It's
> the same issue in other areas of the negotiations. The moment China were to give
> an inch here, they [the US and others] would use it in other areas of the negoti-
> ations. So China is very cautious.[43]

China's stance provokes frustration from many other countries. As one
developed country negotiator put it: "When will we be able to have a
serious adult conversation about having more than three groups of countries [developed, developing, and LDCs]? The fact is China *is* different
than other developing countries. It's clearly different in size, capacity, and
so on."[44]

Many developing countries, whose fisheries are at a vastly lower level
of development than China's, stress their need for SDT. While, in aggregate, the global fishing industry suffers from overcapacity, the fishing
sectors of many developing countries remain underdeveloped, lacking
the industrial capacity even to fish their own waters up to maximum
sustainable yields (UNEP 2011). For such countries, maintaining their
ability to support and develop their fisheries is considered essential. An
ACP negotiator expressed it thus:

> We want to develop our fishery so it creates jobs for us and sustains our people—
> it's a livelihood security issue for us. We want some flexibility because the level of
> development of our fishery is not the same as others that are more developed.
> There are developed countries that have modern fleets, ports, gear, and there are
> developing countries too that are in that category. Many of our countries don't
> provide fishing subsidies because they can't afford them. And even if they did it
> would be miniscule—we're not responsible for the subsidies that cause fish stock
> depletion. It's those distant water fishing nations with big boats, big fleets, and
> equipment.[45]

Many developing countries accordingly argue that new WTO disciplines
should focus on subsidies that support large-scale, industrial fishing on
the high seas, exempting smaller-scale fishing activities within their own
national waters—a position that generally has broad support within the
organization on the basis of equity.[46]

Yet many developing countries are concerned that they may be denied
effective SDT "because of the China factor" (Sen 2018). As one negotiator stated, "Our concern is because the decision on SDT measures in any

agreement is going to be crafted keeping China and other big developing countries in mind, it's going to be more rigid for us and not necessarily provide the kind of flexibility that's important for us."[47] For smaller developing countries, to quote one of their negotiators:

The issue is how to develop rules that work for us little countries that are dependent on fishing, provide us with the flexibility we need, but that can't be given to the bigger developing countries. When I talk to developed countries they say "no, no, no, you are not the target [of efforts to limit SDT]—the target is China and the other big developing countries." But they are now classed in the same category as us and they are refusing to accept any differentiation among developing countries. For as long as they can do that [claim developing country status], they can access the same flexibilities as us. This is the real difficulty at the WTO—it's the big developing countries that oppose any talk on differentiation.[48]

This, many developing country negotiators point out, has been an issue not just in fisheries but "across the negotiations."[49]

As with the dynamics in the agriculture negotiations described in the previous chapter, despite the damaging effects of China's fisheries subsidies, many developing countries are reluctant to openly challenge China because of its economic and political heft. As one small developed country negotiator stated, "There's only one country here that criticizes China, and that's the US, and the smaller you get the more polite you are to China."[50] According to another negotiator,

If you talk to these countries privately, they are quite frank and tell you it's all about China. But in their formal communications, they will never say that directly, instead they will say we need to deal with all subsidies and all members—which is code for we want to deal with China.[51]

A developing country negotiator elaborated:

Developing countries are not yet openly challenging China. ... There's still a lingering solidarity, and developing countries do not want to openly show divisions among themselves. But if you look at some of the proposals from developing countries, there are elements that are subtly going after China's subsidies. The ACP, for example, says "major players" need to reduce their subsidies and if we say "major players" that means China and others. There is no effort to openly go after differentiation. Differentiation is the elephant in the room in the broader scheme of the negotiations. Developing countries would never put in a proposal that frontally targets China or other major developing countries, even if it's in there subtly. The recent ACP proposal said flexibility for a transition period should only be open to developing countries with non-distant water fisheries, making a distinction there between distant water and non-distant water—that's all about China.[52]

Most developing countries are thus highly reluctant to antagonize China and have refrained from directly criticizing its subsidies at the WTO.

## CHINA'S CENTRAL ROLE IN THE POST-DOHA NEGOTIATIONS ON FISHERIES SUBSIDIES

While the fisheries negotiations effectively came to a halt in 2011 with the Doha collapse, there has been a resurgence of negotiating activity since 2015, with the objective of achieving a standalone WTO agreement to restrict harmful subsidies. The primary impetus behind this has come from the UN Sustainable Development Goals (SDGs), adopted in 2015, which recognized the urgent need to control fisheries subsidies and made this a key international priority. In SDG 14.6, states pledged to reach agreement at the WTO by 2020 to eliminate all forms of subsidies contributing to IUU fishing, prohibit harmful subsidies that promote overcapacity and overfishing, and commit not to introduce any new such subsidies. These targets were accompanied by recognition of the need for "appropriate and effective" SDT for developing and least-developed countries. The UN Ocean Conference in 2017 reaffirmed states' commitment to accelerating work towards a WTO agreement on fisheries. As one developed country negotiator stated, "SDG 14.6 has become the de facto mandate. It's the highest levels of government saying this is a task for the WTO and setting a deadline."[53] This new mandate coming from the SDGs allowed a delinking of fisheries subsidies from other parts of the Doha negotiations, providing the impetus for a standalone agreement.

The SDG mandate has created new momentum at the WTO and provided a strong political driver behind moving the negotiations forward. Developing countries, in particular, have been much more active as *demandeurs* for fisheries subsidy disciplines and elevated the development case for such disciplines. Fisheries subsidies have thus become a key focus of post-Doha negotiations at the WTO, "with the aim of showing that the WTO is still relevant and a useful forum for international cooperation and rule-making, and it can contribute to sustainable development and poverty reduction" (Tipping 2017). In the words of the US Ambassador, fisheries subsidies came to be seen as a way to "breathe new energy into the WTO" and "re-establish the negotiating credibility of the organization" (*Inside US Trade* 2016). Despite substantial high-level political support, however, the persistent issue of the extent to which China, as well as other large emerging economies, should be subject to disciplines remains a significant impediment to achieving a fisheries subsidies agreement.

## US-Led Initiatives and the Positions of Other Major Players

Renewed momentum on fisheries subsidies also came from two US-led initiatives. In 2015, pushed by the US, countries involved in the Trans-Pacific Partnership (TPP) agreed to prohibit subsidies for vessels engaged in IUU fishing and fishing that negatively affects overfished fish stocks.[54] The following year, in 2016, the US launched a plurilateral initiative on fisheries subsidies at the WTO, involving fifteen countries, to run in parallel to the multilateral negotiations.[55] The US-led negotiations were directed at reaching an agreement among a subset of WTO members to prohibit harmful subsidies, including those that contribute to overfishing and overcapacity or that are linked to IUU fishing, as well as strengthening reporting and transparency.[56] The plurilateral initiative was intended to build on the fish subsidy provisions in the TPP by bringing additional WTO members to the table.[57] According to the US, the goal of the initiative was "to protect the long-term sustainability of global fisheries and to ensure American fishing industries and workers are on a level playing field with competitors."[58]

Negotiators report that the US "was very keen to get something on fisheries subsidies" and was "pushing an agreement as a big political/moral issue."[59] The plurilateral initiative was seen by many as an effort by the US, and allied states, to claim the moral high ground. It also reflected US frustration with the multilateral negotiating process at the WTO, which had been repeatedly blocked, in its view, by the obstructionist stance of China and other major developing countries. The stated intention of the initiative was to gather "like-minded participants" to negotiate "an ambitious, high standard agreement," while "at the same time working with all WTO members to make progress toward a multilateral agreement."[60] As one former negotiator stated:

the objective is to establish a benchmark of what fisheries subsidies disciplines could or should look like, amongst those that can be more ambitious (they're low-support states, so they can afford to be more ambitious)—to provide a benchmark for where multilateral negotiations could get to and sort of pull them along in that direction.[61]

And, indeed, as the multilateral negotiations on fisheries subsidies intensified, negotiations in the plurilateral group were suspended.

As a result of TPP, as well as other factors, the dynamics in the fisheries negotiations have changed over time. In earlier stages of the negotiations, the primary line of division was between the so-called Friends of Fish, a loose coalition of countries supporting far-reaching prohibitions on fish subsidies, and traditional big subsidizers like the EU, Japan, Korea, and Taiwan.[62] More recently, however, many of the traditional opponents of fisheries subsidy disciplines have moderated their positions and become less likely to block new disciplines. In 2013, the EU undertook substantial conservation-oriented reform of its Common Fisheries Policy (CFP), which included sharply curtailing capacity-enhancing subsidies, reducing the size of the European fleet and subjecting it to strict catch limits, and banning harmful fishing practices. Consequently, in the words of a negotiator for a Friends of Fish country, "The EU is now playing a more constructive role . . . [and] it would be highly unlikely for the EU to block [an agreement]."[63]

Japan has similarly moderated its position. The country's total fish production has been decreasing over the past several decades, and Japan has been implementing policies to reduce the capacity of its fishing fleet—resulting in a net decrease in the number of vessels and volume of fish caught (EU 2016). Today, Japan's fisheries subsidies are only one-fifth the size of China's (EU 2016). Moreover, Japan agreed to the TPP's prohibitions on subsidies for IUU fishing and overfished stocks, as well as its best endeavor commitment to refrain from introducing or expanding subsidies that contribute to overcapacity. As one developed country negotiator stated:

The TPP—agreed to by both the US and Japan—signaled at least a degree of convergence between the two historical *demandeur* and defensive negotiating blocks at the WTO, and indicated Japan's willingness to accept disciplines, even if limited to IUU and overfished stocks, and best endeavor on new subsidies. And the TPP was in the context of a non-multilateral agreement—it is extremely rare to treat subsidies in such an agreement, so this was significant.[64]

As a Friends of Fish negotiator put it, "Japan signed up to TPP—so it has been sort of neutralized—it is not in a strong position to oppose something multilaterally that it already agreed to in the TPP."[65]

Other traditional opponents of disciplines, such as Korea and Taiwan, are not seen as a genuine threat to an agreement. As a negotiator for a developed country *demandeur* expressed it:

Korea and Taiwan are being a nuisance but they are not going to stand in the way. We're in the business of trying to get an outcome based on consensus, but that doesn't mean everyone has to say yes, it just means that no one says no. Korea and Taiwan will never say no. They'll run interference and counter-arguments right through to the end, but you can just push past them. . . . They don't concern me.[66]

In sum, according to a former negotiator, "there's less risk today that defensive developed countries would kick over the table."[67] The traditional antagonists opposing new rules on fisheries subsidies have thus, at least to some extent, been neutralized.

To quote one developing country negotiator: "There is increasingly widespread agreement among almost all members that this issue is long overdue. Even countries that were hesitant before—like Japan—are now on board."[68] Likewise, as a representative for an NGO advising developing countries stated:

There has been a lot of progress in the fisheries subsidies negotiations. Looking back on the negotiations, many countries had very hard positions at the beginning—including even disputing the link between subsidies and overfishing [i.e., Japan]. But over time there has been a growing consensus as the evidence has piled up. Even subsidizing countries now realize this is not sensible—if we continue to subsidize, the stocks will run out. Many countries have changed their positions, creating reasons for optimism about the possibility of getting a deal.[69]

Spurred by the SDG mandate, there was near-universal support from the WTO membership to detach fisheries subsidies from the failed Doha Round and begin renewed negotiations with the objective of creating a WTO agreement to discipline harmful fisheries subsidies.

## Issue Linkage: Sabotaging the Negotiations or Seeking Fairness?

One powerful opponent, however, stood out: China, which sought to thwart efforts to construct a standalone agreement on fisheries subsidies. China, backed by India and Russia, insisted that negotiations on fisheries subsidies must remain linked to progress in other core areas of the original Doha rules negotiations, which must receive the same treatment and be agreed together to arrive at a "balanced outcome" (Fortnam 2017a; Ravi Kanth 2016). China argued that: "Members needed to keep all pillars of Rules—such as fishery subsidies, trade remedies and RTAs—on the same track with a comparable level of ambition. There should be no fast-track for any of those."[70] Specifically, China has an offensive interest in reforming WTO rules on trade remedies—anti-dumping duties, countervailing duties and safeguards. The purported intent of such measures is to protect against "unfair competition"—such as foreign firms "dumping" goods (selling at below cost of production)—by allowing the affected country to impose retaliatory tariffs. However, China argues that such measures are used unfairly to restrict its exports. China is the most frequent target of anti-dumping duties and other trade defense measures, and it has been on the receiving end of a large and growing number of such actions by the US, in particular (Fortnam 2017c; Hopewell 2016).

From China's perspective, the US is the worst offender: it is among the biggest users of trade defense measures and China has been its primary target. Moreover, despite numerous WTO rulings against the US, it has refused to significantly reform its practices. China has long sought to use WTO negotiations to rein in the US's use of anti-dumping and other trade remedies. As a Chinese negotiator explained:

China is always the #1 target for trade remedies—by the US and everywhere, including developing countries like India and Brazil. We know that trade remedies are misused for protectionist purposes. So China has always wanted to improve the rules, as the biggest exporter.[71]

Fisheries and trade remedies were intentionally linked from the start of the Doha Round in the rules negotiations to create potential trade-offs between the two areas. In 2017, amid the escalation of the negotiations on fisheries subsidies, China put forward a new proposal to amend the WTO's trade remedy rules, which the US promptly rejected, indicating that it would not participate in any negotiations to alter them (Fortnam 2017a). From China's perspective, US efforts to push forward an agreement on fisheries, while leaving behind negotiations to reform anti-dumping, were hypocritical. For China, linking fisheries subsidies and trade remedies is an issue of fairness—if it is going to be asked to give something on fisheries, it should get something in return.

China's insistence on linking the new fisheries negotiations to anti-dumping was, however, roundly criticized, viewed by many as an effort to divert attention from its fishing subsidies and "torpedo the fisheries talks" (Fortnam 2017c). Most delegations opposed China's efforts to link fisheries and anti-dumping—even ones who are seeking anti-dumping reform, like many in the Friends of Anti-Dumping (FANs) group. Japan, for instance, on behalf of most members of FANs, explicitly stated that the anti-dumping negotiations should not be linked to talks on fisheries subsidies (Fortnam 2017a). Even the WTO Director General, Roberto Azevedo, repeatedly stressed that members must avoid linking the fisheries negotiations to other issues (Caporal 2017).

Countries feared that if China insisted on linking progress on trade remedy rules with the fisheries subsidies negotiations, a deal on fisheries subsidies would be impossible—due to US opposition to any reform of its anti-dumping policies. As one developed country negotiator stated:

One thing we know is that the Americans will not do anything on antidumping. That has been the one constant point in their position for the last twenty years. Anyone who thinks the US are doing anything on antidumping, they're on drugs. And that goes back before Trump—that has been their position for many years and things have only gotten worse lately (even before Trump) with the controversy over issues like China's market economy status and overcapacity in various sectors. There's not a hope in hell that we're going to get anything on antidumping. So the question is whether China will demand linkage.[72]

In short, as another put it, "The US has said you're wasting your time. There's not going to be any discussion of this."[73] Indeed, even a former Chinese negotiator acknowledged that "everyone knows getting the US to accept something on trade remedies is impossible."[74] Consequently, a developing country negotiator explained: "That's why other members are insisting please let's look at fisheries subsidies separately and not try to link it to anti-dumping."[75] In this way, the US position defined the realm of possibility in the negotiations.

China's insistence on issue linkage was seen by other states as a tactical move: as one negotiator put it, "there's political steam behind the fisheries negotiations now, and they knew it would kill the fisheries negotiations."[76] Chinese negotiators, however, defended their stance as a legitimate negotiating position. As one stated, "people are pushing on fish subsidies but not trade remedies because the US is not even going to move one inch. But no one blames the US and everyone blames China. The US, and partly the EU, are the ones to blame, but, politically speaking, everyone knows the US won't do anything," so instead China gets blamed for pressing the issue.[77]

The fisheries subsidies negotiations morphed into a direct conflict between the US and China, with China signaling that it would only engage in negotiations on fisheries subsidies in exchange for concessions from the US on anti-dumping, and the US indicating it was unwilling to negotiate any new rules on anti-dumping. Many feared that if China held firm in insisting on issue linkage, the fish subsidy negotiations would simply come to a halt. Yet, in the lead-up to the 2017 Buenos Aires Ministerial, China moderated its stance, indicating, as one negotiator summarized, that "it would not block an outcome on fish because there's no outcome on trade remedies."[78] In the words of another negotiator, "China seems to be *allowing* the fisheries subsidies negotiations to move ahead in the absence of progress on the other pillars" (emphasis added).[79] It is an indication of China's power that it, along with the US, now determines whether or not multilateral negotiations at the WTO on a given issue will proceed.

As this shows, the US still sets the terms of what is doable at the WTO, but now so too does China. China's decision to "allow" the fisheries negotiations to continue was interpreted by other states as a strategic move: Buenos Aires was the first WTO ministerial following the election of President Trump and fisheries subsidies was effectively the sole negotiating item on the agenda. As one developed country negotiator stated, "they want the multilateral trading system to continue to function" and "to signal the WTO is still a viable negotiating forum."[80] China, cultivating an image of itself as the new global advocate of free trade amid the abdication of US leadership under President Trump, likely determined it was in its interests not to be seen as blocking the negotiations going into the Buenos Aires Ministerial, confident that the spotlight of criticism would then fall on Trump and the US. Moreover, although China allowed the fisheries negotiations to proceed, it has nonetheless refused to accept any significant disciplines on its subsidies.

## Despite Reforms, China's Expansionist Agenda Continues

While China is making certain reforms to its fisheries policies, stimulating the global expansion of its industry remains a core priority, leaving its resistance to WTO disciplines firmly entrenched. China has been engaged in renewed efforts to improve the state of its domestic fisheries, for example, including cracking down on overfishing through fishing moratoriums and aggressive policing and attempting to repopulate severely depleted domestic fisheries (Chen 2017; Godfrey 2018a). Yet domestic environmental reforms continue to coexist with an expansionist international strategy, prompting accusations that China is "an environmentalist at home, while plundering abroad" (Godfrey 2018a). As one former Chinese negotiator explained:

These are two sides of the same coin—in its domestic waters, its EEZ, there's lots of effort and reforms directed at reducing capacity, cutting subsidies, moving people into other sectors, but on the high seas, China is still supporting its fishing industry a lot. China draws a line between its domestic fishery and the high seas; domestically it's different, but on the high seas, that's where it becomes sensitive. Politically, expanding in the high seas is an explicit policy goal: China says on the high seas it will boldly encourage more boats and fishers to go there, and they should have a reasonable share of high seas fishing.[81]

Indeed, China's most recent 13th five-year plan (2016–20) identifies continued development of its distant water fishery as a major policy goal. As part of its industrial strategy, China is undertaking reforms to upgrade, rationalize, and increase the efficiency of its long-distance fishing fleet, including directing government subsidies towards transitioning to larger and "smarter" vessels and weeding out smaller and weaker firms. The central government recently announced its intention to reduce fuel subsidies by 40 percent by 2019 (FAO 2018); however, China's fuel subsidies remain large even with such a cut, and it appears to be shifting support into other forms of subsidies, such as for vessel upgrading and the expansion of overseas fishing bases (which will themselves reduce the need for fuel subsidies, by reducing the distances Chinese fishing boats need to travel). Similarly, in 2017, China announced plans to cap the size of its distant water fleet at the 2016 level of 3,000 vessels, but industry analysts point out that China is still increasing its total fishing power by simply shifting to "much bigger ships" (Godfrey 2017). In fact, despite capping the total number of vessels in its fleet, China has nonetheless raised its target for fishing catch in international waters by 15 percent by 2020 (Harkell 2018), and the continued development of its overseas fishing bases further shows that China has no intention of slowing the expansion of its international fishing operations (Godfrey 2018b). At the WTO, China's opposition to any restrictions on its subsidies remains as firm as ever. As one developed country negotiator stated, "there is no sign that China's fisheries reforms have affected its position here at all."[82]

As with other areas of international trade negotiations involving China, other states complain that the highly opaque and non-transparent nature of its subsidies acts as a significant impediment to trade negotiations and rule-making on fisheries. Although countries are required to report their subsidies to the WTO, China's notifications have been persistently delayed and contained major omissions: the US and others allege that China has at least thirty subsidy programs for fisheries that it has not reported.[83] The US in particular has repeatedly demanded greater transparency from China, but largely without success. The result is that states are unable to know the exact volume or forms of subsidies China is providing, particularly given the large volume of subsidies provided by sub-national governments, which the central government often fails to notify. While the notification problem is not unique to China, given the magnitude of its fishing industry and subsidies, the absence of clear information presents "a serious problem" in the negotiations, in the words of one negotiator.[84] As another stated, "All we can rely on are various estimates that are out there ... We are sort of negotiating in the dark."[85]

## China's Resistance to Disciplines

Throughout the post-Doha negotiations, as during the Doha Round, China has shown that it is unwilling to accept even the most minimal prohibitions on its subsidies. In advance of the 2015 Nairobi Ministerial, the Chair of the negotiations put forward a draft text that would have had members commit merely to refrain from introducing or expanding subsidies that contribute to overcapacity and overfishing, but this was rejected by China (*Bridges Daily Update* 2015). Two years later, fisheries subsidies was seen as the issue that held the most promise for a substantive outcome at the Buenos Aires Ministerial (Hannah, Scott, and Wilkinson 2018). Emphasis was placed on seeking agreement to prohibit subsidies to IUU fishing and fishing of overfished stocks, which were seen as leading candidates for an agreement at the Ministerial because of the particularly egregious nature of such subsidies. There were also hopes of a best endeavor (non-binding) standstill agreement on subsidies contributing to overfishing or overcapacity.[86]

Prior to the Ministerial, however, China tabled a proposal to selectively ban subsidies for IUU fishing, indicating that it wanted the prohibition to be limited solely to cases of IUU fishing, rather than any more comprehensive elimination of subsidies.[87] And its proposal came with several caveats, such as that governments, rather than independent experts, decide what constitutes IUU fishing, and that disputed territories, like the South China Sea, be exempt from any phase-out of subsidies. China's proposal was widely seen as an attempt to water down the prospective rules and curb broader subsidy disciplines that would have a significant effect on its distant water fishing fleet. It was considered unacceptable to the US and others, who argued that it effectively gave subsidizing countries a veto and fell far short of creating "meaningful disciplines" on subsidies (Reuters 2017a). Concerned about damage to its international reputation, China has recently made signs of some efforts to crack down on illegal fishing within its own fleet (by temporarily removing access to fuel subsidies, for example) (Harkell 2018). However, its willingness to accept international disciplines (however limited) on IUU, as well as its new steps at the national level to constrain IUU fishing, are seen as part of an effort to buffer its international image, while trying to stave off more serious prohibitions on subsidies that lead to overcapacity and overfishing, which remain the key target of other states (Hancock 2018b).

An agreement at Buenos Aires to prohibit subsidies for fishing of stocks that are already overfished would have been significant, given that over

30 percent of fish stocks are overfished (*Bridges Weekly* 2017e). However, while China indicated it would be willing to support a prohibition
on subsidies that contribute to IUU fishing, it refused to accept a prohibition on subsidies to overfished stocks (Fortnam 2017b). As one
developed country negotiator stated, "China is saying it is willing to do
something on IUU and transparency. I would struggle to say that's ambitious with a straight face—it's close to meaningless in fact."[88] Negotiators
report that a prohibition solely on IUU fishing would be a very limited
outcome: a very "narrow prohibition," reflecting an "extremely low"
level of ambition.[89] IUU fishing, as one negotiator stated, "is still only
one small sliver of the whole fisheries subsidies problem," or, as another
put it, "a tiny drop in a vast ocean."[90]

There are also major questions about the enforceability of an IUU
prohibition, which many believe would be ineffective without broader
restrictions on capacity-enhancing subsidies. As a negotiator explained,
"No country has a budget line for IUU fishing. It's overcapacity that leads
to IUU fishing, so if you want to combat IUU fishing, you need to tackle
subsidies that generate overcapacity. You're not going to put a stop to
IUU fishing through dealing with IUU subsidies."[91] If the WTO were to
prohibit subsidies to vessels that have been found guilty of IUU fishing,
that is an extremely small number of boats: only 309 vessels in the world
(out of nearly 3 million) are IUU-listed by regional fisheries management
organizations (RFMOs), which are the international organizations
responsible for managing fishing on the high seas.[92] As one negotiator
acknowledged, "you could easily say this is ridiculous—it's not enough to
make a difference."[93] An Ambassador for an island developing country
echoed this in stating: "This is peripheral stuff. It's not getting at overfishing or the overcapacity problem properly—and that's what is really at
stake for us."[94]

However, progress on subsidies for overcapacity and overfishing is
seen as so far out of reach that these issues were not even discussed at
the Buenos Aires Ministerial. And even with the level of ambition severely
reduced, members failed to agree on any concrete measures at Buenos
Aires. Instead, after nearly two decades of negotiations on fisheries subsidies, and despite the renewed mandate provided by the SDGs, which
stressed the urgent need for substantive disciplines, the only thing states
could agree on was to continue negotiating—as one negotiator put it, "in
other words, basically doing nothing."[95]

Fisheries subsidies is currently one of the sole areas of active multilateral negotiations at the WTO. Yet many negotiators indicate that it is

"difficult to see any sort of meaningful outcome" in the fisheries negotiations.[96] Negotiators report that even if states are able to reach some form of a fisheries agreement, such as on "low hanging fruit" like IUU fishing, "the question is how significant it will be."[97] As one stated, a prohibition on subsidies for IUU fishing, "that's such a political no brainer, it should be the relatively easiest thing to get an agreement on," but after that "it just gets progressively harder to agree on anything."[98] In sum, as an LDC negotiator put it, "it will be extremely difficult to get a deep and meaningful agreement" on fisheries subsidies.[99]

Although there are several areas of contention in the negotiations—with many countries focused on their defensive interests, seeking to place the burden of responsibility on other states and minimize the impact of disciplines on their own activities—by far the most fundamental issue of dispute remains SDT for China. As one negotiator summarized:

The issue of differentiating between large and small developing countries has become the central stumbling block in the negotiations. If some of the world's largest and most powerful, most successful distant water fishers are developing countries, like China, and they refuse to allow any further differentiation, how do we get any kind of a meaningful agreement?[100]

This, she continued, is now the "central challenge in the negotiations." To be clear, China is hardly alone in seeking a carve-out for its own subsidies. But given the magnitude of its subsidies and the global reach of its industrial fishery such an exemption for China would have serious systemic implications, both for the environment and development. It is thus China's subsidies, as one participant put it, that are at the "forefront of members' minds" in the fisheries negotiations (Fortnam 2017c).

## "The Deciders": Centrality of the US and China

The US and China are now both key protagonists in the fisheries negotiations. The US played an essential role in establishing fisheries subsidies as an area of WTO negotiations, and has historically been the leading advocate of a broad and strict prohibition on fisheries subsidies, subject to only narrowly defined exceptions. Now, the prospects of a deal are widely seen to rest on China and its willingness to accept restrictions. As one developing country negotiator put it, "The make or break issue for any fisheries subsidy agreement is whether China will accept disciplines on its subsidies."[101] Another echoed this in stating, "China, along with the US, is now big enough to define the contours of the negotiations and any possible agreement."[102] A former negotiator summed up the current dynamics as follows: "The two big players needed for a deal are the US and China. The US and China are the deciders—the two countries with the power to block any deal. If either China or the US don't agree to what is on the table, others won't either and we won't have a deal."[103]

There is a major gap between the US and China, with little sign of common ground. The US has indicated that it is unwilling to settle for a low-ambition agreement; it expects China to make a "significant contribution" toward a WTO agreement on fisheries subsidies and refuses to allow China's industrial fishery to benefit from SDT exemptions (*Bridges Weekly* 2017e; *Inside US Trade* 2012). Yet China, whose emergence as the world's largest fishing nation has been fueled by heavy subsidies, is seeking a carve-out for virtually its entire fishery. As a former developed country negotiator stated, China "would be quite happy if the WTO didn't come up with fisheries subsidies disciplines."[104] Just as the US is unwilling to consider any new WTO rules that would limit its ability to use trade defense measures, China has made it clear that it is unwilling to participate in any agreement that requires a significant reduction in or constraints on its fisheries subsidies. And, given its newfound economic heft, as one negotiator summarized, "if you're China, you can just block."[105]

In the words of a developed country negotiator, "The way deals are done here is the big guys get around the table and the rest of us go along for the ride. If they want to do a deal, they will."[106] Meanwhile, however, there is a sense that, as one developing country negotiator put it, "the interests and concerns of developing countries are being left behind" in the fisheries negotiations.[107] Another similarly stated: "For smaller states like us, very often we feel like we're being swept along with the tide— collateral damage of a fight between the major powers. Because, realistically, who do we really threaten? What leverage do we have? We don't have any bargaining strength."[108] Despite the pressing importance of the fisheries subsidies issue for many developing countries, the prospects of agreement appear dim.

## CONCLUSION

As this chapter has shown, amid a global fisheries crisis, achieving a standalone WTO agreement to restrict harmful fisheries subsidies has become a major priority of the international community since the collapse of the Doha Round. As the world's leading fishing power, with a heavily subsidized fleet, China has become a critical actor in the fisheries subsidies negotiations. The question of whether China should have access to SDT has become a core issue of dispute in the negotiations, impeding efforts to secure an agreement. There is a fundamental conflict between China's demands for SDT and the insistence of the US and others that all major players must be subject to disciplines, the implications of which go far beyond US–China relations. On the basis of its status as a developing country, China is seeking to exempt its fisheries subsidies from WTO disciplines. However, given the massive size and global reach of its industrial fishing fleet and the large volume of subsidies it is providing, China's subsidies have serious systemic consequences. Allowing China to exempt its subsidies would contravene the purpose of constructing disciplines and have severely negative implications for the sustainability of global fisheries resources and for other developing countries who rely on such resources for economic development, incomes and livelihoods, and food security.

The fisheries subsidies case illustrates how the China paradox—here, the contradiction between its status as a developing country and the fact that it is a globally dominant industrial fishing nation with the world's largest and farthest-ranging fleet—is creating profound challenges for global trade governance. As this case underscores, the issue of how China should be treated in global trade rules has become a central source of conflict in WTO negotiations.

# 4

# Beyond the WTO: Erosion of the Export Credit Arrangement

This chapter examines the impact of China's rise on the global governance of export credit—an important and increasingly contentious area of economic policy and international negotiations, which, to date, has received comparatively little attention from scholars of international political economy. The governments of most major economies use export credit—loans and other forms of financing that assist foreign buyers in purchasing goods and services from national exporters—to promote their exports. If provided at below-market rates, state-backed export credit may act as a subsidy and distort trade. As I will show, the global dynamics of export credit are being transformed by contemporary power shifts, with significant implications for global governance. The existing system of governance for export credit—which limits the ability of states to use export credit to subsidize, and thus artificially boost, their exports—was created under the auspices of the Organisation for Economic Co-operation and Development (OECD) in the 1970s and repeatedly strengthened since then. For decades, export credit has been held up as an example of a successful global governance regime (Levit 2004; Moravcsik 1989; Shaffer, Wolfe, and Le 2015), with its system of disciplines proving highly effective in restricting the use of export credit as a form of state subsidy.

However, I demonstrate that the rise of China—which is not a member of the OECD nor bound by its rules—has profoundly altered the landscape of export credit and disrupted its governance arrangements. Over the past two decades, China has emerged as the world's largest supplier of export credit, providing volumes of financing four times greater than any other state. State-backed export credit is a key tool of China's development strategy, used to foster industrial upgrading and the international expansion of its domestic firms and industries. Yet I argue that the dramatic increase in the use of export credit by China, as well as other major emerging economies, is eroding the efficacy of existing international rules intended to prevent a competitive spiral of state subsidization via export credit. The disruption of the export credit regime highlights the conflict between the liberal principles of the existing global governance architecture and China's economic development objectives.

## LIBERAL GLOBAL GOVERNANCE VERSUS THE DEVELOPMENTAL STATE

Government-supported export financing has far-reaching consequences for international trade patterns (Wright 2011). Yet, despite its importance in the global economy, for the past several decades the governance of export credit at the OECD has been largely overlooked amid emphasis on other aspects of trade policy and negotiations. Most academic literature on this subject dates from the 1970s and 1980s, when the governance regime for export credit was first created. The relative neglect of export credit in international political economy scholarship since then is arguably a reflection of the success of this regime. With a system of international rules in place that worked smoothly and effectively for decades, the global governance of export credit was—until recently—relatively uneventful.

From a liberal perspective, export credit has constituted an example of a highly successful global regulatory regime. Over time, the system of governance created under the OECD virtually eliminated the subsidy component of export credit, limiting state provision of export credit mainly to addressing market failure while preventing states from using export credit to artificially distort markets and trade flows. From the standpoint of neoclassical economics, this is a collectively rational solution, ensuring markets can function efficiently and avoiding a costly and self-defeating subsidy war.

Yet, as I will show, export credit has now become a prime illustration of how liberal global governance institutions are threatened by contemporary power shifts, and particularly the rise of China. China has emerged as the world's largest provider of export credit but refused to participate in the established governance regime or to accept international disciplines on its use of export credit. Given the scale of its export credit activities, China's non-participation threatens to destabilize the set of governance arrangements that worked effectively in this area for decades.

While contemporary power shifts are disrupting the global governance of export credit, this is not due to an unwillingness on the part of the established powers or the existing regime to accommodate China or other rising powers. Although based at the OECD, states are not required to be OECD members to participate in the existing system of rules governing export credit. Indeed, the US and other established powers have been eager either to incorporate China into the current regime or to engage it in the construction of a new one, but China has resisted both options. The issue is thus not an absence of accommodation, but a fundamental incompatibility of preferences. Export credit is a clear case in which China rejects existing governance arrangements, because there is a disjuncture between the goal of the export credit regime and China's development strategy.

For many, this would be a prime illustration of how China is "irresponsible" (Patrick 2010) and acting as a "spoiler" or "shirker" in global trade governance (Schweller 2011). I would argue, however, that the case of export credit governance problematizes such interpretations. From the perspective of the established powers or the regime they have created, it is easy to point to China as the problem and to dismiss its stance—undermining the export credit regime by refusing to participate in it—as irresponsible. However, while contemporary power shifts are disrupting global export credit governance, as I will demonstrate, it is not simply because China is irresponsible or recalcitrant, but because it has objectives that conflict with the overarching goals of the governance regime. The disruption of the international export credit regime is rooted in a fundamental conflict between the interests of the US and China: the US and other established powers have an interest in preserving the liberal regime they created, with states voluntarily cooperating to restrict their use of export credit to prevent a destructive, competitive spiral of subsidization, whereas China and other emerging powers have an interest in maintaining their ability to use export credit as part of their strategies for national development. This is, in short, a clash between liberalism and development.

Export credit thus underscores the inherent tension between liberal global governance institutions and the developmental state that characterizes China and many other emerging economies. From the perspective of the US and other established powers, the export credit regime and its disciplines are essential to fostering an open and fair global trading system, with competition taking place on a level playing field undistorted by state subsidies. But state-backed export credit has historically been a key industrial policy instrument employed by successful late developers (World Bank 1993). From the perspective of China and other emerging economies, a system that constrains their scope for development by requiring them to relinquish their use of an important industrial policy tool cannot be considered fair: what the US and other established powers perceive as a level playing field is, in fact, one that serves to perpetuate their industrial and economic supremacy. There is thus an inherent conflict between the objectives of the established powers and those of emerging challengers. While driven by its developmental objectives, China's stance nonetheless threatens to undermine the existing liberal governance regime for export credit.

### WHAT IS EXPORT CREDIT?

Trade finance is a critical, but understudied, aspect of the global political economy (Blackmon 2017). Approximately 80 percent to 90 percent of world trade relies on some form of financing, with over $10 trillion in trade finance provided annually (Akhtar 2015). Most trade finance comes from the private sector, but states also play a vital role in financing trade.[1] Every major economy has an export credit agency (ECA) that provides various forms of financing to facilitate and expand exports, including direct loans to foreign buyers, insurance and loan guarantees, working capital financing, and finance for large-scale infrastructure and industrial projects. Each ECA functions as a public or semipublic bank, borrowing from the national treasury or capital markets and using the funds to finance exports (Moravcsik 1989). To quote one official, "If trade is the engine that drives the increasingly integrated global economy, export credit is the fuel that powers it" (Konno 1998: 95).

States have used official export credit as a tool to encourage exports and stimulate their economies since the early 1900s. The volume of capital provided in this way is substantial: approximately sixty ECAs are now in operation worldwide, providing $300 billion in trade-related finance annually (Akhtar 2015; Exim 2015). In some countries, state-backed export credit supports as much as 20 percent of exports, and total ECA authorizations account for more than 5 percent of GDP (NAM 2014). Officially supported export credit occupies a crucial niche, filling gaps in the availability of private financing. ECAs play a major role in financing capital goods exports—"big-ticket" exports, such as aircraft, satellites, transportation equipment, manufacturing and agricultural machinery, energy and mining equipment, power plants, and major infrastructure projects—which often involves long-term financing of complex, multi-billion dollar sales (Hufbauer, Fickling, and Wong 2011). In such sectors, ECA support can help make transactions more commercially attractive by mitigating risks of financing or providing another source of funding to diversify risks.

State-backed export finance is a key policy tool used by states to promote their national economic interests. To provide an illustration of how this operates: in the United Kingdom, for example, UK Export Finance (UKEF) supports the aerospace sector by supplying financing to facilitate the sale of Airbus jets to foreign buyers. Given the size of these transactions, the purchasing airlines rarely pay cash and instead require loans to make the purchase possible. UKEF can step in to provide direct loans when commercial financing is unavailable, or to guarantee (and thereby reduce the cost of) commercial loans. Such state-backed financing is particularly important in facilitating sales to emerging markets, where less-developed banking and capital markets limit the availability of private financing. By facilitating the sale of Airbus jets, government-backed export credit helps to support an important industrial sector in the British economy. Aerospace is just one example of the types of industries supported by UKEF and its counterparts around the world.

For many countries, state provision of export credit is a core part of their industrial policy and national export strategies, and its importance has only been amplified since the 2008 Global Financial Crisis. During the crisis, when the availability of commercial credit contracted dramatically, government-backed export credit played a critical role in filling the gap in trade finance, keeping international trade moving and preventing the financial crisis from spiraling into a worldwide depression (Auboin 2015; Blackmon 2016). National ECAs thus serve as a vital source of counter-cyclical lending. In addition, the implementation of new Basel III financial regulations diminished the availability of private lending for certain forms of trade, increasing the need for state-backed export credit (Akhtar 2015). And, since the crisis, many states have increasingly come to view export credit as an important instrument to foster domestic economic growth by boosting exports.

The principal governance issue related to export credit arises from the fact that it may be subsidized by states as a means to promote exports. Since an ECA is a state agency with access to capital at low government rates, state-backed export credit is usually offered at interest rates below those that would be charged on the market for similar loans, if such loans are available at all (Moravcsik 1989). However, an ECA may also go further and subsidize interest rates directly, by lending at rates below its own cost of borrowing. Given that financing often represents a significant

portion of a large capital goods transaction or infrastructure project, even
modest government credit subsidies can be a decisive factor in awarding a
bid. Like other forms of export subsidies, without global regulation, the
natural tendency would be for states to offer increasingly higher subsidies
in an effort to give their exports an advantage in global markets, distorting trade flows and triggering a costly subsidy war that would drain
national budgets and reduce aggregate welfare (Coppens 2014; Levit
2004; Wright 2011).

## THE GLOBAL GOVERNANCE OF EXPORT CREDIT

The use of export credit by states is governed by a set of rules established
at the OECD, an international institution comprised primarily of
advanced-industrialized states, and thus often described as a "rich man's
club." Efforts to establish disciplines on government-backed export financing began in the 1970s. Many states were already providing subsidized
financing at below-market rates, but the oil shocks provoked the outbreak
of an export credit war (Moravcsik 1989). Rising oil prices resulted in
large trade deficits in most OECD countries, which prompted heightened
competition over export markets. Governments increasingly turned to
using subsidized export credit in a competitive race to "win" exports,
leading to rising levels of subsidization across the advanced-industrialized
countries. In a context of high interest rates, supporting large export
contracts became increasingly expensive for states, burdening national
budgets amid growing deficits (Vassard 2015).

The US led the creation of the current international regime governing
export credit (Moravcsik 1989; Vassard 2015). As Andrew Moravcsik
(1989: 199) details, the hegemonic power of the US played a crucial role
in the creation of the regime and lent decisive support to liberalization
efforts. The US's interest in eliminating subsidies provided "the catalyst
that sparked serious negotiations" and the US assumed leadership of the
negotiations, with its initiatives driving the formation, and subsequent
extension, of the export credit regime. There was a relatively large degree
of consensus among states on the desirability of an international regime,
but where necessary, at several crucial junctures, the US used the exercise
of coercive power to overcome resistance from recalcitrant countries, such
as France and Japan, with more interventionist economic models and
greater support for subsidies.

The OECD Arrangement on Officially Supported Export Credits (the
"OECD Arrangement") was created in 1978.[2] Its disciplines place strict

limits on the financing packages that ECAs may offer to borrowers. Its highly specific and technical provisions define the most favorable terms under which credit may be granted (including minimum interest rates and premiums, term-to-maturity, down payment, repayment schedules, and guidelines for classifying risk). These conditions are designed to adjust automatically based on changes in capital markets and commercial interest rates. The Arrangement includes disciplines on tied aid, as well as additional sector-specific understandings governing the terms and conditions of export financing for commercial aircraft, ships, nuclear power plants, renewable energy, and railway infrastructure. Since its creation, the Arrangement has been continuously revised and updated to tighten its disciplines, close loopholes, and adapt to changing circumstances (Moravcsik 1989; Vassard 2015). In addition to being the key driver behind the Arrangement's creation, the US was also the primary force behind this continual strengthening of its disciplines, designed to bring the global provision of export credit closer to market principles (Coppens 2014; Hall 2011).

Transparency is a critical aspect of the governance regime for export credit. The Arrangement sets out clear and detailed procedures for mandatory notification and exchange of information on credit practices. The system provides for what participants describe as "real time transparency"—a procedure and forum for reporting on impending transactions, exchanging confidential transaction data, and resolving disagreements before a transaction is completed. A participant is allowed to deviate from the terms of the Arrangement if they follow its notification process, providing other participants with the opportunity to match the terms of that bid by offering the same level of support; this threat of matching acts as a powerful enforcement mechanism for the Arrangement's provisions (Coppens 2014). In this way, the OECD Arrangement ensures the predictability of export credit policies and practices among its participants. As described by a senior OECD official, "everyone knows what the best terms available are, so no one worries about what terms competing governments might offer. ... There are no secret financing terms and, thus, no competitive advantages to be gained from deviating from the rules" (Drysdale 2015). The transparency and monitoring mechanisms built into the OECD regime reduce information asymmetry, encourage participants to conform to its disciplines, and provide confidence that others are doing the same.

The OECD Arrangement is not a formal treaty and has no formal enforcement mechanisms; instead, it is an informal, consensus-based "gentleman's agreement." Yet, despite its status as mere "soft law," the Arrangement has proven to be a highly effective regulatory regime. As Janet Koven Levit (2004: 68) demonstrates, the Arrangement has succeeded in achieving "thorough, deep, sustained compliance" among its participants. OECD and ECA officials themselves report that non-compliance is extremely rare. Many argue that its soft law status has, in fact, been an advantage—ensuring that the Arrangement is flexible and adaptable and can more easily be reviewed, modified, amended, and strengthened (Bonucci 2011; Levit 2004). The Arrangement has built trust among its participants and a shared understanding of appropriate practices that has significantly shaped state behavior (Shaffer, Wolfe, and Le 2015).

As a result, the existing regulatory regime for export credit is widely identified as an example of effective international economic cooperation (Levit 2004; Moravcsik 1989; Shaffer, Wolfe, and Le 2015). The OECD Arrangement has generally met its objective of eliminating competition among states based on export credit financing, in order to ensure that exports compete in global markets on the basis of price and quality rather than subsidized financing (Wright 2011).[3] In the words of one trade official, "over years and years of tightening its disciplines, the Arrangement has evolved to largely eliminate the subsidy component of export credit."[4] Its rules have enabled ECAs to fill gaps in the availability of commercial financing and facilitate the expansion of trade without distorting global markets. To quote a negotiator, the OECD Arrangement has been "very effective in terms of creating a level playing field and creating a situation where governments are complementing rather than competing with or crowding out the private sector."[5] In short, as one OECD official summed it up, "The export credit world has been really peaceful because of the Arrangement."[6]

WTO rules on export subsidies prohibit subsidized export credit; however, as detailed below, in practice, export credit is extremely difficult to police via the WTO. The smaller forum of the OECD became the institutional home of the export credit regime because it offered a more nimble and effective means of governing export credit (Moravcsik 1989). The Arrangement is not a universal agreement, but a form of club governance. It operates as a system of mutual self-restraint in the provision of state-backed export credit: while its participants are in direct competition with one another for export markets, they nonetheless came together to establish and abide by a common set of rules governing the terms of that competition. OECD membership is not required to join the Arrangement: any significant export credit provider is eligible to participate.

Export credit is what Robert Keohane (1982: 351) calls a "control-oriented regime," in which, through a set of institutionalized arrangements, "members maintain some degree of control over each other's behavior, thus decreasing harmful externalities arising from independent action as well as reducing uncertainty stemming from uncoordinated activity." Control-oriented regimes, like that for export credit, seek to regulate the behavior of their members. The condition for a mutual-control regime to be effective, however, is that *all* significant actors within the issue-area being regulated must be members of the regime (Keohane 1982: 353). When the Arrangement was created, and for several decades afterwards, it covered all of the world's major export credit providers—which were then exclusively rich countries. Since developing countries were not significant providers of export credit, there was no reason for them to be subject to such disciplines and their non-participation did not undermine the regime's functioning.[7] Now, however, the club model of governance for export credit centered on the advanced-industrialized states of the OECD is coming under strain, as major providers of export credit—such as China—emerge outside the club and show little interest in joining.

## CHANGING GLOBAL DYNAMICS OF EXPORT CREDIT

In recent years, the global landscape of export credit has changed dramatically due to an explosion in export credit provision by China and other emerging economies. Between 2000 and 2014, the BRICs (Brazil, Russia, India, and China) increased their official export financing from less than 3 percent to 40 percent of the world total (Exim 2015). The vast majority of this increase has come from China, which constitutes 90 percent of the medium- and long-term trade-related official support activity of the BRIC countries and is now the world's largest export credit provider. In 2014, China supplied $58 billion in export credit support—far more than the $12 billion provided by the US and, indeed, more than *all* the G7 rich countries *combined*—plus an additional $43 billion in overseas investment financing to promote its exports (see Figure 4.1). As one US export credit official stated regarding China's provision of export credit: "They just dwarf everyone else."[8]

The expansion in China's use of export credit is closely tied to its evolving development strategy. After forty years of rapid economic growth, China is reaching the limits of a growth model centered on low-wage, labor-intensive production of basic consumer goods, as the country faces slowing growth, rising labor costs, tighter resource and

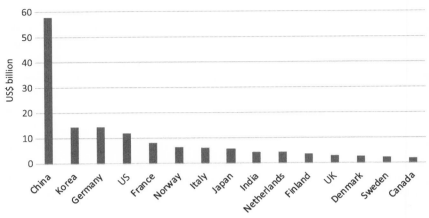

FIGURE 4.1 Export credit volumes, 2014.
Source: Exim 2015

environmental constraints, and increasing competition from lower-wage countries. According to Chinese policymakers, "China has entered a critical stage of economic restructuring" in which it faces "the challenge of optimizing and upgrading its industrial structure" in order to avoid getting stuck at its current income level and continue its process of development (DRC 2014). Their hope is that "if China manages to optimize and upgrade its industrial structure, gathers new momentum for a steady economic growth and gains a new competitive edge, it will escape the middle-income trap and develop into a high-income country." China's officials see industrial upgrading as "the only way out" of under-development, but also as "a long uphill battle," in which the state must play an active role (DRC 2014).

The Chinese government identifies advanced manufacturing as "the way out for China as it seeks a new economic driver and a new global competitive edge" (Jing and Man-ki 2015). China is seeking to transform its economy and move into more technology-intensive and higher-value-added industries. With its "Made in China 2025" industrial strategy, China has targeted ten priority sectors: information technology, robotics, aerospace, vehicles, rail equipment, advanced materials, power equipment, ocean-engineering equipment and ships, biopharmaceuticals and medical equipment, and agricultural machinery (Hopewell 2018; Kennedy 2015). China's stated goal is to enable its manufacturing sector to "catch-up" with advanced-industrialized countries by 2025 and ultimately to be a world-leading manufacturing power by 2049.

Export credit is a key part of China's developmental state toolkit. It is one of the prime means by which China is deploying its newfound financial power to give its firms a competitive advantage in global markets, while fostering industrial upgrading and the development of strategic sectors. The country has three ECAs—China Exim Bank, China Development Bank, and Sinosure—and, as one US trade official put it, "Now China is sitting on huge reserves, and they probably more than anyone can afford to subsidize."[9] Promoting China's exports through state-backed export credit is a strategy that comes from the State Council and is implemented by these state-owned policy banks (CDB, Exim Bank) and insurer (Sinosure) in close coordination with Chinese firms (Downs 2011). China's policy banks are funded through bond issues (80 percent of which are bought by China's state-owned commercial banks), and also receive periodic cash infusions from state coffers and China's massive foreign exchange reserves; in 2015, for example, China Exim Bank and CDB received capital injections totaling $93 billion (Kong and Gallagher 2017). Since the late 1990s, China has undertaken substantial administrative reforms to improve the performance of its policy banks, building highly effective institutions for delivering export credit: its ECAs are well-resourced and professionalized, with considerable expertise (Downs 2011; Sanderson and Forsythe 2012). China has thus developed substantial institutional capacity and capability in this area. On export credit, there is a convergence between the strategic objectives of the Chinese government and the commercial interests of its firms. Its ECAs and business work closely together to structure and execute transactions, which advance both national and corporate interests concurrently (Downs 2011).

A representative of a rival ECA characterized China's strategy as follows:

What China does is develop an industry domestically, then uses export credit to make markets for them abroad. There's a strategically well-implemented plan to start an industry, grow that industry and then internationalize it, and these are the three agencies that do it for them. And what we've seen is that when they pick a sector, they can dominate it. They start domestically, then use below-market financing to start moving into emerging markets in Africa, Latin America, and poorer parts of Asia, then into industrialized countries like the US, EU, Canada. They're not in it for the short-term game. They're in it for the long-term, fifty years down the road, when they'll be dominating every sector economically. There is a plan and they've done it damn well so far—and there's no sign anyone is about to slow it down.[10]

As a result, he continued: "Frankly, everyone can see what's coming and everyone is scared to death." While other successful recent developers, such as the East Asian newly industrialized countries (NICs)—Korea, Singapore, Taiwan, and Hong Kong—also made use of export credit as part of their development strategies (World Bank 1993), China has been characterized as conducting "the most aggressive export credit financing campaign in history" (Ezell 2011). And this strategy is proving highly effective. To quote one WTO official: "In almost every capital goods sector, China is going from a bit player to being one of the biggest."[11]

Export credit has been the driving force behind the expansion of China's activities in Africa, Latin America, and elsewhere (Bräutigam 2009; Gallagher, Irwin, and Koleski 2012). While often mistakenly described as aid, most of China's lending to Africa and other parts of the developing world is in fact export credit—loans tied to the export of Chinese goods (Bräutigam 2009). Chinese ECAs are aggressively using export credit for export promotion purposes, offering preferential loans in exchange for resources or low-cost loans on very extended repayment terms on projects to gain market share. In 2013, for instance, its Exim Bank announced that China would provide $1 trillion in financing through 2025 for transportation infrastructure projects in Africa (Akhtar 2015). China's massive new Belt and Road Initiative provides similar avenues for using its financial might to support its industries and the "going out" of Chinese enterprises abroad (Ferdinand 2016).

Although considerably smaller in scale, other emerging economies are using export financing strategically in key sectors to significant effect—including Brazil in construction, Russia in nuclear energy, and India in transportation and energy. Given the extremely large volumes of financing it is providing, China's use of export credit is seen as a serious competitive challenge to the US, EU, and other advanced-industrialized states and the most significant threat to the export credit regime.

## EROSION OF THE EXPORT CREDIT GOVERNANCE REGIME

While the global regulatory regime centered on the OECD Arrangement worked very effectively to govern export credit until recently, its disciplines are now being undermined by the substantial increase in export credit provision by China and other emerging economies. The international export credit regime addresses what Arthur Stein (1982) calls a "dilemma of common interests," where cooperation is necessary to avoid an undesirable outcome (in this case, a war of competitive subsidization that could destabilize the trading system) but individually each state has an incentive to deviate (by providing credit subsidies to support their exports). As Stein (1982: 312–13) states, "All regimes intended to deal with dilemmas of common interests must specify strict patterns of behavior and insure that no one cheats." This requires institutional structures for policing compliance: the regime must specify "what constitutes cheating, and each actor must be assured of its own ability to spot others' cheating immediately," through "verification and monitoring procedures" that ensure cheating is "observable." Accordingly, the export credit regime has developed a detailed set of rules defining the terms on which states are allowed to provide export credit, with extensive monitoring procedures to ensure compliance. For the regime to work, however, states need assurance that their competitors are not cheating; China's absence therefore presents a significant problem.

Information-sharing is recognized as one of the most important functions of regimes (Keohane 1984). Uncertainty about other states' behavior, and the difficulty of observing others' actions clearly, is a significant obstacle to international cooperation (Koremenos, Lipson, and Snidal 2001). International regimes reduce risk and uncertainty by increasing the flow of information among member states, making regimes most valuable in cases where information is asymmetrically distributed (Keohane 1984). In the case of export credit, where states have extensive information about their own activities but not those of others, a central function of the Arrangement is providing increased transparency and information-sharing among participants: indeed, its "detailed transparency provisions" have been identified as the "most important part of the regime" (Moravcsik 1989: 204). By requiring states to provide information about their export credit activities, the transparency provisions of the regime act as both a method of monitoring and an incentive for compliance with its disciplines and have therefore played a crucial role in ensuring its stability.

The Agreement's information-sharing requirements provide a powerful deterrence against cheating by giving other participants the opportunity to match the terms of any bid a state is providing. Since China is not subject to the regime's reporting requirements, however, states have no means to verify and monitor its behavior and no assurance that it will not subsidize. As an ECA official stated:

If you want to provide export credit, you provide a confidential notification to Arrangement participants with the details of the transaction, with all the specific terms of the transaction going out to all of your competitor ECAs. So participants are constantly monitoring each other's activities. The only recourse is matching, but everyone agrees this surveillance mechanism works. Because the moment you break the terms, your competitors will just do the same thing. Whereas if China wants to break the terms, it just does it. There's nothing to stop them—and we won't even know it's happening.[12]

Other states cannot know the frequency with or extent to which China is breaching the Arrangement, but they know China has strong incentives to do so. Moreover, China's unwillingness to join the regime heightens distrust by signaling to participants that it wants to remain free to deviate from Arrangements terms, intensifying fears that China is using export credit to undercut their exports.

Because China is not bound by the information-sharing requirements of the export credit regime, other states lack reliable, comprehensive information about China's activities. According to an OECD study, "there is a scarcity of concrete information about the Chinese export credit programs, both about the types and volumes of export credit support and the terms and conditions for them" (Skarp 2015). As one negotiator indicated, "In terms of the terms and conditions they offer, we just don't know. We don't have access to that information."[13] Given the highly opaque and non-transparent nature of China's financing, publicly available data on its export credit practices are extremely limited, and the terms and conditions of specific transactions are usually not known. States are forced to rely on anecdotal evidence, gleaned from rare instances where Chinese lending terms have been leaked or otherwise become publicly available.

Based on this information, many OECD countries believe that China is using its ability to extend credit on more favorable terms to gain an advantage over participants in the Arrangement and related sectoral understandings. According to an ECA official, "What China is doing is riskier transactions, with fewer rules, at slightly less cost, with longer terms and a lot more flexibilities—when you combine all of those things, it can be quite an attractive package."[14] Moreover, he continued, "They don't have to go far off the market in any one term to get an overall package that is very attractive, plus they use all these side programs as further inducement [e.g., combining export credit with development aid]."[15] Since financing can often account for as much as 40 percent of the cost of a project, attractive export credit terms can be enough to give China's exports a significant competitive edge (Pomfret 2010).

The issue is not just the interest rate that China is charging. The interest rate is only one factor in determining the competitiveness of a loan, and thus whether state-backed lending will distort trade. Relaxing other terms and conditions of lending to depart from prevailing market conditions

TABLE 4.1 *OECD Arrangement requirements*

| OECD Arrangement major disciplines |
|---|

- *Minimum interest rate:* commercially indexed rates calculated monthly by the OECD for each participant based on the interest rate on its government bonds + 1% (Commercial Interest Reference Rates, CIRRs).
- *Minimum premium rate to cover credit risk:* ECAs are required to charge a premium, in addition to interest charges, to cover the risk of non-repayment of export credit; calculated based on country risk and commercial risk associated with the buyer.
- *Maximum loan repayment period:* 8½ years for loans to developed countries and 10 years for loans to developing countries; 12 and 14 years for rail infrastructure; 12 years for non-nuclear power plants; 18 years for nuclear power plants.
- *No grace period:* the first installment of principal and interest payment must be made within 6 months of the start of the credit, and a maximum of every 6 months thereafter.
- Minimum 15% down payment.
- Maximum support of 85% of export contract value.

| OECD Arrangement Rules on Tied Aid (Helsinki Package) |
|---|

- Tied aid not permitted for commercially viable projects or countries above lower middle income.
- Requires a minimum concessionality level of 35% (50% for LDCs).

can also act as a subsidy and be used to gain a competitive advantage. This is why the Arrangement regulates each of the key terms and conditions of export credit—including the interest rate, premium rate, repayment period, grace period, down payment, and portion of the contract supported—to ensure a level playing field among participants (see Table 4.1). For a non-participant like China, deviating from the Arrangement on any of these terms can be used to underbid competitors who are required to abide by its rules.

Since it is not bound by Arrangement rules, China is able to offer more flexible financing packages and more favorable terms. While it is believed that China's standard interest rate on export credit is generally similar to Arrangement or market terms, there are many instances (see examples below) where China has strategically provided lower interests rates (EU 2011). Even a slightly lower rate can give Chinese exports a significant advantage: a difference of just 1 percent to 2 percent in the interest rate increases total financing costs by 18 percent to 30 percent for a twelve-year loan (Gallagher, Irwin, and Koleski 2012). The other key element of pricing is risk premiums. Under the Arrangement, the minimum interest rate a lending country must charge is based on its *own* cost of borrowing (i.e., a flat rate, irrespective of the transaction or borrower); the regulation of risk premium fees is therefore an essential part of the Arrangement, which makes government-backed financing mimic the market by requiring ECAs to charge higher costs for riskier transactions. Since the premium rate charged by an ECA is often the largest component in the overall price of financing, a low (or no) premium rate could be the decisive factor in awarding a bid, making the Arrangement's risk premium rules essential to ensuring a level playing field (Gonter 2011). These fees can be considerable: on a ten-year loan, for example, risk premium rates average between 6 percent and 19 percent of the value of the loan, depending on the creditworthiness of the buyer.[16] OECD countries are concerned that Chinese ECAs often do not charge risk premiums, and when they do the fees do not approach the levels required by the Arrangement (Exim 2015). The lack of adequate fees to cover credit risk would represent a significant subsidy by the Chinese government, lowering the cost of financing for Chinese exporters and providing them with an advantage compared to those in the OECD.

In addition, China is also believed to gain an advantage through longer grace and repayment periods than permitted under the Arrangement (EU 2011). Extended repayment periods, like interest-rate subsidies, increase the attractiveness of financing. Importers, who evaluate financing in terms of its present value, prefer longer repayment periods, which allow them to discount the loan over a longer period, as well as shifting risk to the lender (Moravcsik 1989). While the Arrangement stipulates a maximum repayment period of 8.5 or 10 years for most loans, China's loans usually come with a maturity of 12 to 15 years (Bräutigam 2011), and it is not unusual to see Chinese loans with terms of 20 years or more, and even as high as 28.5 years (Bräutigam and Gallagher 2014). By offering longer loan tenure periods, China is able to provide more competitive financing, giving its exporters an advantage. Similarly, loans with longer grace periods are also less costly to service. While the Arrangement prohibits grace periods, China's loans often include a grace period of 2 to 5 years (Bräutigam 2011), which makes their terms considerably more favorable.

China also appears to violate Arrangement rules through its use of "mixed credits," or blended financing—combining standard export credit with development finance (grants or concessional loans at below-market rates) on the same transaction to produce an attractive financing package that gives its exporters an advantage in winning export contracts. Tied aid

(aid tied to the procurement of goods and services from the donor country, which can be used to circumvent the objectives of export credit disciplines) and mixed credits are strictly regulated by the Arrangement. The Arrangement's Helsinki Rules are intended to minimize the trade-distorting effects of tied aid and ensure it is directed towards genuine development purposes, by mandating minimum concessionality levels, preventing such financing from being used for projects in higher-income countries that can be financed commercially and ensuring it is instead exclusively used to support developmental projects in lower-income countries (see Table 4.1). The Arrangement substantially curtailed the practice of using tied aid for export promotion by OECD countries (Hall 2011; Tvardek 2011). However, China's tied aid frequently takes the form of low-concessionality loans, which are most distortionary from a trade perspective and violate the terms of the Arrangement (Exim 2016). China issues many large loans with tenors between twenty and twenty-five years, a seven-year grace period, and interest rates between 0 percent and 3 percent—terms which "likely fall outside the range permitted by OECD disciplines" by violating the minimum 35 percent concessionality requirement (Exim 2014). Furthermore, under the Arrangement, tied aid is only permitted for lower-middle- and low-income countries and non-commercially viable projects. However, China has contravened Arrangement rules by extending concessional loans to commercially viable projects in upper-middle-income countries (EU 2011). Through its use of tied aid and mixed credits, China is thus providing more attractive financing terms than available under the Arrangement (EU 2011; Exim 2018).

Rail equipment exports provide an illustration of how China's ability to provide more favorable credit terms advantages its firms and buoys its industrial upgrading. Representing an annual market of $120 billion, this is one of the ten priority industries that the Chinese government has targeted for overseas expansion as part of its effort to transform China into one of the world's most competitive advanced manufacturers. China has the world's largest high-speed rail network and its firms now participate in hundreds of overseas rail projects. In 2015, China's two state-owned railroad equipment makers (CSR Corp. and CNR Corp.) merged to create CRRC Corp., a $130 billion giant that is now the world's second-largest industrial company, behind GE, and dwarfs rivals such as Siemens and France's Alstom. The motive behind the merger is to leverage economies of scale that will allow China to compete overseas even more aggressively. China's rail exporters have been targeting emerging markets in Africa, Latin America, and Southeast Asia, while also winning high-profile contracts in advanced countries. According to analysts, although China's rail technology is less sophisticated, its main competitive strength is that its technology is offered as part of a package that includes attractive export credit financing (*Bloomberg* 2015).

Although it is extremely rare for the pricing terms of Chinese bids to become publicly available, one of the few cases where such terms are known was a $500 million sale of rail locomotives to Pakistan: while the Arrangement would require a minimum-risk premium fee of approximately 21 percent, China Exim Bank offered a fee of just 8 percent (*Financial Times* 2011). In another instance for which terms are known, CDB extended a $10 billion line of credit to Chinese rail equipment companies for sales to Argentina at LIBOR+6 percent, well below market rates that would be at least LIBOR+9.35 percent (Gallagher, Irwin, and Koleski 2012). The loan also involved a nineteen-year repayment period, violating the maximum loan tenor permitted by the Arrangement. The Arrangement provides repayment terms of up to twelve years for railway infrastructure exports to developed countries and up to fourteen years for developing countries, but China's repayment terms for its rail exports often exceed twenty years (Akhtar 2015). These differences in interest rates, fees, and repayment terms provide China's exports with a significant advantage over its OECD competitors and have helped to fuel the global expansion of its rail industry.

Rail is just one of many industries in which China is using more-favorable export credit terms to give its firms a competitive edge in global markets. The telecommunications sector provides another example. China Development Bank has provided one company alone—Huawei Technologies—with a massive $30 billion line of credit, enabling it to offer financing rates and terms that are unmatchable by competitors. While transaction details are usually masked in secrecy, Brazil's largest landline telephone company, Tele Norte, publicly confirmed that it chose to purchase network equipment from Huawei rather than competing European and American suppliers specifically because of access to that financing, which CDB offered with an interest rate of about 4 percent (compared to market rates of about 6 percent) and a two-year grace period on payments (Akhtar 2015). America Movil, the largest mobile phone carrier in Latin America, likewise confirmed that access to below-market financing from CDB was its major reason for choosing Huawei for a $1 billion deal to upgrade its network (Hufbauer, Fickling, and Wong 2011). Huawei's cheap credit line from CDB is seen as playing a similarly critical role in enabling the company to increase its sales to India from $50 million to $2.5 billion in just one year (Ezell 2011). Fueled by such support, Huawei has become the world's largest telecommunications equipment manufacturer, overtaking Ericsson, the European-based multinational, in 2012. The global expansion of ZTE, China's other major telecom equipment manufacturer, has been similarly driven by $25 billion credit lines from CDB and China Exim Bank. An EU investigation found that "such facilities are a major selling point which enables ZTE to clinch deals on its export markets ahead of its competitors, while shifting the entirety or majority of its risk of payment onto the Chinese policy banks" (Dalton 2011). China is thus using attractive export credit terms to fuel the global expansion of national champions.

Other instances of China undercutting the terms of the Arrangement abound. China Exim Bank provided a $45 million loan to Jamaica for construction of a convention center at 2 percent interest with a twenty-year repayment period (Gallagher, Irwin, and Koleski 2012); however, the Arrangement would require a minimum interest rate of approximately 5 percent, along with a 20 percent premium fee and a maximum loan tenor of ten years.[17] A Chinese company was awarded a contract to build a €170 million bridge in Serbia, without any call for tender, based on a loan from China Exim Bank providing an interest rate of 3 percent and a fifteen-year repayment period (OA 2010). The Arrangement would require a minimum 5 percent interest rate plus premium fees of approximately 12 percent to 25 percent and a maximum ten-year repayment period. Similarly, a $1.25 billion contract to modernize and expand a Serbian coal power plant was awarded to a Chinese company, CMCEC, with financing provided by China Exim Bank at 3 percent interest over fifteen years (OA 2010). The Arrangement, in contrast, would require approximately 4 percent interest plus premium fees of 12 percent to 25 percent and a maximum twelve-year repayment period. Other projects in Eastern Europe awarded to Chinese firms with ECA backing including several $500 million to $750 million power plants, a €3 billion high-speed rail link between Belgrade and Budapest, and a €600 million highway. In violation of the terms of the Arrangement, China is generally charging between 2 percent to 2.5 percent for these loans, with twenty- to thirty-year repayment periods (Karnitschnig 2017). Eastern Europe is seen as a strategic entry point for Chinese companies in the European market, and Chinese ECAs are reportedly using aggressive financing practices to undercut competitors and expand their foothold in these markets (OA 2010; EU 2011).

It is not necessary for all, or even most, of China's export credit to be subsidized for it to pose a competitive threat to OECD countries or jeopardize the Arrangement. By operating outside the Arrangement, China has maximum flexibility to adjust the terms and conditions of its financing, based on competitive conditions and its strategic interests. As one ECA official stated: "They like their flexibility and use it tremendously."[18] Chinese rates and lending terms vary considerably: Chinese ECAs may often provide financing not far from Arrangement or market terms, but, for strategically important transactions, they are able to undercut the Arrangement and use discounted financing to gain a competitive advantage (Exim 2006). This is akin to a "loss leader" strategy— where an initial subsidy serves as an investment in winning subsequent sales—with China using cheap credit selectively to win key contracts that enable its firms to gain a foothold in a new market, establish their technology and technical standards, and develop brand recognition.

OECD ECAs are receiving mounting complaints from their exporters that they are losing contracts to Chinese firms because of the more favorable financing packages the latter are able to offer. According to an American business representative, "US multinationals are facing with greater frequency the problem of subsidized export credit financing from China in international tenders" (Schewel 2011b). In the words of the US Export–Import Bank Chair: "They're winning deals in part because they're not playing by the rules" (Reddy 2011). As one ECA official stated, "We've seen them coming in to areas where they are competing with our exporters, often with very cheap money, and often with tied agreements."[19] Another summarized: "Everyone feels under attack."[20]

Given the massive volume of financing it is providing, incorporating China into global rule-making and disciplines on export credit is a key priority of the US, EU, and other advanced-industrialized states (see, for example, European Commission 2015; United States 2015a). As the head of the US Export–Import Bank put it, "it's important that they play by the rules that everybody else is playing by" (Schewel 2011a). However, such efforts have proven largely unsuccessful. Although the US strongly pressed China to join the Arrangement, China refused. Beijing has indicated that it will not join a set of rules that it played no role in creating and that do not reflect its development objectives. China's position, as articulated by Chen Deming, former Minister of Commerce, is that the OECD Arrangement "aims to solve the problem of international competition among developed countries and does not fully reflect the development concerns of developing countries" like China (Deming and Peiru 2016: 209). As a developing country, he argues, China's provision of export credit is distinct, and it is not appropriate for China to join the Arrangement. Thus, as OECD negotiators put it, "China has shown no interest in coming here" or "subjecting their export credit to these disciplines."[21]

Participants fear that China's absence significantly undermines the Arrangement and reduces its effectiveness. As one ECA official stated, "the big question on everyone's mind now is whether the Arrangement is becoming obsolete."[22] A negotiator summed up the problem as follows:

You have this Arrangement that's worked well for decades and over time has gotten better and better as its disciplines bite more and more. The problem is that they were universal rules—everyone who exported capital goods was a member—but now the world has completely changed. ... China has traditionally been an exporter of consumer goods, but now there is almost no sector where China is not a major exporter of capital goods. What happens to your export credit Arrangement if China is not a participant? If the Arrangement is going to operate in a meaningful way, it has to involve all the major exporters of capital goods, meaning it has to involve China. Everyone who exports capital goods needs to be part of the system or it can't work.[23]

Similarly, another participant echoed this in stating that, for the Arrangement to work effectively, "The major providers of export credit need to be there. The Arrangement becomes pretty irrelevant pretty quickly if the world's biggest exporter won't participate. There's no point agreeing on reciprocal restraint if it doesn't include all actors."[24] This has already begun to hamper the ongoing process of negotiations to continually strengthen the Arrangement. Negotiators report that there are now many issues that "members don't want to talk about" because "why would they agree to rules when China is not there and China is the biggest producer?"[25] States are reluctant to commit themselves to new disciplines that will not also bind China.

### International Working Group on Export Credits

Thwarted in its efforts to convince China to join the Arrangement, the US tried a different tack. In 2012, the US drove the creation of a new International Working Group on Export Credits (IWG), involving eighteen major developed and developing countries, including China, to negotiate a successor to the OECD Arrangement. This was a US-led initiative pushed at the highest levels that came out of the bilateral US–China Strategic and Economic Dialogue (S&ED). After many years of pressure by the US, following a meeting between President Barack Obama and soon to be President Xi Jinping, the two countries jointly announced

agreement "to establish an international working group of major providers of export financing to make concrete progress towards a set of
international guidelines on the provision of official export financing."[26]
The resulting IWG came to include the nine participants in the OECD
Arrangement (the US, EU, Canada, Japan, Korea, Norway, Switzerland,
New Zealand, and Australia) as well as nine non-participants (the BRICS,
plus Indonesia, Israel, Malaysia, and Turkey). It was China that insisted
on the participation of the eight other emerging economies, in order to
ensure balance between developed and emerging economies and bolster
its side in the negotiations by ensuring that it would not be outnumbered
by the Arrangement participants. As a result, compared to the Arrangement, the IWG is considerably more inclusive, in that nearly half of its
participants are developing countries.

From the perspective of the US and other developed countries, the IWG
was a second-best solution: as one negotiator stated, "we had dreamed of
dragging China into the OECD Arrangement, but the failure of that effort
is what led to the IWG."[27] Seeking to rein in export credit provision by
China, the IWG represented an attempt by the US to maintain a liberal
regime of export credit governance by replacing the Arrangement with a
new version that would incorporate the major emerging economies. The
US identified this as a key strategic priority in its economic relations with
China and, negotiators report, "pushed China very hard" to enter into
and engage in the negotiations.[28] As one US official stated, "Everyone's
hopes are resting on the IWG—that it will be able to control China's
ability to take everyone's lunch."[29] Other advanced-industrialized states
have placed similar emphasis on the IWG as a means to create new, more
universal rules on export credit.

Yet, given the centrality of export credit to their development strategies, China and the other emerging economies have little incentive either
to join existing governance arrangements or subject themselves to new
disciplines that could inhibit their future growth prospects. A representative of the US Chamber of Commerce expressed it thus: "Their economies
depend on their ECAs. I don't see a world where they're suddenly going to
say 'OK, we don't need our ECAs'. That's just not realistic."[30] A party to
the negotiations provided a similar assessment:

China has vast resources—the amount of money available now is almost beyond
belief. Their view is "why the hell should we agree to not use these resources?
These guys are trying to constrain our ability to achieve our rightful place in the
world." They don't see anything in it for them. It's not in their interest to accept
these constraints. They provide so much export credit it's astounding. Beside the

Chinese, the US Exim Bank looks like a corner bank in Ames, Iowa. China is doing this on a scale that just dwarfs what's happening in the rest of the world. Why should they let anyone stop them?[31]

Not only does export credit form part of China's industrial upgrading strategy, but as China's growth has slowed in recent years it has increasingly sought to export its excess capacity. In this context, China has little or no interest in accepting restrictions on its use of export finance.

Consequently, despite significant pressure from the US, as well as other advanced-industrialized states, there has been little progress in the IWG. The IWG has held meetings every three to six months, but has been working at a "glacial pace" and yielded "negligible results" (Bergsten 2014). According to participants, this is primarily due to resistance from China: "China has been foot-dragging in meetings, slowing the process down and refusing to put any real proposals on the table. If China wanted to do a deal, than we could move quickly, but the fact is it doesn't."[32] Negotiators indicate that China has been "throwing up all kinds of process-based hurdles and obstructions" and "its actions indicate that it is not interested in moving forward."[33] As a result, there has been "very little movement" and, indeed, "very little in the way of real negotiations."[34]

For the first three years of the IWG, China refused to engage in negotiations on a set of general, horizontal rules—the approach favored by the majority of participants. Instead, China insisted that the IWG should begin only with "discussions" of export credit practices in two specific industrial sectors. At China's insistence, the sectors chosen were shipbuilding—although the US and several other IWG members have no export credit activities in that sector—and medical equipment—a sector without any significant export credit intervention (as one participant put it, "not even a real sector," from the perspective of export credit).[35] China also insisted on keeping core issues related to export credit provision— such as interest rates, premiums, and transparency—out of the discussion. As a result, according to negotiators, the sectoral negotiations were "essentially useless" and "didn't really mean anything."[36] It was not until 2015 that China even agreed to begin discussions on a general, horizontal system of rules. In the words of one Western ECA official, "Now they've agreed to go to horizontal negotiations—it took 3 years to get to where we should have started in the first place."[37] And negotiators report that even now: "There's nothing *in* the negotiations yet," and no prospect of any agreement on the horizon.[38]

As a result, many participants have significantly lowered their expectations for the IWG. In the words of one senior US ECA official,

What the US, EU and other OECD members want is a new version of the Arrangement—a comprehensive set of rules that incorporates the emerging economies. But that's exactly what China is *not* going to participate in. They're not going to play that game—negotiating a new version of the Arrangement. The best we can likely aim for is improved transparency. That alone would be quite an accomplishment in the world we have today.[39]

For the US and other advanced-industrialized states, improved transparency, even simply about what programs China is using, is an important objective of the IWG. But negotiators report that even this has been a "huge struggle."[40] So far within the IWG, it is only the OECD members that have shared detailed information about their export credit programs—something they are already required to do under the OECD Arrangement—while China has refused to provide comparable information on its own programs. Information exchange has been largely one-sided, with little reciprocity: China, officials from OECD states complain, has "tried to suck in as much information as possible from us about how we do export credit while giving us as little information as possible about their own activities."[41]

One trade official thus summed up the IWG negotiations as follows: "The process has been going on for years and there has been zero progress."[42] Efforts by the US and other advanced-industrialized states to engage China and other emerging economies in multilateral negotiations to create new restraints on export credit—or even to share basic information about their practices—have proven fruitless. While formally cooperating in the negotiations, China's behavior has served primarily to thwart rather than advance the goal of arriving at a new set of disciplines. It is a sign of China's newfound power that it has been able to exert such control over the agenda, process, and pace of the negotiations and refused to be pressured or coerced into accepting rules that it views as against its interests.

From its position as global hegemon, the US was the driving force behind the creation of the Arrangement and the continual strengthening of its disciplines; however, its current inability to press China into existing or new governance arrangements that would control its use of export credit suggests an important weakening of US power in the face of a rising China. Moreover, at the same time that the US faces a growing competitive challenge from China and other emerging powers, its role as the traditional leader of export credit governance has also been undermined by domestic political conflicts over its own ECA. A campaign by the ultra-free-market Tea Party movement to eliminate the US Export–Import Bank has severely constrained the US's provision of export credit, further diminishing its leverage in international negotiations (Chin and Gallagher 2015; Hopewell 2017c).

The international regulatory regime for export credit has worked well for decades, but what was once a highly effective governance mechanism is now in danger of being subverted by the rise of new powers outside of that system. In the contemporary world of export credit, to quote one ECA official, "China is the 800-pound gorilla."[43] Its substantial economic and political power has enabled China to act outside the bounds of the Arrangement and to resist pressures from the US and other traditional powers to agree to the creation of a new set of disciplines that would restrict its use of export credit. As one trade official bluntly put it, "China is the new actor breaking everything to pieces."[44] Among export credit practitioners, the rise of China and other emerging economies is therefore widely seen as the greatest single challenge to the existing governance regime.

## INADEQUACY OF WTO DISCIPLINES

Amid the weakening of the OECD Arrangement's authority and the inability to reach agreement on a new version to replace it, one might expect the US and other advanced-industrialized states to turn to the WTO as an alternative means to compel China and the other emerging economies to rein in their use of export credit. However, for the purposes of disciplining export credit, the WTO is a poor substitute for the Arrangement. Official export credit is covered by the WTO Agreement on Subsidies and Countervailing Measures (ASCM), which disciplines the use of export subsidies and the actions countries can take to counter the effects of these subsidies. The OECD Arrangement is incorporated into the ASCM as a carve out to the illustrative list of prohibited export subsidies in Annex 1 (item (k)) (Shaffer, Wolfe, and Le 2015). This operates as a "safe harbor clause," ensuring that any use of export credit by a WTO member that is in conformity with the Arrangement's disciplines will not be considered a prohibited export subsidy under WTO rules (OECD 2011: 232; Wright 2011). Consequently, any WTO member who acts within the conditions set out in the Arrangement, regardless of whether they are a participant to it, is deemed to be in compliance with their WTO obligations (Shaffer, Wolfe, and Le 2015).

This means that, technically, the Arrangement's disciplines are incorporated into WTO rules. However, they are nearly impossible to enforce at the WTO. Part of the reason the OECD Arrangement was created in the first place is that the dispute-settlement mechanism provided in the WTO, and its predecessor the GATT, is largely ineffective for disciplining export credit (Moravcsik 1989). First, WTO dispute settlement is generally considered too cumbersome and not fast enough to work well in this area. Given the lengthy nature of the WTO dispute-settlement process, which often takes many years for a case to reach a conclusion, even if a country were to succeed in winning a determination that a competitor's financing for a specific transaction constituted a prohibited export subsidy, the case would not be concluded until years after that transaction had been completed and its exporter had lost the contract.

Second, in contrast to the real time transparency provided by the Arrangement, the WTO contains no comparable mechanism for the routine exchange of detailed and confidential transaction data. While Arrangement participants are required to share extensive information about their practices with one another, the export credit practices of non-participants are generally secretive and non-transparent, with the result that their competitors lack detailed information about their export credit policies and programs as well as the specific terms of individual transactions. This lack of information renders it extremely difficult to challenge export credit practices at the WTO.

Third, each time a state provides export credit, whether or not it is considered a subsidy will depend on the specifics of that transaction. As one trade official stated, in order to challenge a state's export credit policies at the WTO, "you would need to bring a systemic case, but the terms and conditions of each transaction are different, so it is difficult if not usually impossible to bring a systemic case. Since it is very difficult to challenge a whole program, you would be left challenging individual transactions."[45] Consequently, there have to date been only two cases on (non-agricultural) export credit in the history of WTO dispute settlement—out of a total of over 500 disputes.[46]

There are thus fundamental differences in how disciplines work in the Arrangement compared to the WTO, with crucial implications for the governance of export credit. As one WTO official stated,

The Arrangement works very well. Our rules are completely different in how they work and what they do. Short of prohibiting all use of export credit, there's little the WTO can do. Our structure and the way our rules work are not well-suited to this issue. The system at the WTO really only works for broad systemic issues, and it is almost completely useless for dealing with export credit because it's ex-post. Our system would never provide the day-to-day working and certainty of the OECD Arrangement.[47]

As a result of the way its rules and dispute settlement mechanism are designed and function, the WTO is ill-equipped to regulate export credit and cannot provide a viable alternative to the OECD Arrangement.

Thus, while it would be theoretically possible to use the WTO's dispute-settlement mechanism to challenge the use of export credit by China and other emerging economies, WTO trade lawyers indicate that in practice this would be "extraordinarily difficult if not usually impossible."[48] As one indicated:

China's use of export credit is potentially actionable at the WTO, yes. But the reason they created the system for governing export credit in the OECD in the first place is because our rules [at the WTO] have some profound weaknesses. Here, it's a two- to three-year process to take a case, plus eighteen months of implementation, so maybe five years later—long after you have lost the contract—you could get a finding that the exporting country violated its WTO obligations. But, by then, it's not like the transaction and the financing can be undone. So, in theory, one could challenge China on export credit, you could litigate it for five years, but what would you have at the end of five years?

In sum, "China could be vulnerable to a WTO challenge, but it would be expensive, take years to occur, and be very hard to get a meaningful victory."[49] The WTO system is thus inadequate for disciplining state-backed export credit and provides little means for the US and other traditional powers to compel China to restrict its use of export credit.

### CONCLUSION

As this chapter has shown, the global governance of export credit has been destabilized by the rise of China. Analysis of the OECD Arrangement and IWG negotiations suggest that contemporary power shifts are making multilateral cooperation to govern export credit increasingly difficult and that the capacity of the US hegemon to steer global rule-making in this area is diminishing in the context of growing multipolarity. The rise of China and other emerging economies as major providers of government-backed trade financing has proven highly disruptive to the transparent, rule-bound, orderly system for the governance of export credit. Reluctant to relinquish an important industrial policy tool that is vital to its continued development, China has resisted external disciplines on its use of export credit. But its unwillingness either to join existing governance arrangements or to subject itself to new disciplines threatens what has until now been a highly effective regulatory regime and risks prompting a reemergence of destructive competition via export credit subsidies. The case of export credit thus throws into stark relief the tension between the development objectives of China and other emerging powers and the American-led liberal international economic order. And, as the following chapter will demonstrate, the failure to effectively incorporate China into the global governance of export credit has broader implications that go beyond trade or international economic relations, narrowly defined—it also has important consequences for issues at the intersection of trade and other policy objectives, such as environment.

# 5

# Negotiating in the Dragon's Shadow: Export Credit for Coal Plants

This chapter examines the US-led effort to establish new global rules on export credit for coal-fired power plants—a trade issue with important environmental implications. The development of overseas coal power projects is a large and lucrative industry, and one in which a number of the world's leading economies have significant export interests at stake. Government-backed export credit for coal power plants supports the export of technology and equipment, as well as engineering and construction services, by providing financing at below-market rates and in instances where commercial financing may not otherwise be available. As such, it operates as an export subsidy and plays a significant role in promoting the expansion of such plants abroad. Export credit has therefore been a key target of efforts to reduce global fossil fuel subsidies, amid concerns about the effects of climate change.

Coal power is the most polluting fossil fuel technology. Coal plants represent the single largest source of global carbon emissions from combustion and are a key driver of climate change; they emit twice as much, for example, as natural gas plants (NRDC 2017). Climate scientists have established that the use of coal must be rapidly phased out if the world is to have any possibility of curbing climate change. In the 2015 Paris Agreement, arising from the 21st Conference of the Parties (COP21) to the United Nations Framework Convention on Climate Change (UNFCCC), more than 190 countries committed to seeking to limit the rise in average world temperature to well below 2 degrees Celsius, and to make best efforts to limit it to 1.5 degrees. According to research by the International Energy Agency, to have a 50 percent chance of limiting the rise in global temperatures to 2 degrees would require immediately halting all new coal plant construction and retiring two-thirds of existing stock by 2040 (IEA 2014b). New coal plants currently planned will result in six times more carbon pollution than is possible to keep warming to 1.5 degrees Celsius.[1]

Motivated by environmental concerns, the US spearheaded an initiative in 2013 to negotiate a multilateral agreement that would prohibit the use of export credit for coal-fired power plants. Given China's resistance to export credit disciplines and the lack of progress in the International Working Group on Export Credits (IWG) detailed in the last chapter, the US was forced to pursue new disciplines on coal financing within the context of the OECD Arrangement. This meant, however, that any resulting rules would not cover China, which is now the world's largest exporter and financer of overseas coal power projects. While China was not a party to the negotiations, I argue that its absence profoundly affected the dynamics of global trade negotiations on export credit for coal plants and undermined US efforts to secure an ambitious agreement with a stringent set of disciplines.

This case, I argue, underscores the centrality of China and the difficulty for the US and other states of trying to conduct any major multilateral trade negotiation, and construct effective global trade rules, without it. Although the US was able to successfully lead the creation of a new multilateral agreement restricting export credit for coal-fired power plants, the impact of the agreement is severely limited by the fact that China is not a participant: the new rules leave out the biggest player in this sector, responsible for nearly half of all export credit for coal plants worldwide. Furthermore, even though China was not a participant, it nonetheless cast a major shadow over the negotiations. OECD countries that export coal plants were understandably reluctant to agree to restrict their use of export credit when China—the dominant player in the field and their chief competitor—would face no similar restrictions on supporting its exports. The fact that China would not be bound by the agreement, and therefore able to continue to promote its exports with cheap state-supported financing and guarantees, would give its exporters a significant competitive advantage over those from the OECD. China's growing role in this sector and its absence from the negotiations thus significantly complicated efforts to secure effective international disciplines on export credit for coal plants and ultimately contributed to lowering the level of ambition in the final agreement. While the US had sought a broad prohibition on export credit for coal plants, it was ultimately only able to secure an agreement by including large carve-outs necessary to appease countries concerned about Chinese competition. The OECD coal agreement was thus a product of American power and leadership, but also one that demonstrates the diminished capacity of the US to exercise global leadership and steer global rule-making on trade and environment in the context of a rising China.

## TRADE AND ENVIRONMENT GOVERNANCE UNDER THE OECD ARRANGEMENT

Seeking to incorporate environmental objectives into the global governance of export credit is not new but has considerable precedent. There has long been recognition that export credit—as a form of export subsidy—lies at the intersection of trade and environment. Many of the projects financed by export credit agencies (ECAs), such as large dams, power plants, mines, oil and gas, and dredging for ports, have potentially significant environmental and social implications. Beginning in the 1980s, prompted by the role of export credit in a number of high-profile, controversial projects, such as the Three Gorges Dam in China and the Bataan nuclear power plant in the Philippines, ECAs came under increasing scrutiny and faced mounting pressure from public stakeholders and NGOs not to support projects that harm the environment or adversely affect local communities. Civil society actors waged a large-scale transnational advocacy campaign that pressed OECD countries to accept that ECAs should promote compliance with international environmental and social standards (Maurer and Nakhooda 2003; Schaper 2007; Wright 2011). In the mid-1990s, at the instigation of the US, the participants in the OECD Arrangement began a process of expanding its rules to address the potential environmental and social impacts of the projects they finance. This ultimately resulted in the establishment of the OECD Common Approaches for Export Credits and Environmental and Social Due Diligence ("Common Approaches") in 2003, and subsequent negotiations by states to revise and deepen its rules in 2005, 2007, 2012, and 2016.

The Common Approaches seek to ensure that all officially supported medium- to long-term export credit transactions (i.e., with repayment terms of two years or more) are reviewed for their potential environmental impacts, and any negative impacts are mitigated or eliminated in order to achieve a high level of environmental protection (Karkovirta 2011). Part of the goal of creating common environmental procedures is to maintain a level playing field among participants by harmonizing environmental and social standards, in order to ensure that no country gains a competitive advantage by attaching lower environmental standards to its provision of export credit and to thereby prevent "a race to the bottom." Although, like the rest of the Arrangement, it is a non-binding, consensus-based set of rules, compliance is reviewed regularly and monitored by the OECD Secretariat, and these reviews have shown a high degree of ECA compliance with the Common Approaches (OECD 2016).

The Common Approaches have been progressively strengthened over time and expanded to include a range of issues, such as measures to combat bribery, provisions on responsible lending to low-income countries, screening and due diligence for project-related human rights impacts, and greenhouse gas reporting (OECD 2016a). In 2005, Arrangement participants established a sector-specific agreement on renewable energy and water projects, which was revised in 2009 and subsequently expanded to include climate change mitigation in 2012 and adaptation in 2014 (OECD 2014b). This agreement permits more favorable export credit terms and conditions for this sector (such as longer repayment terms, which lowers the cost of such projects), in order to encourage a move toward renewable technologies and away from more traditional, carbon-intensive means of energy production (OECD 2011: 82). With the new sector-specific agreement on coal-fired power plants, in contrast, the objective was the reverse: to create restrictions limiting the use of export credit in this sector.

Over time, the OECD Arrangement has thus evolved from an instrument designed to address the subsidy component of export credit to a considerably broader and more complex regime addressing multiple aspects of export credit provision, including its environmental, social, and human rights implications. This process is far from complete and there remains considerable room for further strengthening and improving the system of environmental governance created at the OECD (Gelder, German, and Bailis 2012; Ruggie and Nelson 2015). But the Common Approaches and other related measures (such as the environment-related Sector Understandings) have nonetheless been identified as "a major step forward" in creating international standards for environmental and social due diligence on export credit, improving the environmental practices of ECAs, and moving toward the "greening" of export credit (Eberlein et al. 2010; see also Atzl 2014). The OECD rules have thus represented an essential global mechanism for governing the environmental and social aspects of export credit and protecting against its potentially adverse effects.

Importantly, the creation of the Common Approaches and the subsequent strengthening of its disciplines were initiated and driven by the

American hegemon, working in alliance with a network of NGOs (Schaper 2007). In the 1990s, the US was the first country to put in place a comprehensive set of national environmental standards for its ECA and, as more recently with the coal agreement, it effectively sought to extend those standards internationally to other export credit providers via the OECD (Wright 2011). Such measures were not unopposed: many states had no interest in constraining their exporters' access to export credit based on environmental criteria. Nevertheless, however, using a combination of moral authority and political pressure, the US was able to overcome resistance and succeeded in creating common international rules governing the environmental practices of ECAs (Schaper 2007). Without question, American leadership was crucial to the establishment and progressive expansion of the OECD's environmental and social governance measures for export credit.

The contrast with contemporary US efforts to create new rules for coal power plants is striking—and demonstrates the new limits on the reach of US power. With the creation of the OECD Common Approaches, the US led the establishment of a universal set of rules—universal in the sense of applying to what were then all major providers of export credit. Yet, as the following analysis will show, American efforts to exercise similar leadership in the environmental governance of export credit today have been weakened by the rise of China. As a result of China's emergence as the dominant player in this sector and its refusal to participate, the new rules cover only about half the universe of export credit for coal plants. The US's inability to create a similarly universal set of rules governing support for overseas coal plants illustrates new constraints on American influence and authority in global rule-making on trade and environment.

## EXPORT CREDIT FOR COAL POWER PLANTS

In the context of growing concern about climate change, there has been increasing pressure to institute global regulation of export credit for coal plants. Over the past decade, ECAs have become the largest source of public financing for overseas coal-fired power plants. Support from ECAs now greatly exceeds financing for these types of projects by multilateral finance institutions like the World Bank (FOE 2016). While funding for coal projects from the multilateral development banks has fallen, this has been more than offset by an increase in funding from ECAs (IEA 2017b). ECA support plays an important role in bringing coal-fired plants online worldwide. OECD ECAs helped finance more than $35 billion worth of coal plants between 2007 and 2014 (*Washington Post* 2015). According to leaked OECD documents, export credit provided by OECD countries supported nearly one-quarter of the annual new global coal power capacity installed outside of China between 2005 and 2012 (*Washington Post* 2015).

As with other industries, the primary purpose of ECA financing for coal power plants is to boost national exports and enhance the competitiveness and profits of their domestic firms and industries. ECA-supported coal projects typically back engineering, procurement, and construction (EPC) contracts awarded to domestic companies, including the export of technology and equipment such as boilers and steam turbines. These companies are usually large multinationals, such as Mitsubishi, Toshiba, Hitachi, and Marubeni in Japan, Doosan in South Korea, Alstom in France, Siemens in Germany, and General Electric in the United States. ECAs provide support for coal-fired power plants through direct project finance or loan guarantees (insurance to cover the overall risk of an investment at a lower cost and longer tenor [typically twelve to twenty years] than commercial insurance).

New coal projects often rely on ECA support because they require very large amounts of capital. The construction of a 600-megawatt coal-fired power plant, for example, typically costs between $500 million and $1.3 billion (NRDC 2016a). The availability of finance thus becomes a critical factor in the development of coal plants. ECAs typically provide financing at lower interest rates and with longer repayment terms than commercial sources; by providing financing at below-market rates, government-backed export credit acts as an important form of subsidy. In addition, the backing of an ECA can make it considerably more attractive for private financial institutions to participate in a project and bankroll the remaining finance. Loan guarantees provided by ECAs help to mitigate the level of commercial and political risk in a project; this can include protection against potential cash flow problems arising from the insolvency of project participants, or cover in case a buyer defaults on repayments, currency convertibility issues emerge (such as exchange rate fluctuations or exchange controls), or there is disruption arising from political and civil unrest. As such, the involvement of an ECA can be vital for projects that are deemed too risky for private commercial banks to finance alone (IEA 2017b). ECA support thus makes projects possible that might otherwise not be commercially viable if reliant solely on private sector financing.

Within the OECD, prompted by environmental concerns, countries have been committing to a coal phase out, shuttering coal plants and prohibiting the construction of new coal plants domestically. Yet, via their ECAs, many OECD countries are nonetheless supporting their industries to export the same technology abroad—overwhelmingly to developing countries. Critics therefore argue that ECA support provides "a hidden lifeline" that works to prop up declining, highly polluting industries in rich countries by offshoring emissions (NRDC 2017). A representative from the Overseas Development Institute, for instance, described export credit for coal plants as "dirty money" that helps advanced countries "export their dead-end technology to developing countries" (quoted in *The Guardian* 2015a).

Environmentalists have argued for an immediate and comprehensive ban on ECA support for new coal capacity. As one NGO representative stated: "At a time when the world is in a climate change crisis, to be pumping billions of dollars of subsidies into projects that increase greenhouse gasses is the worst possible policy imaginable."[2] Another echoed this: "The fact that ECAs basically guarantee a company that it can build its coal plant without losing money makes it more profitable, more viable, and more attractive. The impact of this finance on the climate is huge. If you could cut ECA support, then these investments would be much less attractive."[3] He continued: "This is government money. If governments seriously wants to address climate change they have to address this."[4]

Globally, the coal industry, not surprisingly, has strongly opposed efforts to curb ECA financing for coal-fired power plants. The industry argues that coal plants are necessary to address energy poverty by expanding access to affordable and reliable energy in poor countries, and that restricting or ending export credit for coal-fired power plants would undermine economic development (ACCF 2015). There is a significant deficit in global energy supply: a total of 1.2 billion people around the world lack electricity, the majority of whom are located in sub-Saharan Africa, where only 32 percent of the population has access to electricity (IEA 2015). One of the UN Sustainable Development Goals (SDG7) is to ensure access to "affordable, reliable, sustainable and modern energy for all" by 2030. Coal advocates make the case that emerging economies need to expand their power supply in response to growing demand and coal is their best option due to its cost efficiency and reliability. In the words of the head of the World Coal Association, "the WCA is concerned over the impact" that restrictions on ECA support for coal would "have on supporting economic development and improving energy access in many developing and emerging economies" (*Financial Times* 2015a). According to the association, higher-efficiency coal technology "has a vital role to play" in cutting emissions while delivering improved energy access, and export credit for higher-efficiency coal plants could help engineer a shift towards those technologies: "export credits are a key mechanism to ensure that [efficient] technologies are used rather than cheaper but higher-emission plants" (*E&E News* 2015c). The coal industry thus maintains that export credit for coal is beneficial not only for development but also for the environment.

Although the coal industry has been aggressively promoting higher-efficiency coal plants—so-called clean coal—as a solution to global energy needs, experts argue that this is a fiction (Littlecott 2015). As Oxfam, the international development NGO, puts it, the notion of "clean coal" is "in one word: deluded. No matter how it is spun, there is no such thing as 'clean coal', for it will always be one of the more damaging, polluting and, above all, expensive energy investment choices that could be made" (quoted in *E&E News* 2017). While expanding energy access is a global development priority, environmental and development NGOs argue that export credit for coal plants is not the answer.

Concerns about development are not what drive decisions by ECAs to support the export of coal plants. ECAs are not development agencies—they have no development mandate, and they do not apply criteria of poverty alleviation or energy access to their lending decisions. The provision of export credit is driven by commercial considerations and the interests of national exporters. Consequently, export credit for coal does not target energy poverty. Contrary to claims that export credit for coal helps to improve energy access for the poor, ECA financing has rarely supported electrification efforts in the poorest countries: between 2007 and 2015, for instance, not a single coal project backed by OECD export credit was in a low-income country, where the need for access to energy is greatest (NRDC 2016b). Instead, the main destination for export credit for coal plants is emerging economies (such as India, South Africa, Vietnam, Indonesia, Turkey, the Philippines, Chile, and Eastern Europe) (OECD 2014a). If the large volume of coal plants currently planned in these countries goes ahead, as World Bank President Jim Kim succinctly stated, "we are finished ... That would spell disaster for us and our planet" (*Eco-Business* 2017).

Furthermore, development NGOs argue that coal plants are not the most effective means to address energy poverty. With 80 percent of people who lack access to energy living in remote rural areas far from the grid, the most efficient and cost-effective way of providing them with access to electricity is through smaller-scale, decentralized—primarily renewable—energy sources, rather than extending grid services centered on large-scale power plants such as those fueled by coal (CAFOD 2016; ODI and Oxfam 2015). According to the International Energy Agency, the vast majority of energy investment is needed in distributed ("mini-grid" or "off-grid") energy projects, which are generally cheaper, more reliable, and most likely to directly benefit the poorest communities; yet currently only 1 percent of finance is allocated to such projects (IEA 2017a; SEFA 2017).

NGOs argue that export credit for coal plants does little to support energy access for the poor in developing countries and, instead, worsens conditions for local communities through deadly pollution. Coal power plants emit an array of toxic air pollutants (including sulfur dioxide, nitrogen oxides, particulate matter, and mercury) that negatively impact the local environment and public health. Pollution from coal plants causes a broad range of severe health problems, including respiratory ailments, stroke, cardiovascular disease, other heart-related diseases, and neurological conditions. In Southeast Asia alone, it is estimated that air pollution from coal plants is responsible for 20,000 premature deaths a year; and if all coal projects currently planned or under construction are actually built that figure will increase to 70,000 per year by 2030 (Koplitz et al. 2017). An estimated 100,000 people die annually from coal-fired power plants in India, where air pollution is now the third largest cause of death (*Business Standard* 2019; CNN 2017). The expansion of coal-fired power in South and Southeast Asia is thus having severe public health consequences. Coal plants also often have negative impacts on local economies, with, for example, toxic waste from plants poisoning water supplies and damaging the livelihoods of fisherfolk or pollutants contaminating arable land and crops and destroying the livelihoods of agricultural producers (UNESCO 2016). As a result of their severe environmental, health, and social impacts, plans for new coal plants in developing countries often engender intense opposition and protest from local communities (*Economic Times* 2016; Mathiesen 2016). In addition, many developing countries—and the poorest members of their populations—are the most vulnerable to the effects of climate change, of which carbon emissions from coal plants are a major driver (Oxfam 2017).

While coal plant exporters tout coal as an inexpensive energy source, opponents argue that the true cost of a coal plant is far higher when the large negative externalities it generates—including environmental degradation, pollution, and health impacts, as well as climate change implications—are taken into account. NGOs maintain that, based on a full cost analysis that includes these negative externalities, coal plants are far less competitive compared to alternative energy sources (OCI and WWF 2015). Indeed, in recent years, the cost of renewable energy, such as wind and solar, has plummeted. The world average cost of solar energy, for instance, has fallen from $750/MWh in 2000 to just $100/MWh today (WEF 2016).[5] As a result, renewables are becoming competitive with, and sometimes even cheaper than, coal power. It is estimated that renewable energy has already reached cost parity with conventional sources in more than thirty countries, and two-thirds of the world should reach this point within the next couple of years (WEF 2016). Solar is now the cheapest source of electricity in India, for example—as much as 50 percent cheaper than new coal power, according to some estimates (*Bloomberg* 2017).

Solar energy is projected to fall to half the price of electricity from coal within approximately one to two decades. Yet in order for the new coal-fired plants being built today to make an adequate rate of return they will need to burn coal for the next thirty to forty years—the average lifespan of a coal plant. Critics therefore argue that ECA support for coal-fired power plants means locking countries into a heavily polluting energy source for decades, when lower-cost alternatives are rapidly becoming available. New coal plants are at risk of becoming "stranded assets" unable to recover their original investment costs (Littlecott 2015). The International Energy Agency's World Energy Investment Outlook estimates that $120 billion worth of coal power plants around the worlds could be "stranded"—where the costs of the plants will exceed the long-term returns (IEA 2014a). Environmental groups thus argue that financing coal infrastructure that will be around for decades is a "carbon trap"—locking recipient countries into many years of harmful air pollution, water impacts, and greenhouse gas emissions (NRDC 2016a).

One of the Paris Agreement's stated objectives is "[m]aking finance flows consistent with a pathway towards low greenhouse gas emissions and climate resilient development." Yet ECA finance for energy has overwhelmingly flowed towards pollution-heavy energy sources, such as coal. OECD countries provide five times more export credit funding for fossil-fuel technology than green energy (Reuters 2015). Environmental NGOs contend that providing access to low-interest financing and loan guarantees for coal-fired power plants unfairly favors coal over clean energy alternatives. As a result, environmentalists argue, ECA support for coal rather than renewables is undermining the global transition to clean energy.

While exporters profit from ECA support for coal plants, critics argue that recipient countries are left to grapple with the financial, public health and environmental impacts (NRDC 2016a). Development and environmental NGOs complain that, by supporting coal plant exports, in the words of one campaigner, "governments are prioritizing the corporate profits of the coal industry over the climate and interests of the poor" (*The Guardian* 2015a). NGOs assert that, as one representative put it, "the main beneficiaries" of OECD export credit for coal plants "are OECD dirty industry, not energy poor nations" (*The Guardian* 2015b). It was these concerns about the negative environmental impacts of coal power projects that led the US under the Obama Administration to seek to establish new global rules restricting export credit for coal plants.

## CHINA'S SUPPORT FOR OVERSEAS COAL PLANTS

US-led efforts to secure new global disciplines on export credit for coal plants have, however, been profoundly undermined by the rise of China, which has dramatically transformed the competitive dynamics in this sector. Prior to 2000, China had virtually no coal power equipment exports (Hannam 2016). But, in less than two decades, it has become the world's largest exporter. In parallel with the growth of its exports, China has also become the largest financer of overseas coal-fired power plants. Between 2000 and 2016, it is estimated that China has provided over $40 billion to such projects (*Financial Times* 2017). The biggest recipients of Chinese export credit for coal plants have been India, Indonesia, Vietnam, Ukraine, and Pakistan. China acquired its technology through licensing and joint ventures with major foreign manufacturers, such as Mitsubishi, Toshiba, and Hitachi (Japan), Alstom (France), and Siemens (Germany) (Yue 2012). Now, it is constructing coal plants more cheaply and outbidding those firms (IEA 2017b). Its coal plant exports are aided by attractive financing from China's ECAs, along with its state-owned commercial banks. Over the past two decades, China Exim Bank and the China Development Bank have doubled their financing for energy projects in developing countries, and more than half of this has gone to coal power projects (Sherwin 2016). China's support for coal plant exports has become a large and growing contributor to the coal-intensification of the developing world: Chinese firms operating abroad have been involved in 41 percent of global coal capacity addition outside of the OECD and China since 2005, and 47 percent since 2010 (Hannam 2016).

In recent years, China has been engaged in a deep reform of its domestic energy policies. Prompted in part by a smog and air pollution crisis, which has been particularly acute in Beijing and Northern China, air quality has become a major political priority for the Chinese Communist Party (Hart, Bassett, and Johnson 2017). China declared a "war on pollution" with plans to improve air quality and reduce $CO_2$ emissions (Umbach and Yu 2016). Since 2013, China has set caps on and reduced its own domestic coal consumption, halted or postponed planned new coal plants, accelerated closure of older plants using dirtier technology, and made huge investments in the expansion of its renewable and low-carbon energy generation capacity, such as wind and solar (Forsythe 2016).

China's anti-pollution measures and excess coal power capacity—with many plants operating at only 40 percent to 50 percent capacity—have led to a decrease in investment and idle construction and manufacturing capacity in the sector (Hao 2017). With reduced demand for new coal projects domestically, China's energy firms are looking to foreign markets for growth, backed by substantial support from the Chinese ECAs. Shanghai Electric Group, for example, one of the country's largest electrical equipment makers, has announced plans to build coal power plants in Egypt, Pakistan, and Iran with a total capacity of 6,285 megawatts—almost ten times the 660 megawatts of coal power it has planned in China. The China Energy Engineering Corporation, which has no public plans to develop coal power in China, is building 2,200 megawatts of coal-fired power capacity in Vietnam and Malawi (Tabuchi 2017). Although China has made a massive investment in a shift to renewable energy domestically—investing an extraordinary $366 billion in renewables between 2014 and 2016—its overseas energy finance is still overwhelmingly dominated by coal (providing over twenty-three times more to overseas coal projects than renewables from 2013 to 2016) (NRDC 2017). While increasingly restricting coal power and seeking to promote a green energy transition at home, China has been vigorously pushing the expansion of coal power overseas by heavily financing coal projects that provide export opportunities to its coal-plant equipment manufacturers and state-owned enterprises undertaking engineering, procurement, and construction contracts. This has led to accusations that China is now following the example set by the OECD countries by "outsourcing its pollution" (Sherwin 2016) and "exporting carbon emissions" (Hao 2017). In addition, while China has shifted toward building the most efficient "ultra-supercritical" coal plants domestically due to concerns about air pollution and efforts to reduce its own emissions, nearly all of its exports are dirtier plants using less-efficient "subcritical" or "super-critical" technology. As one environmentalist put it, "we know what they are building abroad is lower technology than what they are building in China."[6]

China now plays a massive role in financing coal plants in the developing world. Dispensing cheap loans for the construction of coal plants forms part of China's broader overseas investment strategy and serves both geoeconomic and geopolitical objectives—contributing to domestic economic growth, while also bolstering the country's influence and leverage at the regional and global levels (Umbach and Yu 2016). ECA-backed exports of Chinese coal-fired technology are expected to expand further via China's Belt and Road Initiative (Sherwin 2016). Announced in 2013, the Belt and Road Initiative calls for up to $900 billion in infrastructure investments overseas, including power plants. It is intended to create additional new opportunities for Chinese companies and encourage the continued expansion of exports and is thus viewed as an important driver of China's future growth and economic development, as well as a means to pull neighboring countries more tightly into its sphere of influence.

## THE NEGOTIATION OF RULES ON EXPORT CREDIT FOR COAL PLANTS

The negotiations to establish new global rules governing the use of export credit for coal-fired power plants began in 2013, two years before the Paris climate change meetings. The US was the driving force behind the negotiations, seeking to establish an ambitious and expansive multilateral agreement that would virtually eliminate export credit support for overseas coal plants. This was intended to be a signature initiative of the Obama Administration in the lead up to the Paris climate talks and a centerpiece of US leadership on trade and climate change. However, the negotiations took place in the shadow of China's emergence as the world's largest financer of overseas coal plants, which significantly shaped their dynamics. The coal agreement has been described by states involved as "highly complex and controversial" and probably "the most political negotiation" to take place at the OECD on export credit in years.[7]

In June 2013, in response to environmental pressure and growing concern about climate change, President Obama announced a new US Climate Action Plan (United States 2013d). Emphasizing its obligation to act as a global leader in reducing carbon emissions, the US committed to end public financing for new conventional coal-fired power plants except in the poorest countries and under very strict circumstances:

the President calls for an end to US government support for public financing of new coal plants overseas, except for (a) the most efficient coal technology available in the world's poorest countries in cases where no other economically feasible alternative exists, or (b) facilities deploying carbon capture and sequestration technologies.

The US also clearly indicated that it intended to seek to extend the reach of this initiative globally: "As part of this new commitment, we will work actively to secure the agreement of other countries and the multilateral development banks to adopt similar policies as soon as possible." For the US, its objectives thus went beyond domestic policy change—it was seeking to exercise global leadership on climate change by promoting international cooperation and shaping the behavior of other states.

The US announcement set off a cascade of activity. The World Bank, in which the US has the largest voting share, followed a month later by announcing in July 2013 its own phase-out of coal support, except in "rare and exceptional" circumstances, typically for only the poorest countries that have no alternative to coal. In October 2013, the US issued revised guidance for US positions in the multilateral development banks to reflect its new stance on financing for overseas coal plants (United States 2013b). And in December 2013, implementing the President's Action Plan, the US Export–Import Bank became the world's first ECA to adopt a policy curbing coal plant financing (United States 2013a).

Calling for other states to join it in ending overseas coal financing, the US launched a major push to establish new rules on export credit for coal plants as part of the OECD Arrangement. With the impetus originating from the US president, who identified it as a key diplomatic priority, negotiators described this as a "full court press" by the US.[8] The Americans aimed to secure an agreement before the 2015 COP21 UN climate negotiations in Paris, as an important signal that the world's major advanced economies were committed to taking meaningful, concrete action on climate change, to help build momentum and ensure a high level of ambition for the Paris agreement. As one participant stated, "the US had a very strong position and wanted to move forward aggressively."[9] The US objective was to make coal plants ineligible for government export subsidies or multilateral assistance. Effectively, the US wanted to multilateralize its domestic policy changes, by making them the basis for new global rules in this area. As Phillip Hannam (2016) aptly put it, "the US hoped to copy and paste its own new domestic carbon guidelines" into global rule-making. Since private banks often follow the OECD's guidelines in their own lending practices, many also hoped that new rules governing state-backed export credit could have a broader ripple effect (Eilperin 2015).

The US preference was to negotiate restrictions on overseas coal financing within the International Working Group, in order to ensure that the resulting new rules would encompass China and the other major emerging economies. As one participant summarized, given China's emergence as the world's biggest export credit provider and its refusal to participate in the Arrangement, "the OECD Arrangement is an increasingly obsolete forum. The IWG—that's the way forward and where standards should be developed. With China participating in the IWG, that would be the place to create more effective international mechanisms."[10] When the IWG began, the US and other advanced-industrialized states hoped it would mirror the Arrangement by going beyond dealing with solely the financial terms of export credit to address a range of related "good governance" issues, and ultimately incorporate similar provisions to those in the Arrangement, including for environmental and social due diligence processes, anti-bribery measures, and sustainable lending practices.

For many OECD countries and their exporters, bringing China into a common set of disciplines on environmental and social governance of export credit is an important objective. There are widespread concerns about the environmental and social implications of China's lending practices (Gallagher, Irwin, and Koleski 2012; Sanderson and Forsythe 2012), and competing exporters allege that China's less stringent (and more opaque) policies give its exporters an unfair advantage over those from the OECD who face more cumbersome and costly standards imposed by their ECAs and are sometimes denied financing for projects that fail to meet environmental, social, or human rights standards. OECD ECAs stress the importance of a level playing field and are keen to ensure China is "playing by the same set of rules."[11] Yet hopes that the IWG would be an effective forum for addressing good governance soon evaporated. As one negotiator stated, when the IWG initially began, various OECD countries "suggested the IWG deal with good governance. That will happen when pigs fly. China won't even negotiate standard export credit terms."[12]

It quickly become apparent that China was stalling the IWG process and was highly resistant to agreeing to bind itself to new disciplines on export credit. From the perspective of the US and other OECD participants, the IWG negotiations were moving excruciatingly slowly and the prospects of the IWG yielding an agreement—even solely on financing terms, never mind good governance—anytime in the near future were increasingly dim. By 2013, when the US launched its coal initiative, it had already become clear that the IWG was not a viable forum for pursuing an agreement to restrict overseas coal financing. From the US's perspective, a multilateral agreement on coal encompassing China would obviously have been vastly preferable. But, given its intense resistance to any constraints on its use of export credit, trying to get China to agree to multilateral disciplines on export credit for coal was, as one OECD negotiator stated, simply "impossible."[13] The US was thus forced instead to pursue disciplines via the more limited forum of the OECD. For the US, the OECD was decidedly a second-best option but the only realistic one available given Chinese resistance to export credit disciplines within the IWG. Negotiators indicate that China was invited to the meetings at the OECD where the coal agreement was negotiated, but it declined to attend.[14] The inability of the US to get China to cooperate in the construction of new rules on export credit for coal, and the fact that the US was forced to turn to the more limited forum of the OECD Arrangement, where any resulting agreement would fail to capture the world's biggest source of export credit for coal plants and nearly half of such financing, is itself a sign of the new constraints on the US's ability to lead the construction of global rules on trade and environment.

Nevertheless, the US determined that it wanted a broad prohibition on export credit for coal plants within the OECD and went about building support for its position. Several OECD countries quickly followed the US's lead by limiting or halting lending for coal power projects and backing the establishment of new multilateral rules to restrict financing by other states. Five Nordic countries—Denmark, Finland, Iceland, Norway, and Sweden—issued a joint statement with the US in September 2013 committing to ending public financing for new coal-fired power plants overseas, except in rare circumstances (United States 2013c). The UK made a similar statement in November 2013 (Department of Energy and Climate Change 2013), and the Netherlands joined the US coal ban in March 2014 (Netherlands 2014). The European Bank for Reconstruction and Development (EBRD) and the European Investment Bank (EIB) also adopted similar restrictions (*Trade Finance* 2015). One by one, the US thus steadily brought states and other actors onside, convincing them to support its initiative and building a growing coalition in favor of restricting export credit for coal plants. Resistance, however, came from the major exporters of overseas coal-fired power plants within the OECD—Japan, South Korea, and parts of the EU—which were strongly averse to any restrictions that would not also bind China.

## The Specter of China

While China did not participate in the negotiations, even in its absence it had a significant effect on the negotiations. Participants described China as "the red dragon in the room" during negotiation of the OECD coal agreement.[15] About a dozen OECD countries provide ECA support for coal-fired power plants and, of that, five countries (Japan, South Korea, France, Germany, and the US) accounted for nearly all (94 percent) of the support provided in terms of credit value (OECD 2014a). Globally, however, China is the largest provider of public financing for new foreign coal power plants, and its financing level is approximately 70 percent more than Japan, the second largest provider (see Figure 5.1). Chinese financing accounts for about 41 percent of the global total, followed by Japan (24 percent), South Korea (14 percent), Germany (12 percent), France (5 percent), and the United States (5 percent) (Ueno, Yanagi, and Nakano 2014). The fact that China would not be participating in the agreement and be bound by its rules undermined US efforts to convince

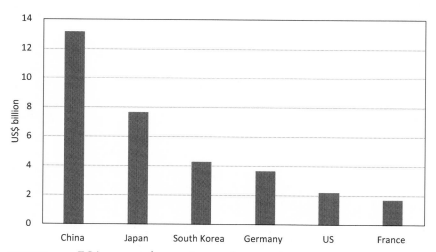

FIGURE 5.1 ECA support for overseas coal power plants, 2007–2013 (US$ billion).
Source: Data from Ueno, Yanagi, and Nakano 2014

the OECD's largest backers of overseas coal plants to agree to more stringent disciplines.

Exporters from these OECD countries were highly resistant to disciplines on export credit, given the intense competition they face from China. The US was effectively asking these states to relinquish an important export subsidy for their industry, while the world's dominant player in the sector and their key competitor—China—would remain free to support its exports with no limits or restrictions whatsoever. Countries such as Japan, Korea, Germany, and France maintained that placing restrictions on their use of export credit, if China was not constrained by similar rules, would unfairly disadvantage their exporters. The fact that China would not be bound by the OECD agreement on coal power plants would give its exporters a significant competitive edge, as they would be able to continue to access cheap state-supported financing and guarantees for their projects, while their competitors would be cut off from such financing. The goal of OECD export credit disciplines—including their environmental provisions—is to create a level playing field among exporters, but, without China's participation, OECD exporters feared they would instead be ceding the field to China.

These concerns were especially acute for Japan and Korea. China's rise has fundamentally changed the competitive environment in the sector, with China increasingly outcompeting the traditionally dominant exporters, Japan and Korea, based on price and financing, pushing Japan and Korea to the number two and three spots, and causing them to lose significant market share. Already under threat from Chinese competition, Japanese and Korean companies exporting coal plants would be in an even weaker position without access to export credit. Not only are Japan and Korea the largest coal plant equipment exporters after China, and thus the OECD countries with the greatest export interests at stake, but among the advanced-industrialized states they are probably the countries that have already been most directly and profoundly affected by Chinese competition in their key areas of export interest. In one sector after another, China has increasingly threatened their competitive advantage in the industries they have historically dominated. As one ECA official stated:

Now Korea and Japan are running around like chickens with their heads cut off. In shipbuilding they used to dominate, then China came in; and it's the same in nuclear power plant construction, and in steel, and in coal plants. China is a big competitive threat to Japan and Korea. In almost every area of their competitiveness, they now have to face China.[16]

In this context, to voluntarily agree to restrictions on their use of export credit in the face of intense competition from China in the global market for coal-fired power plants was thus anathema to Japan and Korea. They were understandably extremely reluctant to relinquish a key tool they have used to support their exporters amid growing Chinese competition. As one negotiator summarized, for Japan, its position was: "We sell the best technology, and if we withdraw, China will take these markets."[17] In the words of another participant, "Japan and Korea were worried that if we tie our hands on this, it just opens the door to China."[18] By relinquishing their use of a major export subsidy, Japan and Korea would be tying their own hands in the face of intense competition from China and putting their exporters at a significant disadvantage.

What is more, exporters from Japan, Korea, and Europe argued that if access to export credit for OECD coal exporters was restricted or eliminated, not only would China move in to replace them, but it would do so with older and less-efficient technology. As a result, they contended, new OECD regulations on export credit for coal plants—which would not include China—could actually have the effect of increasing greenhouse gas emissions. Figure 5.2 indicates the different types of coal plant technologies and their relative efficiencies. Subcritical plants use the oldest and least efficient technology and have not been the global standard since the 1950s; supercritical plants have been the global standard since the 1960s and ultra-supercritical since the 1990s (Hannam 2016). Globally, new coal plants completed and planned in recent years have been split relatively evenly among the three technologies (see Figure 5.3).

OECD exporting countries argued that China's technology is less advanced, and it exports more dirty, higher-emission coal plants. Nearly all of China's exports are subcritical or supercritical, whereas, in the case of Japan, for example, a much larger portion of its exports are ultra-

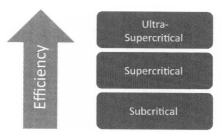

FIGURE 5.2 Coal plant efficiency.
Source: Kiko Network et al. 2017

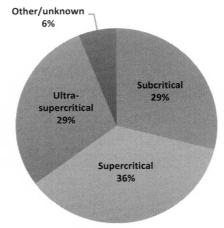

FIGURE 5.3 Global coal plants completed or planned, 2010–2018.
Note: Includes coal plants in China.
Source: Kiko Network et al. 2017

supercritical (Kiko Network et al. 2017; Ueno, Yanagi, and Nakano 2014). The share of ultra-supercritical technology in Japan's exports is growing significantly and projected to continue to increase; this has been established as a key economic policy objective and is being aggressively promoted by the government through export credit and other forms of overseas financing.[19] Japan therefore argued that:

self-restriction by the OECD countries on the official support to coal-fired power plants is most likely to invite private funds or non-OECD official development funds to fill the gaps, and more importantly, to introduce low-efficient technologies in some emerging countries, rather than high-efficient technologies with higher initial costs. In short, self-restriction of the OECD's official support could "crowd-in" low-efficient technologies, resulting in the increase of the global $CO_2$ emission compared to the status quo.[20]

Exporters in France and Germany made similar arguments about the superior efficiency of their technology compared to China, and the effects of potential OECD restrictions (*Trade Finance* 2014). As one negotiator summarized: "We knew that since coal power plants will be built in places like South Africa, Indonesia and India, if we don't fund these, it's China that will build them. And they build more-polluting coal-fired power plants."[21] Another participant echoed this in stating, "if we're not going to be able to finance exports of our technology, then China will come in and take over markets; they'll use less-efficient technology and build more-polluting plants."[22] Consequently, as one negotiator explained, "our industry was arguing that, from a pollution perspective, it's only going to make things worse," if the OECD countries put in place restrictions that did not also bind China.[23]

As one negotiator put it, "the China bogeyman" thus became a predominant factor shaping the negotiations.[24] In the context of Chinese competition, OECD exporting countries argued strongly against the stringent restrictions sought by the US and others. The fact that China would not be party to the agreement and bound by its rules made it extremely difficult to convince Japan, South Korea, and other high-support countries to agree to disciplines. The two major European exporters, France and Germany, were eventually convinced by late 2014 to support disciplines on coal financing, due to a combination of domestic, EU, and international pressure motivated by environmental concerns. As one negotiator stated, "the US was applying a lot of political pressure and the fact it was the run up to Paris [COP21] created even more pressure" for states to signal that they were taking action on climate change by reaching an agreement on export credit (particularly France, who was hosting the UN climate talks in Paris).[25] However, Japan and Korea—who had greater commercial interests at stake—remained firmly opposed. Notably, these are not countries that typically take an obstructionist stance towards the US in multilateral trade negotiations. As one experienced negotiator, who has spent over thirty years engaged in multilateral negotiations at the GATT/WTO and OECD, summarized: "Japan in international trade negotiations tends to go with the flow."[26] In this case, however, as one participant stated, Japan and Korea were "being terribly obstinate in blocking progress in the negotiations because of their concerns about competition from China."[27] Even though it was not a participant, China thus cast a powerful shadow over the negotiations.

By 2015, the last holdouts were Japan and Korea, along with Australia (which, while not an exporter of coal plant equipment, is one of the world's largest coal exporters and a vocal champion of coal power).[28] Then, in September 2015, just two months before the Paris climate summit, following bilateral meetings, the US and China reached agreement on a joint presidential statement on climate change (United States 2015b). Among other issues—including each country's statement of its intended nationally determined contributions (NDCs) for COP21, which for China included a commitment to lower $CO_2$ emissions by 60 percent, promote renewables, and initiate a national emissions trading scheme—the agreement between the two countries specifically included reference to overseas public financing and climate change. The US confirmed that it had "ended public financing for new conventional coal-fired power plants except in the poorest countries." China pledged to "strengthen green and low-carbon policies and regulations with a view to strictly controlling public investment flowing into projects with high pollution and carbon emissions both domestically and internationally." This was heralded as a major breakthrough and a sign that, while not a party to the OECD negotiations, China had nonetheless agreed to take similar steps to restrict its use of export credit for overseas coal plants.

But, as environmental groups have since pointed out, China's purported commitment on overseas financing was vague and undefined, more a general statement of intent than a concrete plan of action, and certainly not binding or enforceable.[29] It was not clear, for example, what "with a view to strictly controlling public investment" would actually mean precisely and in practical terms, nor "high pollution and carbon emissions"—would this, in terms of the emerging framework at the OECD, refer to and encompass medium-efficiency supercritical plants? Higher-efficiency ultra-supercritical? As one representative of an environmental NGO stated, "it was extremely vague, with nothing concrete and no way to enforce it."[30] Indeed, he continued, "we followed up with the US government to ask about how it would be implemented, and no one could say." And, looking back today, several years later, the agreement has had no discernable impact on China's export credit policies or practices.

Nonetheless, however, while the US–China agreement may ultimately have had little real impact on China's policies, it served as a critical turning point in the OECD negotiations and played a pivotal role in driving the negotiations to a conclusion. As one US official stated, the US–China agreement "sort of unlocked the final stages of this agreement in the OECD" (quoted in *E&E News* 2015c). Another participant explained further: "it was a very useful thing to use within the negotiations. It created this sense of 'If even China can commit [to restricting overseas investment for high-emissions projects], then why can't the OECD, why can't Japan?'"[31] The high-level joint statement by the US and China helped to increase pressure on Japan—the biggest supplier of export credit for coal within the OECD and the strongest opponent of restrictions—by making it appear increasingly isolated amid a broader global shift to pro-climate policies. In the words of one negotiator, "it put political pressure on Japan to reach a compromise with the US. It didn't want to be blamed for impeding the agreement."[32] An environmental campaigner put it as follows: "Japan is very sensitive to their reputation.

As long as they can do bad stuff without being put in the international spotlight, they'll do it. But if there is reputational risk, if they fear it will reflect badly on them, they'll move."[33]

The US–China climate agreement thus served as the decisive factor that caused Japan, as well as Korea and Australia, to surrender their resistance and capitulate to the US-led OECD coal agreement. In October 2015, just a month after the US–China announcement, the US and Japan reached a compromise. In the words of one participant,

This was a major, major US push. And Japan understood that if it continued holding a conservative position before COP21, it would suffer significant reputational damage. It wanted to show that it was moving forward on coal. Ultimately COP21 and the major US push finally pushed them to agree.[34]

The US–Japan compromise ultimately formed the basis of the final agreement, with additional concessions to Korea and Australia.

## THE SECTOR UNDERSTANDING ON COAL-FIRED POWER PLANTS

After two years of intense negotiations, states reached agreement on the new Sector Understanding on Export Credits for Coal-Fired Electricity Generation Projects (CFSU) in November 2015. The negotiations went right down to the wire, with the agreement concluded just two weeks before the start of the COP21 Paris climate negotiations. The agreement serves as an annex to the OECD Arrangement and took effect on January 1, 2017 (OECD 2015a). It applies to the US, EU, Japan, South Korea, Australia, Canada, New Zealand, Norway, and Switzerland.

The agreement creates partial restrictions on the use of export credit financing for coal-fired power plants, but not an outright ban. The agreement draws distinctions based on plant size, the technology employed, and conditions in the recipient country (see Table 5.1). It allows support for the most-efficient "ultra-supercritical" plants in all countries. It prohibits export credit for large plants employing less-efficient "supercritical" and "subcritical" technologies. It allows support for medium-size "supercritical plants" in the world's poorest countries (those listed as eligible for the World Bank's International Development Association (IDA) concessional lending) and countries facing energy poverty challenges (defined as those with a national electrification rate of less than 90 percent), as well as for smaller "subcritical" plants in IDA-eligible countries. For eligible support, it imposes a ten- to twelve-year repayment

TABLE 5.1 *Key provisions of the Sector Understanding on Coal-Fired Power Plants*

| Plant Size/ Technology | Large (Unit > 500 MW) | Medium (Unit = 300–500 MW) | Small (Unit < 300 MW) |
|---|---|---|---|
| Ultra-supercritical | Permitted | Permitted | Permitted |
| Supercritical | Ineligible | Only in IDA-eligible or energy-poor countries | Only in IDA-eligible or energy-poor countries |
| Subcritical | Ineligible | Ineligible | Only in IDA-eligible countries |

*Efficiency →* (vertical label at left)

period. The restrictions will not apply to any plants equipped with carbon capture and storage (CCS) capabilities, as provided under the existing climate sector understanding.[35]

The Sector Understanding represents the first time countries have reached multilateral agreement to restrict export credit financing for coal-fired power plants. According to the OECD Secretariat, over two-thirds of the coal-fired power projects receiving official export credit support from Arrangement participants between 2003 and 2013 would not have been eligible for such support under the new rules (OECD 2015b). US officials estimated that approximately 80 percent of coal plants in the current OECD ECA pipeline will become ineligible for financing under the agreement (*E&E News* 2015c). The agreement is thus expected to make the "vast majority" of about 1,000 planned coal plants ineligible for export credit by OECD countries (*Financial Times* 2015b). These figures are substantiated by independent analysis conducted by environmental groups such as the World Wildlife Fund.[36]

Outside of China (where most new coal plants are ultra-supercritical but produced domestically and therefore do not involve export credit), the global coal plant pipeline overwhelmingly consists of subcritical and supercritical plants. Most plants being built fall into the "large" category: a typical coal-fired generating unit is 500 MW in size, and most power stations have two or more such units (Shearer et al. 2017). The bulk of planned coal projects are large, supercritical plants (*E&E News* 2015a), which under the new rules are now prohibited from receiving official export credit, as are large and medium subcritical plants. Thus, under the new agreement, as one participant stated, OECD export credit for "the sub- and supercritical pipeline is very much reduced."[37] The agreement is therefore viewed as an important step forward on the path of transitioning away from coal to clean energy. One NGO summarized its impact as follows: "It is very significant. The most dirty, inefficient coal plants are now banned by the sector understanding. Only very efficient plants were allowed in. And there is evidence it is already biting. This is a good step—but it does not go far enough."[38]

The OECD coal agreement was a product of US power but also shows the contemporary limitations of that power amid a rising China. The coal agreement was conceived and executed by the US, which used its leadership and influence to persuade other states to cooperate. As one participant stated, "It was the US pushing the agreement, very strongly. The agreement came about because of a strong push by the Obama Administration. This was the result of a major diplomatic push by the US at the highest levels."[39] The US instigated and drove every step of the negotiations, built a growing coalition of support for its initiative, steadily overcame opposition, got countries onside, and pushed them to agree. Simply put, without the US, there would never have been an agreement on export credit for coal plants, or even such an initiative in the first place. Yet, while the US claimed the resulting agreement as a victory, the reality is that it fell significantly short of US objectives.

First, the biggest gap in the Sector Understanding is that it does not cover China. As one environmental campaigner stated: "Obviously it matters immensely that China was not part of the agreement because China is spending enormous amounts of money on export credit for coal plants."[40] To this date, China's financing remains entirely unconstrained. Environmental NGOs report that the provisions of the 2015 US–China climate agreement pertaining to export credit "really haven't been implemented in any way [on the Chinese side]—no change in China's export credit policies for coal is evident."[41] Since that September 2015 commitment by China, the China Development Bank (CDB) alone—just one of China's three ECAs—has approved more than $2.1 billion in coal financing (Sherwin 2016). Most see little chance of China joining the OECD coal agreement or agreeing to accept global rules limiting its overseas financing for coal plants. As one negotiator stated:

Definitely on the domestic level, they have restricted coal, but this has led to a push to export abroad. Now China is building coal plants all over the world, even in the Balkans in Eastern Europe. There are huge interests in China that want to continue building coal. There is little incentive for the Chinese government to restrict finance for coal abroad. It's against the interests of its own industry and companies.[42]

Another echoed this, stating: "Any restriction on China's export credit would have to come from China. It's not willing to be pushed into anything" by external forces seeking to impose disciplines on its use of export credit for coal.[43]

Second, what the US was pushing for, and what environmentalists argue is needed, is a full ban on export credit support for coal-fired power plants, except in very rare and strictly constrained circumstances. Instead, the coal agreement still allows export credit for many types of new coal plants: financing for ultra-supercritical plants in any country, regardless of income or development level, is permitted and financing for small and medium supercritical plants is allowed in many of the major emerging economies that are the site of most of the world's coal plant construction. The final agreement is thus a significantly watered-down version of what the US had originally sought to achieve.

Environmentalists argue that the distinction drawn in the agreement between subcritical, supercritical, and ultra-supercritical technology is misleading because all coal plants are carbon intensive, regardless of their technology. There is, in fact, very little difference in their carbon emissions, and even the most efficient coal plants pollute almost as much as low-efficiency plants. The simple fact is that: "Adding *any* more new coal plants, no matter what their efficiency, is not in line with the internationally agreed objective of keeping global warming below 2 degrees" (WWF 2015). As an NGO representative elaborated:

Any coal plant you build has an incredibly negative impact on the planet. A coal plant is in operation for thirty to forty years. And even an ultra-supercritical plant pollutes three to four times more than a gas plant. You cannot invest one more new dollar in coal infrastructure, otherwise you will miss the 2 degree target. Ultra-supercritical may emit a little bit less $CO_2$ than supercritical, but it's still way more than a gas plant or, of course, renewables like wind and solar that don't emit at all. From the perspective of science, we cannot build any new coal plants at all.[44]

In this context, as one environmental campaigner argued, "continuing to provide public subsidies for coal plants overseas is simply indefensible" (*E&E News* 2015b). By for the first time establishing restrictions governing the use of export credit for coal-fired power plants and creating disciplines where none existed before, the Sector Understanding represents a preliminary move towards establishing global disciplines on subsidies for fossil fuels; yet its impact is undermined by the substantial carve-outs that were needed to appease concerns among OECD states about Chinese competition.

For its participants, as the Chair of the negotiations stated, the Sector Understanding is seen as "a *first important step* towards aligning export credit policies with climate change objectives" (*Trade Finance* 2015, emphasis added). The agreement contains a mandatory, built-in review process, to begin by mid-2019 "with the objective of further strengthening its terms and conditions in a second phase beginning no later than 1 January 2021" (OECD 2015a). According to the provisions of the agreement, the review will take into account advances in technology and climate science. It will also consider "developments in the export credit financing policies and practices of non-OECD countries, especially the major exporting countries of coal-fired power plants, recognizing the important role that Participants can play in encouraging the Participation of non-OECD countries in this area" (OECD 2015a). However, given little sign of change in China's export credit policy, or willingness to negotiate global rules that would constrain its use of export credit, there are unlikely to be conditions for strengthening the agreement. And other emerging economies, notably India, also appear to be following China in seeking aggressively to expand their export of coal-fired power plants, including financing projects that have been declined by Western lenders on environmental and social grounds (Hopewell 2019).

Environmental NGOs argue that strengthening the OECD's disciplines on coal plants is "extremely important."[45] In addition to expanding those disciplines to eliminate all financing for coal plants, they would also like to see restrictions on export credit for other coal-related activities, such as exploration and mining, and for other fossil fuels, such as oil and gas. ECAs annually fund a whopping $32 billion worth of projects in the oil and gas sector (FOE 2017). But, without the participation of China, the prospects for significantly strengthening or expanding the agreement's disciplines are limited.

The OECD coal agreement was a US-driven initiative that relied heavily on American leadership. As one OECD official stated, "It was only adopted because of a major push from the US."[46] But we should be careful not to idealize the US's position or its role. As a smaller exporter of coal equipment than countries like Japan or Korea, the US had more limited commercial interests at stake, making it easier for it to take a more progressive position on the issue. And, having already made its own policy changes in this area, it now wanted to impose them on the rest of the world—as one analyst stated, "copying and pasting" its domestic policies into global rules. But, as this analysis has shown, in seeking to do so, the US bumped up against significant constraints caused by the rise of China.

In contrast to the other cases analyzed in this book, this is a case where the US *was* able to successfully drive forward and secure the conclusion of a new multilateral agreement governing trade. Each of the previous cases—the Doha Round, the post-Doha WTO negotiations on agriculture and fisheries, and the IWG—represented an effort to negotiate an agreement that included China, and in each the result was a stalemate and the failure to reach an agreement. In this case, if China had participated in the coal negotiations, the result would likely have been the same: a stalemate with no agreement, as occurred in each of the other negotiations analyzed in the preceding chapters. As one participant stated:

If China had been part of the Sector Understanding coal negotiations, it would probably have resulted in a stalemate, or a completely watered down and meaningless agreement. Because there is no way China would agree to anything. China will always use the argument that the rich countries should go first, like in the climate change negotiations. If they had participated, China would never have agreed to the same guidelines that were produced.[47]

Instead, amid China's refusal to participate in the export credit regime, the negotiations proceeded without China. However, while the US was able to secure an agreement, it is one that excludes the most significant player in this sector. Rather than establishing a set of universal rules encompassing all major players, the effect of the agreement was automatically truncated by the fact that China is not a participant. The coal agreement was an American initiative and would not have come about without US leadership, but it also demonstrates the limits of US leadership in the context of a rising China. The US effectively faced a choice between two suboptimal outcomes: an agreement covering approximately half the universe of export credit provided for coal plants, or no agreement at all. In short, half the world or nothing.

This case also provides another indication of the EU's status as a peripheral power compared to either the US or China. The contrast between the US and EU in the coal negotiations is striking. As is frequently the case in multilateral trade negotiations, internal divisions within the EU—in this case, between countries providing financing for their coal plant exports and those seeking to restrict such financing—prevented it from playing a leadership role akin to that of the US, whether for or against new disciplines. One the one hand, Germany, and to a lesser extent France, had a strong industry that wanted to continue exporting their technology with full government support. Many Eastern European countries, including Poland, Hungary, the Czech Republic, and Slovakia, were also opposed to any restrictions, because they are heavily dependent on coal for their own energy supply. On the other hand, others such as the UK, Scandinavian countries, and the Netherlands, driven by environmental considerations, took steps at the national level to restrict coal and were eager to see similar restrictions at the global level. As a result, it took a long period of time for the EU even to agree on a common position, which was not arrived at until after summer 2015, a full two years after the negotiations began (EU 2015). Consequently, to quote one participant, EU countries wanting disciplines on export credit for coal "hid behind the US" and let them do the pushing.[48] As has often been the case at the WTO, including during the Doha Round and in the post-Doha negotiations on agriculture and fisheries subsidies, its internal disagreements prevented the EU from taking a strong position in the OECD coal negotiations and rendered it a more marginal actor than would be expected given its economic size. Like the previous cases discussed in the book, here too, internal divisions effectively neutralized the EU and rendered its role largely secondary to the two primary forces affecting the negotiations— the US and China. Although China was not a participant, its absence loomed large in influencing the negotiation of the OECD coal agreement.

## CONCLUSION

This case has highlighted the difficulty of negotiating multilateral trade rules today without the participation of China. Driven by the US, the OECD engaged in a major international negotiation intended to produce a new set of rules that would limit the ability of states to subsidize the export of coal plants, given their profoundly negative implications for the global environment and climate change. This represented one of the first efforts to establish concrete global disciplines on subsidies for fossil fuels, but, as this analysis has shown, it was significantly undermined by the fact that China refused to participate. Even fifteen years ago, China's absence from the negotiating table would not have been an issue; but in just a short period of time its rise has fundamentally changed the competitive dynamics in this sector. In this context, the fact that China—the largest financer and exporter of coal plants—would not be party to the agreement and bound by its rules made it considerably more difficult to conduct the negotiations and build effective disciplines.

The resulting agreement was a US-led initiative and the product of an intense diplomatic lobbying effort by the US, but it also highlights the limitation of US power amid the rise of China. The fact that China, which alone accounts for nearly half of all export credit provided for overseas coal plants, is not a participant substantially reduces the impact of the new rules. In addition, the agreement itself falls far short of what the US had originally sought to achieve. While the US was pushing for a complete ban on export credit for coal-fired power plants, with exemptions only for the poorest countries, instead the final agreement contained major carve-outs necessary to appease concerns that disciplines applying solely to OECD countries would unfairly disadvantage their exporters in a trade sector where they are in direct competition with China. The fact that the rules would not be universal, capturing all the major competitors in the field, but instead would leave out China, overwhelmingly the largest player, acted as a significant impediment to securing stronger disciplines. Thus, as this case has demonstrated, even when China is not part of the negotiation of new multilateral agreements governing trade, it casts a powerful shadow over such negotiations.

Under President Trump, the US now appears to be abandoning any effort to play a leadership role on trade and environment. In a 180 degree change in US policy, Trump has withdrawn the US from the Paris Agreement and, expressing strong support for the US coal industry, is making significant changes to domestic coal policy within the US. The US has clearly now become one of the chief obstacles to progress in addressing climate change and other global environmental concerns. But what this analysis has shown is that, even when the US was previously attempting to play a constructive leadership role in the global governance of trade and environment, by leading the creation of new restrictions on export credit for coal-fired power plants, its ability to do so was significantly constrained by a rising China.

Now, in the absence of US leadership, there is speculation that China may assume the mantle of leadership on fighting climate change. Indeed, China appears to be actively cultivating an image of itself as a new global leader on the environment, which could yield substantial reputational gains and serve as an important source of soft power. Certainly, many of China's domestic policy changes—including aggressively curbing pollution and carbon emissions, shuttering coal plants, and promoting renewable energy sources—will make a significant contribution to addressing climate change. Yet, despite these positive signals domestically, there are no indications of any change in its policy for overseas coal finance.

# Conclusion

This book has challenged two core assumptions in contemporary debates about the rise of China: (1) the US maintains its dominance in the international system, with China's economic and military power capabilities too far below those of the US for it to pose a serious threat to American hegemony and (2) a rising China can be integrated into the US-led liberal international economic order because China has benefited from the existence of that order and has an interest in maintaining it. Drawing on an analysis of the global trade regime, which is at the center of the US-led liberal international economic order, I have argued that China's rise has proven far more disruptive—both to US power as well as to global trade governance and rule-making—than many anticipated.

First, contrary to those who argue that China does not possess sufficient power to threaten US hegemony, I have shown that China's ascent has substantially weakened American control over the governing institutions of the trading system and its power to write the rules of global trade. A key aspect of American hegemony to date—its ability to lead or dominate global institutions—has been severely undermined by the rise of China. If the US once "ran the system" (Ikenberry 2015a), this book has demonstrated the extent to which that has now been disrupted. Regardless of whether or not China will ever overtake the US as hegemon, it is clear that China's rise has *already* sharply curtailed the US's power over the institutions and rules that govern the global economy.

The world's two dominant powers are locked in a competitive struggle over the global institutions and rules governing trade. This is a struggle over institutional power and who gets to set the rules of the game. The US and China are not only competing for economic dominance, I argue, but also engaged in a pitched battle to set the rules of that competition, with each seeking to shape the rules to reflect and advance its own interests.

Drawing on the five cases analyzed, I have demonstrated that the US's ability to exercise power in and through international institutions has been severely constrained by the rise of China. Each of these cases—the Doha Round, agricultural subsidies, fisheries subsidies, export credit, and export credit for coal-fired power plants—were negotiations launched and led by the US. And in all of these cases the US has been barred from obtaining its objectives by China. Despite intense efforts, the US has been unable to force China to undertake greater commitments to liberalize its market in the Doha Round or to accept disciplines on its use of agricultural subsidies, fisheries subsidies, export credit, or export credit for coal power plants. China has refused to defer to American power in the trade regime or to simply be a rule-taker, but instead has repeatedly blocked or impeded US-led initiatives to secure international agreements across a wide range of different areas. The US's influence and authority in global trade governance has been substantially weakened by China's emergence as a countervailing power. These cases demonstrate the diminished capacity of the American hegemon to lead and steer global trade governance in the context of a rising China, and thus highlight new limits and constraints on US power. Unlike previous rising powers, such as Japan, China has consistently thwarted US efforts to construct new global trade rules, producing a recurring impasse across a broad range of different areas of global trade governance.

The fact that China has constrained the US's institutional power does not imply that it has gained such power of its own. China is refusing to be a rule-taker in the global trade regime, but that does not mean it has become a rule-maker. Within the trading system, China's power is primarily structural in nature, derived from the weight of its market in the global economy. None of China's behavior would be as challenging were it not for its market size. However, while China has developed immense structural power, thus far it has developed only very limited institutional power—it has been able to prevent the adoption of rules it opposes but not to construct new rules. In other words, China has demonstrated the ability to *block* multilateral trade rules but not to *create* them. Elsewhere, it is clear that China is working to develop greater institutional power through initiatives like the Belt and Road Initiative and the Asian Infrastructure Investment Bank (Hameiri and Jones 2018; Wilson 2017). But there is, as of yet, no sign of China replacing the US as rule-maker within the multilateral trading system or assuming the dominant role in constructing global trade rules.

Second, this book has also challenged the optimistic assumption that global institutions will continue to function effectively amid the rise of China. Analysis of the trade regime indicates that US–China conflict has become a persistent and recurrent dynamic across multiple and diverse areas of global trade governance. It is proving extremely difficult for the global trading system to adapt to, manage, and accommodate growing economic rivalry between the US and China—the clash of a hegemon and its emerging challenger. The clash between these two powers is blocking global rule-making in trade and undermining the institutions designed to prevent global trade wars.

It is frequently assumed that if rising powers are supporters of established governance institutions and successfully incorporated into their decision-making structures, then those institutions will continue to function smoothly and effectively. Yet, as I have demonstrated, analysis of China's impact on global trade governance refutes this view. As the world's largest exporter, China is a beneficiary and supporter of an open, rules-based trading system, and trade is an area of global economic governance where the US has actively sought to incorporate China.

In the case of the WTO, the US invited China into the power structure of the institution, gave it a seat at the table that reflected its economic weight, and actively sought to engage it in the process of global rule-making. China has thus been integrated into the WTO and its core power structure, but the result has been a direct confrontation between the US and China over the rules of global trade that has paralyzed the institution. The clash between the trading system's two dominant powers has produced a repeated stalemate, which has effectively brought the core negotiating function of the WTO to a halt. This was evident first and foremost in the breakdown of the Doha Round, which collapsed due to US–China conflict. But the same fundamental conflict between the US and China has persisted since the Doha collapse and continues to impede the construction of global trade rules, as evident in the deadlock in the post-Doha negotiations on agricultural subsidies and fisheries subsidies, which had both been identified as priority targets for standalone agreements and intended to demonstrate the continued relevance of the WTO as a rule-making institution.

Nor are these dynamics limited to the WTO. Analysis of the OECD Arrangement on Export Credit indicates that similar disruptions are occurring in other areas of global trade governance. Despite considerable US pressure, China has resisted incorporation into the export credit regime by refusing to participate in existing or new disciplines on export credit, which it views as fundamentally against its development interests. As this case highlights, there are areas of global trade governance where China has strategic reasons to resist incorporation—and China has shown that it has sufficient power to repel efforts by the US to compel it to participate. The result, however, is that China's rise is undermining the liberal regime for governing export credit that for decades has been essential to preventing a competitive spiral of state subsidization via export credit. Likewise, in recent US-led negotiations to restrict export credit for coal-fired power plants, China's unwillingness to participate hampered efforts to secure an ambitious international agreement with meaningful disciplines, underscoring the challenge of constructing effective global rules on trade without the participation of China.

In short, in the case of the WTO, China has been incorporated, but the result has been deadlock, paralyzing the negotiating function of that institution; in the case of the export credit regime, China has refused to be incorporated, undermining its rules; and in the case of the agreement on export credit for coal plants, China's absence made the construction of effective disciplines impossible. The rise of China, and its resulting confrontation with the US, has thus created serious difficulties for the functioning of the global trade regime, eroding the efficacy of existing trade rules and institutions and preventing the construction of new and stronger rules to govern global trade.

The struggle between these two dominant powers is obstructing global rule-making in the realm of trade. Such rule-making is not only vital to the governance of the global economy but, as several of the cases analyzed in this book have demonstrated, it is also essential to addressing pressing global problems that are in critical need of international cooperation. The failure to agree new disciplines on agricultural subsidies and fisheries subsidies, for instance, has severely negative implications for developing countries, which are the chief victims of such subsidies, and for efforts to foster global development. Likewise, the inability to construct strong and effective disciplines on fisheries subsidies or export credit for overseas coal plants has harmful ramifications for international efforts to protect the global environment by preventing overfishing to conserve the world's fish stocks or reducing greenhouse gas emissions to combat climate change.

## HOW SHOULD CHINA BE TREATED IN THE MULTILATERAL TRADING SYSTEM?

At the core of the clash between the US and China is a struggle over whether, and how, the rules of the international trading system will apply to China. As this analysis has shown, the question of how China should be classified and treated in global trade governance has become the primary issue of dispute in the trade regime, and it is proving to be a difficult and intractable source of conflict. China's rise represents a new and unprecedented bifurcation of economic power and development status. The *China paradox*—the fact that China is now both a major economic power and a developing country with relatively low per capita incomes—has created significant challenges for global trade governance.

Despite its considerable aggregate economic might, in terms of the average standard of living of its population, a vast gulf still separates China from the US and other advanced-industrialized states. Yet while China remains a developing country and continues to face significant development challenges, it is now an extremely large and immensely powerful force in the global economy and seen by the US and many other states as a major competitive threat. From China's perspective, protecting its policy space—and specifically its ability to use interventionist trade policy measures such as subsidies—is essential to continuing its process of economic development. China's interest in maintaining its scope for continued development has, however, thrown it into conflict with the US. China insists that, as a developing country, it should be entitled to special and differential treatment, but the US is unwilling to extend such treatment to a major economic competitor and its chief hegemonic rival and has instead demanded universal rules and reciprocal concessions from China.

This fundamental conflict over how China should be treated in the multilateral trading system has paralyzed global rule-making in trade. Exempting China from global trade disciplines is highly contentious in the context of its growing rivalry with the US, but it is also controversial due to the broader global impacts of its policies. Although China may still be a developing country, it is now the world's largest trader and second largest economy. Given the enormous size of its economy and the extremely large volume of subsidies it is providing, its policies have serious systemic consequences for global markets and trade. The problem with providing SDT for China is thus that China is clearly not like other developing countries. Simply put, China is now so big that its policies have an outsized effect on the global economy. As a result, exempting China from global trade disciplines threatens to jeopardize efforts to achieve crucial global development and environmental objectives.

China is now the world's largest subsidizer of agriculture and fisheries, provider of export credit, and supplier of export credit for coal power plants. But China has refused to accept disciplines on its use of such subsidies. Given its scale, the magnitude of its subsidies, and their impact on global markets, this creates a systemic problem: it is not possible to construct effective disciplines in any of these areas without China's participation. And exempting China would severely undermine the efficacy of any new rules.

Considerable attention has focused on China's industrial subsidies, driven primarily by the economic interests and competitiveness concerns of the US and other advanced-industrialized states. But, as I have shown, China is now making extensive use of other forms of subsidies—such as for agriculture and fisheries—that have harmful effects on other developing countries. China's agricultural subsidies are reducing the incomes of poor farmers elsewhere in the developing world. In the case of fisheries, China's subsidies are contributing to the rapid depletion of the world's fish stocks, with severely negative implications for the sustainability of global fisheries resources and for developing countries who depend on such resources for food security and livelihoods. China's trade policies thus have significant implications for development in the rest of the Global South. The cases of agricultural subsidies and fisheries subsidies indicate a deep tension between China's strategies for pursuing its own developmental objectives and the interests of other developing countries. It is other developing countries who are most vulnerable to, and least equipped to absorb, the negative external effects of China's policies.

As analysis of the post-Doha negotiations at the WTO highlights, China is now playing a major role in blocking pro-development reform of the trading system. Its stance in obstructing disciplines on agricultural subsidies and fisheries subsidies has profoundly negative implications for the developing world. The rise of China as a dominant economic power is thus reshaping the fault lines of global trade politics, rendering the old North–South framing of the conflict over global development in the multilateral trading system increasingly outdated and inaccurate. While the US and other advanced-industrialized states have historically been seen as the principal impediment to making the multilateral trading system work for developing countries, it is no longer just the US or other rich countries that are barring important changes to global trade rules that would benefit developing countries but now also China.

China's rise is having similarly important implications for the global politics of trade and environment. China is increasingly positioning itself as a global environmental leader in arenas such as the international climate change negotiations; yet, at the same time, China is undermining efforts to promote environmental sustainability in the multilateral trading regime. China's trade policies are having increasingly harmful effects on the global environment, but China has fiercely resisted external disciplines on the grounds of its developing country status. By refusing to accept disciplines on its environmentally harmful subsidies—such as its fisheries subsidies or its subsidies for exporting coal power plants—China is impeding efforts to use global trade rules and institutions to help combat climate change and achieve the UN Sustainable Development Goals. Of course, China is hardly unique among the major economic powers in blocking or undercutting global environmental initiatives that run counter to its economic interests. However, China's emerging environmental leadership elsewhere in global governance is undermined by its much more self-serving behavior in the trade regime, where it is obstructing reforms of the trading system that are crucial to the goal of protecting the environment and promoting sustainable development.

## IT'S NOT JUST ABOUT THE MONEY

As this book has shown, US–China rivalry now factors heavily in multilateral trade negotiations, even in potentially unexpected areas such as agriculture and fisheries. In each of the cases analyzed, what is complicating multilateral trade negotiations is that they are not simply about the commercial interests at stake: the larger economic and geopolitical rivalry between the US and China is playing a significant role in shaping their objectives and the dynamics of negotiations. Both the US and China evaluate any prospective new trade rules through the prism of their rivalry.

The US abandoned the Doha Round—the same round it had fought fiercely to launch in the face of intense opposition from other states only a decade before—just as the round was on the verge of being concluded. In the context of its growing rivalry with China, the proposed Doha agreement—with its large SDT carve-outs for China—had become politically unacceptable. Thwarted in its efforts to change the terms of the deal by securing greater concessions from China, the US balked and walked away from the agreement on the table. The US now views all multilateral trade negotiations through the lens of its rivalry with China: the US's central objective—whether at the WTO or beyond—is to bind China to more stringent trade rules, but that has repeatedly proven beyond its power.

For China, its trade policies and position in international trade negotiations—including the explosive growth of its subsidies and its refusal to accept external disciplines—are driven not only by economic objectives, such as raising incomes and supporting industrial development, but also by strategic considerations arising from its growing rivalry with the US. This is perhaps most striking in the case of agriculture. In addition to combating rural poverty, China's highly trade-distorting agricultural subsidies are also motivated by the desire to bolster its domestic food supply. Chinese leaders are acutely aware that its access to essential goods, such as food, could become a geopolitical weapon and be cut off in the event of a future security conflict with the US. Put simply, as a rising power in an international system dominated by the US, and with global agricultural exports heavily controlled by the US and its allies, Beijing does not believe it can rely on global markets to ensure the security of its food supply. Hence China is using subsidies and other protectionist trade policies to increase domestic food production, in an effort to achieve a high degree of self-sufficiency. This security imperative of ensuring self-sufficiency in key strategic commodities naturally conflicts with the goal of establishing a liberal and open global economy, with free trade based on comparative advantage.

Likewise, in the case of fisheries, China's subsidies are not solely about supporting rural incomes and employment, but also consolidating the global dominance of its fishing industry by facilitating its continued outward expansion. This is part of a broader geopolitical strategy, aimed at advancing China's goal of becoming a global maritime power and challenging American hegemony in the world's oceans. In both agriculture and fisheries, it is this combination of economic and geopolitical motives that makes China deeply resistant to efforts to discipline its subsidies at the WTO. Similarly, China's use of subsidized export credit is an important part of its strategy to attempt to catch up with and ultimately surpass the US as the world's dominant industrial power. For China, efforts by the US to curb its export credit or other industrial subsidies—whether via the OECD Arrangement or equivalent disciplines, the WTO, or other means—are viewed with immense suspicion, as an attempt to arrest China's economic development in order to maintain the US's own industrial and economic supremacy. The intersection of economics and geopolitics thus profoundly complicates contemporary efforts to construct global trade rules.

A distinct and historically specific feature of the current US–China rivalry is that it is, in part, taking place within multilateral economic institutions. During the Cold War, the US's chief geopolitical rival—the Soviet Union—lay outside the capitalist global economy and its governing institutions, leading its own rival communist bloc. And, if anything, the presence of an external, existential threat to the world's capitalist democracies helped to increase cohesion within, and commitment to, the US-led liberal international economic order (Zeiler 1999). In contrast, however, the chief threat to American hegemony today, China, has been integrated into, and is operating within, the liberal trading order. The US–China relationship is one characterized by economic interdependence, fueled by trade, but they are also geopolitical rivals, with each viewing the other as a looming security threat.

With China's accession to the WTO—the ultimate signal of China's integration into the liberal economic order—the US had envisioned that this would help to neutralize the China threat, by pulling China into its orbit and in the direction of democracy and free market capitalism. Instead, however, American hopes that global economic integration and growing prosperity would propel domestic economic and political reforms, effectively remaking China in the US's own image, have proven false. Today, China appears wedded more deeply than ever to authoritarianism and a statist model of capitalism to which the US objects. Moreover, with trade fueling a massive increase in its economic might, China's perceived threat to the US has only grown, and it has become increasingly assertive both in its own neighborhood and on the international stage. In contrast to its past rivalry with the Soviet Union, the fact that the US's current rival is inside rather than outside the multilateral trading system is making it far more difficult to govern the trading system and agree on international trade rules. Moving beyond a narrow conception of great power rivalry as a struggle to amass economic and military power, or competing spheres of influence, this book has shown that an important aspect of the contemporary rivalry between the US and China is a struggle for control over the rules of the game—the rules of economic competition in the capitalist global economy.

## THE AMERICAN DISRUPTOR

As this book has shown, growing conflict between the US and China has proven highly disruptive for global trade institutions. The Trump administration has now thrown the trading system into further upheaval.

Remarkably, the US has become the chief threat to the liberal global trade regime constructed under US hegemony.

China is broadly satisfied with the existing rules governing global trade, which have enabled its economic rise by giving it access to global markets, while still allowing considerable scope for interventionist state policies to facilitate its economic development, industrial upgrading, and catch-up. Consequently, China has little desire to alter the rules—indeed, just the opposite, its interest is primarily in maintaining the status quo. Instead, it is the US that has become increasingly dissatisfied with the rules of the trading system—and precisely because they are not working adequately to contain China's rise or enable the US to maintain its economic supremacy. Hence US complaints that the WTO has proven inadequate to address China's "unfair" trade practices, such as heavy industrial subsidies, forced technology transfer, and intellectual property infringement, which the US fears are being used to erode its economic primacy. It is the US—who sees its dominance increasingly under threat from a rising China—that has become the dissatisfied, revisionist state in the international trading system.

By uniting growing anxieties about American hegemonic decline with widespread domestic discontent over increasing economic dislocation, precariousness, and inequality, Trump has created a powerful narrative to account for the US's current economic and social ills, stoking a sense of US victimization while directing popular anger toward "unfair trade" with China and others. Under Trump, the US has abandoned its traditional support for the liberal trading order, forsaking any commitment to multilateralism and a rules-based trading system, and instead resorting to aggressive unilateralism and protectionist measures—including arbitrarily imposing or threatening to impose tariffs on imports from a wide swath of countries, threatening to withdraw from trade agreements, and using strong-arm tactics to bully other countries into making one-sided trade concessions to the US. These actions are widely seen as a violation of WTO rules and threaten to plunge the world into a global trade war. However, the Trump administration is threatening to withdraw from the WTO and blocking appointments to its Appellate Body—which acts effectively as a "supreme court" for global trade—as the terms of its current judges expire. Without the Appellate Body judges needed to adjudicate disputes, the WTO dispute-settlement system risks grinding to a halt. The US has been frustrated with the Appellate Body both for constraining the US's ability to use trade defense measures such as anti-dumping duties—of which China is its primary target—to block imports, and for limiting the application of WTO subsidy rules to China's state-owned enterprises (Shaffer 2018). But by blocking Appellate Body appointments, the US is jeopardizing the WTO's entire system for settling trade disputes. Trump's policies pose a profound threat to the trade regime and the stability of the global economy.

The current shift in the US's orientation towards the international trading system cannot simply be explained by the "idiosyncrasies" of the Trump administration or the rise of populism. It is also, in part, a response to the decline of US institutional power documented in this book, which has led to an erosion of American support for the multilateral trading system it once led. As its control over the institutions and rules governing trade has diminished, the US has grown increasingly dissatisfied with the global trade regime. Under Trump, the US is now actively sabotaging that order, by blatantly violating its rules and principles and endangering its mechanism for peacefully resolving trade disputes among states based on the rule of law rather than the raw use of power.

We are seeing a fundamental change in the nature of US power. A distinct and defining feature of American hegemony is that it has been exercised in and through international institutions: the US constructed the institutions governing the global economy and these institutions served as an important means for the US to consolidate its power in the international system and advance its economic and strategic interests. Yet the US is now abandoning those same institutions, as its power within them declines. The US is forsaking trade multilateralism and instead resorting to aggressive unilateralism based on the raw use of coercive power. What is occurring is thus a decline of American hegemony—in the Gramscian sense of its ability to lead through consent rather than just coercion, which in the case of American hegemony has meant exercising power through the leadership of multilateral institutions that depended on the participation of other states—and a reassertion of US power in a different form. This is, in short, a shift from hegemony to domination. Discarding even the pretense of international cooperation and consent, the US, which remains the dominant power in the international system, has openly embraced economic coercion—based on its continued economic might and the enduring importance of its market in the global economy—as its primary strategy for international economic relations.

Trump's policies are dramatically escalating tensions among states. With his erratic and often contradictory behavior, Trump lacks a coherent strategy on trade. His tariffs and threats have targeted not just China but all of the US's major trading partners, including many of its closest strategic allies. And with his constant flip-flops and reversals on China, Trump appears unclear whether his goal is to secure fundamental structural changes in the Chinese economy, potentially with the intention of arresting China's rise, or if he is merely seeking to ameliorate the US trade deficit by compelling China to buy more American exports of soybeans, energy, and aircraft. Trump's blatant disregard for global trade rules, his reckless approach to managing US trading relations, and his bullying and overt hostility towards many of the US's key allies and trading partners are doing irreparable damage to the US's international standing and endangering the open and rules-based multilateral trading system. Since a hegemon needs followers, Trump's strategy of isolating the US and alienating its allies is likely only to accelerate American hegemonic decline.

At precisely the same time that China's rise has fueled American anxieties about its ability to maintain its economic primacy and its dominant position in the international system, the rise of China has demonstrably weakened American control over the rules and institutions that govern global trade. In response, the US is now undermining global trade institutions. The US's growing use of coercive power in trade represents a serious threat to the liberal international economic order. Growing US–China rivalry is clearly producing growing disorder and instability in the global trading system.

# Notes

NOTES TO INTRODUCTION

1  IMF data, 2015.
2  Merchandise exports, World Bank data, 2015.
3  World Bank data, 2016.
4  IMF data, 2015. In contrast, purchasing power parity (PPP) rates, which account for variation in the price of goods and services between different countries, provide a more accurate comparison of their standard of living.
5  Where necessary to protect the confidentiality of interview respondents, potential identifying information such as their country or interview location has been omitted.
6  UN Stats Database.
7  World Bank data, 2017.


NOTES TO CHAPTER 1

1  World Bank data.
2  Interview, Geneva, March 2009.
3  Interview, Geneva, March 2009.
4  Interview, Geneva, March 2009.
5  Interview, Geneva, July 2016.
6  Interview, New Delhi, March 2010.
7  Interview with NGO representative, Geneva, May 2009.
8  Interview, Beijing, July 2009.
9  Interview, Geneva, April 2009.
10  Interview, Geneva, May 2009.
11  More recently, in 2019, in exchange for US support of Brazil's bid to join the OECD, Brazilian President Jair Bolsonaro agreed to forgo SDT in future WTO negotiations.
12  Interviews with negotiators, Geneva, September 2008–June 2009.

13 World Bank data, 2015.
14 World Bank data, 2013.
15 Interview, Geneva, December 2017.
16 Interview, Geneva, July 2017.
17 Fourth Revision of Draft Modalities for Non-Agricultural Market Access, WTO Negotiating Group on Market Access, TN/MA/W/103/Rev.3, December 6, 2008.
18 Revised Draft Modalities for Agriculture, WTO Committee on Agriculture Special Session, TN/AG/W/4/Rev.4, December 6, 2008.
19 Interview, Geneva, April 2009.
20 Interview, Geneva, May 2009.
21 Interview, Geneva, July 2016.
22 Interview, Geneva, July 2017.
23 Interview, Geneva, July 2016.
24 Interview, Geneva, July 2017.
25 Interview, Geneva, July 2017.
26 Interview, Washington, DC, July 2015.
27 President's trade agenda, Office of the US Trade Representative, Washington, DC, 2011.
28 World Bank and WTO 2016.
29 Interview, Geneva, March 2009.
30 Interview, Geneva, July 2016.
31 Interview, Washington, DC, July 2015.
32 Interview, Washington, DC, July 2015.
33 Interview, Geneva, May 2009.
34 Interview, Geneva, December 2017.
35 Interview, Geneva, July 2017.
36 Interview, Geneva, July 2017.
37 Interviews, Geneva, July 2017.
38 Interview, Brussels, December 2017.
39 World Bank Data, 2009.
40 Quoted in *Le Temps*, "La Chine n'est pas encore un pays développé," March 3, 2016.
41 Interview, Geneva, July 2017.
42 Quoted in *Le Temps*, "La Chine n'est pas encore un pays développé," March 3, 2016.
43 Interview, Geneva, July 2016.
44 Interview, Geneva, July 2016.
45 Interview, Geneva, July 2016.
46 Interview, Geneva, July 2017.
47 Interview, Geneva, July 2016.
48 Interview, Geneva, March 2009.
49 Interview, Washington, DC, July 2015.
50 Interview, Geneva, July 2017.
51 Interview, Geneva, July 2017.
52 Interview, Geneva, July 2017.

## NOTES TO CHAPTER 2

1 Interview, Washington, DC, July 2015.
2 Interview, Geneva, July 2016.
3 Interview, Geneva, July 2016.
4 Interview, Washington, DC, July 2015.
5 US Grains Council, "Focus on Competitiveness: Rising Demand; Intense Battle for Market Share," Press Release, February 22, 2012.
6 House Agriculture Committee Hearing, Washington, DC, June 3, 2015.
7 US Wheat Associates, China Trade Enforcement Fact Sheet, 2016.
8 *DS511: China—Domestic Support for Agricultural Producers* and *DS517: China—Tariff Rate Quotas for Certain Agricultural Products.*
9 World Bank data, 2017.
10 Interview, Geneva, July 2017.
11 Interview, Geneva, July 2016.
12 FAO and World Bank Data.
13 Interview, Geneva, July 2017.
14 Interview, Geneva, July 2016.
15 Interview, Geneva, July 2016.
16 Interview, Geneva, July 2017.
17 Interviews with negotiators, Geneva, July 2016.
18 Interview, Geneva, July 2016.
19 Interview, Geneva, July 2016.
20 For developing countries, investment subsidies generally available to agriculture and agricultural input subsidies generally available to low-income or resource-poor producers are exempt from domestic support reduction commitments.
21 Interview, Geneva, July 2016.
22 Interview, Geneva, July 2016.
23 Interview, Geneva, July 2016.
24 Interview, Washington, DC, July 2015.
25 Revised Draft Modalities for Agriculture, WTO Committee on Agriculture Special Session, TN/AG/W/4/Rev.4, December 6, 2008.
26 Interview, Washington, DC, July 2015.
27 Doha Work Programme, Ministerial Declaration, Hong Kong Ministerial Conference, WT/MIN(05)/Dec, December 22, 2005.
28 TN/AG/W/4/Rev.4.
29 Interview, Geneva, July 2016.
30 Speech by USTR Michael Froman, Geneva, October 17, 2016.
31 Speech by USTR Michael Froman, Geneva, October 17, 2016.
32 Speech by USTR Michael Froman, Geneva, October 17, 2016.
33 Interview, Geneva, July 2016.
34 Interview, Washington, DC, July 2015.
35 Interview, Washington, DC, July 2015.
36 Interview, Washington, DC, July 2015.
37 Interview, Washington, DC, July 2015.

38 The Cairns Group is a group of twenty agricultural exporting countries, composed of Argentina, Australia, Bolivia, Brazil, Canada, Chile, Colombia, Costa Rica, Guatemala, Indonesia, Malaysia, New Zealand, Pakistan, Paraguay, Peru, the Philippines, South Africa, Thailand, Uruguay, and Vietnam.

39 Interview, Geneva, July 2017.

40 Interview, Geneva, July 2016.

41 Interview, Geneva, July 2016.

42 Interview, Geneva, July 2016.

43 Effectively Constraining Trade-Distorting Domestic Support Using Fixed Caps, Submission by New Zealand, Australia, Canada, and Paraguay, JOB/AG/100, July 17, 2017.

44 Proposal on Domestic Support, Public Stockholding for Food Security Purposes and Cotton from Brazil, European Union, Colombia, Peru and Uruguay, JOB/AG/99, 17 July 2017; Effectively Constraining Trade-Distorting Domestic Support Using Fixed Caps, Submission by New Zealand, Australia, Canada and Paraguay, JOB/AG/100, July 17, 2017; WTO Agriculture Negotiations Communication from Argentina, Plurinational State of Bolivia, Brazil, Chile, Ecuador, Paraguay, Peru and Uruguay, TN/AG/GEN/42, March 10, 2017.

45 Interview, Geneva, July 2017.

46 Interviews, Geneva, July 2016 and 2017.

47 Interview, Geneva, July 2016.

48 Interview, Geneva, July 2017.

49 Interview, Geneva, July 2016.

50 Interview, Geneva, July 2016.

51 Interview, Geneva, July 2016.

52 USDA data.

53 Interview, Geneva, July 2016.

54 Interview, Geneva, July 2016.

55 Interviews, Geneva, July 2017.

56 Interview, Geneva, July 2016.

57 Interview, Geneva, July 2016.

58 Interview, Geneva, July 2017.

59 Interview, Geneva, July 2016.

60 Interview, Geneva, July 2016.

61 Interview, Geneva, July 2016.

62 Interview, Geneva, July 2017.

63 Interview, Geneva, July 2016.

64 Interview, Geneva, July 2016.

65 Interview, Geneva, July 2016.

66 Interview, Geneva, July 2016.

67 Interview, Geneva, July 2016.

68 Interview, Geneva, July 2016.

69 Interview, Geneva, July 2017.

70 Interview, Geneva, July 2016.

71 Interviews, Geneva, July 2017 and 2017.

72 Interview, Geneva, July 2016.

73 Interviews, Washington, DC, July 2015.

74 Interview, Geneva, July 2016.
75 Interview, Geneva, July 2017.
76 Interview, Geneva, July 2016.
77 Interview, Geneva, July 2016.
78 Interview, Geneva, July 2016.
79 Cotton production costs are roughly equal in the US and China at about $2 per kilo, compared to $0.50 in some African countries.
80 Interview, Geneva, July 2016.
81 Interview, Geneva, July 2017.
82 World Bank data.
83 Interview, Geneva, July 2017.
84 Interview, Geneva, July 2017.
85 Interview, Washington, DC, July 2015.
86 Interview, Geneva, July 2016.
87 Interview, Geneva, July 2017.
88 Interview, Geneva, July 2017.
89 Interview, Geneva, July 2017.
90 Interview, Geneva, July 2017.
91 Interview, Geneva, July 2017.
92 Interview, Geneva, July 2016.

## NOTES TO CHAPTER 3

1 Under international law, a country is entitled to claim sovereign rights and authority over the exploitation of all fish resources up to 200 nautical miles from its shore, known as their Exclusive Economic Zone (EEZ). The high seas refers to the ocean beyond any national jurisdiction (i.e., outside any country's EEZ).
2 Interview, Geneva, July 2017.
3 Interview, Geneva, July 2017.
4 Communication from the Chair. Negotiating Group on Rules. TN/RL/W/254, April 21, 2011, pp. 46–67.
5 Communication from the Chair. Negotiating Group on Rules. TN/RL/W/254, April 21, 2011, pp. 46–67.
6 Interview, Geneva, July 2017.
7 Interview, Geneva, July 2017.
8 Interviews with negotiators, Geneva, March 2009, April 2009, and July 2017.
9 Communication from the Chair. Negotiating Group on Rules. TN/RL/W/254, April 21, 2011, pp. 46–67.
10 Draft Consolidated Chair Texts of the AD and SCM Agreements, Negotiating Group on Rules, TN/RL/W/213, Annex VIII, Fisheries Subsidies, November 30, 2007.
11 Communication from the United States. Negotiating Group on Rules. TN/RL/GEN/165, April 20, 2010.
12 Interview, Geneva, March 2009.

13 Submission by India, Indonesia and China. TN/RL/GEN/155/Rev.1, May 19, 2008.

14 Communication from Brazil, China, Ecuador, Mexico, and Venezuela. TN/RL/W/241/Rev.1, October 16, 2009.

15 Communication from Brazil, China, Ecuador, Mexico, and Venezuela. TN/RL/W/241/Rev.1, October 16, 2009.

16 Communication from Brazil, China, India, and Mexico. TN/RL/GEN/163, February 11, 2010.

17 Communication from the Chair. Negotiating Group on Rules. TN/RL/W/254, April 21, 2011, pp. 46–67.

18 Submission by India, Indonesia, and China. TN/RL/GEN/155/Rev.1, May 19, 2008.

19 Statement on the Negotiations on Fisheries Subsidies. Communication from Argentina, Chile, Columbia, Ecuador, Mexico, and Peru. TN/RL/W/234, July 17, 2008.

20 Communication from the Chair. Negotiating Group on Rules. TN/RL/W/254, April 21, 2011, pp. 46–67.

21 Submission by India, Indonesia, and China. TN/RL/GEN/155/Rev.1, May 19, 2008.

22 Communication from Brazil, China, Ecuador, Mexico, and Venezuela. TN/RL/W/241/Rev.1, October 16, 2009.

23 Communication from the Chair. Negotiating Group on Rules. TN/RL/W/254, April 21, 2011, pp. 46–67.

24 Submission by India, Indonesia and China. TN/RL/GEN/155/Rev.1, May 19, 2008.

25 Submission by India, Indonesia and China. TN/RL/GEN/155/Rev.1, May 19, 2008.

26 Communication from the Chair. Negotiating Group on Rules. TN/RL/W/254, April 21, 2011, pp. 46–67.

27 Communication from Brazil, China, Ecuador, Mexico, and Venezuela. TN/RL/W/241/Rev.1, October 16, 2009.

28 Communication from the Chair. Negotiating Group on Rules. TN/RL/W/254, April 21, 2011, pp. 46–67.

29 Communication from the Chair. Negotiating Group on Rules. TN/RL/W/254, April 21, 2011, pp. 46–67.

30 Communication from the Chair. Negotiating Group on Rules. TN/RL/W/254, April 21, 2011, pp. 46–67.

31 Communication from the Chair. Negotiating Group on Rules. TN/RL/W/254, April 21, 2011, pp. 46–67.

32 Communication from the Chair. Negotiating Group on Rules. TN/RL/W/254, April 21, 2011, pp. 46–67.

33 Interview, Geneva, July 2017.

34 Interview, Geneva, July 2017.

35 Interview, Geneva, July 2017.

36 Interview, Geneva, July 2017.

37 Interview, Geneva, July 2017.

38 Interview, Geneva, July 2017.

39 Interview, Geneva, July 2017.
40 See, for example, Textual Proposal for Additional Flexibilities for Small and Vulnerable Economies under Article III of the Proposed Draft Chair's Text on Fisheries Subsidies, Communication from the Small and Vulnerable Economies, TN/RL/GEN/162/Rev.1, April 20, 2011.
41 Minutes of Trade Negotiations Committee Meeting, TN/C/M/37, July 31, 2015: p. 36.
42 Interview, Geneva, July 2017.
43 Interview, Geneva, July 2017.
44 Interview, Geneva, July 2017.
45 Interview, Geneva, July 2017.
46 See, for example, Principles and Elements for Concluding Negotiation on Fisheries Subsidies Rules in the WTO, Submission by Rwanda on Behalf of the ACP Group, TN/RL/GEN/182, November 16, 2016.
47 Interview, Geneva, July 2017.
48 Interview, Geneva, July 2017.
49 Interview, Geneva, July 2017.
50 Interview, Geneva, July 2017.
51 Interview, Geneva, July 2017.
52 Interview, Geneva, July 2017.
53 Interview, Geneva, July 2017.
54 Trans-Pacific Partnership, Chapter 20: Environment, Article 20.16. The TPP was subsequently renamed the Comprehensive and Progressive Agreement for Trans-Pacific Partnership (CPTPP) upon the later withdrawal of the US from the agreement under President Trump.
55 Participants included Argentina, Australia, Canada, Chile, Colombia, New Zealand, Norway, Papua New Guinea, Peru, Singapore, Switzerland, Uruguay, and the US.
56 Joint Statement Regarding Fisheries Subsidies, Washington, DC, September 14, 2016.
57 "Obama Administration Undertaking Global Initiative to Prohibit Harmful Fishing Subsidies," White House Press Release, Washington, DC, September 14, 2016.
58 "Obama Administration Undertaking Global Initiative to Prohibit Harmful Fishing Subsidies," White House Press Release, Washington, DC, September 14, 2016.
59 Interviews, Geneva, July 2017.
60 Joint Statement Regarding Fisheries Subsidies, Washington, DC, September 14, 2016.
61 Interview, Geneva, July 2017.
62 Members of the Friends of Fish included Argentina, Australia, Chile, Colombia, Ecuador, Iceland, New Zealand, Norway, Pakistan, Peru and the US. Occasionally various other states also identified themselves with the group.
63 Interview, Geneva, July 2017.
64 Interview, Geneva, July 2017.
65 Interview, Geneva, July 2017.
66 Interview, Geneva, July 2017.

67 Interview, Geneva, July 2017.
68 Interview, Geneva, July 2017.
69 Interview, Geneva, July 2017.
70 Minutes of the WTO Trade Negotiations Committee, Geneva, TN/C/M/37, July 31, 2015.
71 Interview, Geneva, July 2017
72 Interview, Geneva, July 2017.
73 Interview, Geneva, July 2017.
74 Interview, Geneva, July 2017.
75 Interview, Geneva, July 2017.
76 Interview, Geneva, July 2017.
77 Interview, Geneva, July 2017.
78 Interview, Geneva, July 2017.
79 Interview, Geneva, July 2017.
80 Interview, Geneva, July 2017.
81 Interview, Geneva, July 2017.
82 Interview, Geneva, July 2017.
83 Subsidies: Request from the United States to China Pursuant to Article 25.10 of the Agreement, WTO Submission, Geneva, April 15, 2016.
84 Interview, Geneva, July 2017.
85 Interview, Geneva, July 2017.
86 Draft Ministerial Decision Fisheries Subsidies, WT/MIN(17)/W/4, December 6, 2017.
87 Prohibition of Subsidies to IUU Fishing. Proposal of China. Negotiating Group on Rules. TN/RL/GEN/195, November 1, 2017.
88 Interview, Geneva, July 2017.
89 Interview, Geneva, July 2017.
90 Interviews, Geneva, July 2017.
91 Interview, Geneva, July 2017.
92 RFMO IUU lists and interview, Geneva, July 2017.
93 Interview, Geneva, July 2017.
94 Interview, Geneva, July 2017.
95 Interview, Geneva, July 2017.
96 Interview, Geneva, July 2017.
97 Interviews, Geneva, July 2017.
98 Interview, Geneva, July 2017.
99 Interview, Geneva, July 2017.
100 Interview, Geneva, July 2017.
101 Interview, Geneva, July 2017.
102 Interview, Geneva, July 2017.
103 Interview, Geneva, July 2017.
104 Interview, Geneva, July 2017.
105 Interview, Geneva, July 2017.
106 Interview, Geneva, July 2017.
107 Interview, Geneva, July 2017.
108 Interview, Geneva, July 2017.

## NOTES TO CHAPTER 4

1  Private-sector financing includes loans, letters of credit, guarantees, insurance, and factoring, provided by exporters or financial institutions.

2  The most recent version of the Arrangement is OECD 2018a. Participants are the US, EU, Japan, Korea, Canada, Australia, New Zealand, Norway, and Switzerland. Israel and Turkey are observers.

3  As with any mechanism that restricts export subsidies, the Arrangement could be seen as harming importers, since credit subsidies reduce their costs. However, Arrangement participants are also importers of goods and services backed by foreign ECAs.

4  Interview, July 2016.

5  Interview, July 2015.

6  Interview, June 2016.

7  No developing country has joined the Arrangement, with the exception of Brazil, which is a participant in the Aircraft Sector Understanding but has shown no interest in joining the larger Arrangement. South Korea joined the Arrangement in 1997, once it was already a developed country. Some emerging economies, including Turkey, Poland, Mexico, and Chile, are members of the OECD but not participants in the Arrangement. They are not major providers of export credit and their use of export credit has never been large enough to be seen as a threat to the Arrangement or to concern its participants. Poland, for instance, provides only 0.39 percent of total OECD export credit, Turkey 0.16 percent, and Mexico 0 percent, while Chile does not have an ECA (OECD 2018b).

8  Interview, July 2015.

9  Interview, March 2009.

10  Interview, July 2015.

11  Interview, July 2016.

12  Interview, July 2016.

13  Interview, July 2015.

14  Interview, July 2015.

15  Interview, July 2015.

16  Calculated based on Arrangement Country Risk Classifications (CRCs) as of June 25, 2018.

17  Calculated based on historical CIRR and CRCs.

18  Interview, July 2015.

19  Interview, November 2016.

20  Interview, July 2015.

21  Interviews, June and July 2016.

22  Interview, December 2017.

23  Interview, July 2016.

24  Interview, July 2016.

25  Interviews, June 2016.

26  "Joint Fact Sheet on Strengthening US–China Economic Relations," The White House, Washington, DC, February 14, 2012.

27 Interview, December 2017.
28 Interview, July 2015.
29 Interview, July 2015.
30 Interview, July 2015.
31 Interview, July 2016.
32 Interview, June 2016.
33 Interview, July 2015.
34 Interviews, June 2016.
35 Interview, June 2016.
36 Interviews, June 2015.
37 Interview, July 2015.
38 Interviews, June 2016.
39 Interview, July 2015.
40 Interview, June 2016.
41 Interview, December 2017.
42 Interview, July 2016.
43 Interview, July 2015.
44 Interview, July 2016.
45 Interview, July 2016.
46 Brazil–Canada aircraft and EU–Korea shipbuilding.
47 Interview, July 2016.
48 Interview, July 2016.
49 Interview, July 2016.

NOTES TO CHAPTER 5

1 "OECD Coal Financing Agreement," Presentation by Kate DeAngelis, Friends of the Earth, Tokyo, May 2016.
2 Interview, Washington, DC, July 2015.
3 Interview, Brussels, December 2017.
4 Interview, Brussels, December 2017.
5 Measured as the "levelized cost of energy."
6 Interview, January 2018.
7 European Commission, Report from the Commission to the European Parliament and the Council, Annual Report on Negotiations Undertaken by the Commission in the Field of Export Credits, in the Sense of Regulation (EU) No 1233/2011, Brussels, November 18, 2016, COM(2016) 718 Final.
8 Interview, June 2016.
9 Interview, December 2017.
10 Interview, August 2017.
11 Interview, December 2017.
12 Interview, June 2016.
13 Interview, June 2016.
14 Interviews, June 2016.
15 Interview, November 2016.
16 Interview, July 2015.

17  Interview, June 2016.
18  Interview, June 2016.
19  Interview, January 2018.
20  Japan, August 2015, Joint Meeting: Room Document No.1, ECG and Participants to the Arrangement, Comments on the Revised Chairman's Proposal.
21  Interview, December 2017.
22  Interview, June 2016.
23  Interview, December 2017.
24  Interview, November 2016.
25  Interview, December 2017.
26  Interview, December 2017.
27  Interview, July 2015.
28  Prime Minister Tony Abbott, for instance, proudly proclaimed at the opening of an Australian coal mine: "Coal is good for humanity" (*The Guardian* 2015a).
29  Interviews, December 2017 and January 2018.
30  Interview, December 2017.
31  Interview, December 2017.
32  Interview, June 2016.
33  Interview, December 2017.
34  Interview, December 2017.
35  The Sector Understanding applies solely to export credit, as defined by the OECD Arrangement. It does not cover other forms of financing provided by some ECAs that are not covered by the Arrangement (such as untied loans and guarantees).
36  Interview, December 2017.
37  Interview, November 2016.
38  Interview, August 2017.
39  Interview, December 2017.
40  Interview, January 2018.
41  Interview, January 2018.
42  Interview, December 2017.
43  Interview, January 2018.
44  Interview, Brussels, December 2017.
45  Interview, December 2017.
46  Interview, June 2016.
47  Interview, December 2017.
48  Interview, December 2017.

# References

Aaronson, Susan Ariel, and Jamie M. Zimmerman. 2006. "Fair Trade? How Oxfam Presented a Systemic Approach to Poverty, Development, Human Rights, and Trade." *Human Rights Quarterly* 28(4): 998.

ACCF (American Council for Capital Formation). 2015. "US Coal Plant Financing Policy: A Threat to Long-Term US Interests in the Developing World." American Council for Capital Formation, Center for Policy Research Special Report. February 2015.

Acharya, Amitav. 2014. *The End of American World Order*. Cambridge: Polity.

Akhtar, Shayerah Ilias. 2015. "Export–Import Bank: Overview and Reauthorization Issues." Congressional Research Service. March 25, 2015.

Allee, Todd. 2012. "The Role of the United States: A Multilevel Explanation for Decreased Support Over Time." In A. Narlikar, M. Daunton, and R. M. Stern (eds.) *The Oxford Handbook on The World Trade Organization* Oxford: Oxford University Press.

Altman, Daniel. 2007. "Managing Globalization: Interview with Charlene Barshefsky on Doha." *International Herald Tribune*. January 31, 2007.

Anderson, Kym. 2017. *Finishing Global Farm Trade Reform: Implications for Developing Countries*. Adelaide: University of Adelaide Press.

Anderson, Perry. 2013. "Imperium." *New Left Review* (83): 5–111.

Armijo, Leslie. 2007. "The BRICS Countries (Brazil, Russia, India and China) as Analytical Category: Mirage or Insight?" *Asian Perspective* 31(4): 7–42.

Arrighi, Giovanni, and Beverly J. Silver. 1999. *Chaos and Governance in the Modern World System*. Minneapolis: University of Minnesota Press.

Atzl, Andreas. 2014. "Transnational NGO Networks Campaign against the Ilisu Dam, Turkey." In Waltina Scheumann and Oliver Hensengerth (eds.) *Evolution of Dam Policies: Evidence from the Big Hydropower States*. Berlin: Springer: 201–28.

Auboin, Marc. 2015. "Improving the Availability of Trade Finance in Developing Countries: An Assessment of Remaining Gaps." WTO Working Paper ERSD-2015-06.

Babones, Salvatore. 2011. "The Middling Kingdom: The Hype and the Reality of China's Rise." *Foreign Affairs* 90(5): 79.

———. 2015. "American Hegemony Is Here to Stay." *National Interest*. June 11, 2015. https://nationalinterest.org/feature/american-hegemony-here-stay-13089.

Bair, Jennifer. 2009. "Taking Aim at the New International Economic Order." In Philip Mirowski and Dieter Plehwe (eds.) *The Road from Mont Pèlerin: The Making of the Neoliberal Thought Collective*. Cambridge, MA: Harvard University Press.

Baldwin, Robert E. 1987. "The New Protectionism: A Response to Shifts in National Economic Power." National Bureau of Economic Research Working Paper No. 1823. November 1987.

Ban, Cornel, and Mark Blyth. 2013. "The BRICs and the Washington Consensus: An Introduction." *Review of International Political Economy* 20(2): 241–55.

Barnett, Michael, and Raymond Duvall. 2005. "Power in International Politics." *International Organization* 59(1): 39–75.

Beattie, Alan. 2014. "America's Craven Capitulation in the WTO." *Financial Times*. Beyond BRICS Blog. October 8, 2014.

Beckley, Michael. 2011. "China's Century? Why America's Edge Will Endure." *International Security* 36(3): 41–78.

Beeson, Mark, and S. Bell. 2009. "The G-20 and International Economic Governance: Hegemony, Collectivism, or Both." *Global Governance* 15: 67–86.

Bergsten, Fred. 2014. "Fighting Fire with Fire on Exports." *Washington Post*. September 14, 2014.

Blackmon, Pamela. 2016. "OECD Export Credit Agencies: Supplementing Short-Term Export Credit Insurance during the 2008 Financial Crisis." *International Trade Journal* 30(4): 295–318.

———. 2017. *The Political Economy of Trade Finance: Export Credit Agencies, the Paris Club and the IMF*. London: Routledge.

Block, Fred, and Matthew R. Keller. 2011. *State of Innovation: The US Government's Role in Technology Development*. Boulder, CO: Paradigm Publishers.

———. 2014. "Can the US Sustain Its Global Position? Dynamism and Stagnation in the US Institutional Model." *Political Power and Social Theory* 26: 19–51.

*Bloomberg*. 2015. "With a Rail Merger, China Forging an Industrial Giant Second Only to GE." June 7, 2015.

———. 2017. "Cheaper Solar in India Prompts Rethink for Coal Projects." June 1, 2017.

Blustein, Paul. 2009. *Misadventures of the Most Favored Nations: Clashing Egos, Inflated Ambitions, and the Great Shambles of the World Trade System*. New York: Perseus Books.

Bonucci, Nicola. 2011. "OECD Work on Export Credits: A Legal and Institutional Laboratory." In *Smart Rules for Fair Trade: 50 Years of Export Credits*. Paris: OECD: 49–53.

Bräutigam, Deborah. 2009. *The Dragon's Gift: The Real Story of China in Africa*. Oxford: Oxford University Press.

———. 2011. "Aid 'With Chinese Characteristics': Chinese Foreign Aid and Development Finance Meet the OECD–DAC Aid Regime." *Journal of International Development* 23(5): 752–64.

Bräutigam, Deborah, and Kevin P. Gallagher. 2014. "Bartering Globalization: China's Commodity-Backed Finance in Africa and Latin America." *Global Policy* 5(3): 346–52.

Bremmer, I., and N. Roubini. 2011. "A G-Zero World: The New Economic Club Will Produce Conflict, Not Cooperation." *Foreign Affairs* 90(2): 2–7.

Breslin, Shaun. 2003. "Reforming China's Embedded Socialist Compromise: China and the WTO." *Global Change, Peace and Security* 15(3).

2013. "China and the Global Order: Signalling Threat or Friendship?" *International Affairs* 89(3): 615–34.

*Bridges Daily Update.* 2015. "Bridges Daily Update #5—Overview of Outcomes of WTO's 10th Ministerial in Nairobi." December 19, 2015.

*Bridges Weekly.* 2007. "Fisheries Subsidies Text Represents a Strong Starting Point, Say Delegates." *Bridges Weekly Trade News Digest* 11(44).

2008a. "India, Indonesia and China Present New Proposal on Fisheries Subsidies." *Bridges Weekly Trade News Digest* 12(18).

2008b. "Rules Chair Issues Negotiations Update; Differences Persist." *Bridges Weekly Trade News Digest* 12(20).

2010. "WTO Fisheries Talks Focus on Special Treatment for Poor Countries." *Bridges Weekly Trade News Digest* 14(17).

2017a. "EU, Brazil Call for New WTO Rules on Farm Subsidies, Food Security." *Bridges Weekly Trade News Digest* 21(26).

2017b. "Fisheries Subsidies in the Spotlight Ahead of UN Ocean Conference." *Bridges Weekly Trade News Digest* May 4.

2017c. "Japan Reports Fall in Trade-Distorting Farm Subsidies in New WTO Figures." *Bridges Weekly Trade News Digest.* July 13, 2017.

2017d. "US Initiates WTO Challenge on China's Grain Subsidies." *Bridges Weekly Trade News Digest.* September 15, 2017.

2017e. "WTO Rules on Fisheries Subsidies: Progress and Prospects." *Bridges Weekly Trade News Digest.* November 3, 2017.

Brooks, Stephen G., and William C. Wohlforth. 2016. "The Once and Future Superpower." *Foreign Affairs* 95(3): 91–104.

Brown, Andrew G., and Robert M. Stern. 2012. "Fairness in the WTO Trading System." In A. Narlikar, M. Daunton, and R. M. Stern (eds.) *The Oxford Handbook on The World Trade Organization.* Oxford: Oxford University Press.

Bukovansky, Mlada. 2010. "Institutionalized Hypocrisy and the Politics of Agricultural Trade." In Rawi Abdelal, Mark Blyth, and Craig Parsons (eds.) *Constructing the International Economy.* Ithaca, NY: Cornell University Press: 68–89.

2016. "The Responsibility to Accommodate: Ideas and Change." In T. V. Paul (ed.) *Accommodating Rising Powers: Past, Present, and Future.* Cambridge: Cambridge University Press: 87–108.

*Business Standard.* 2019. "Air Pollution Kills 1.2 mn Indians in a Year, Third Biggest Cause of Death." April 3, 2019.

CAFOD. (Catholic Agency for Overseas Development) 2016. "UK Support for Energy in Developing Countries." In *UK Support for Energy 2010–2017: Protecting the Climate and Lifting People out of Poverty?* https://cafod.org

.uk/content/download/49429/623388/version/4/file/UK%20Support%20for %20Energy%202010-17%20Policy%20Briefing%20web%20version3.pdf.

Campling, Liam, and Elizabeth Havice. 2013. "Mainstreaming Environment and Development at the World Trade Organization? Fisheries Subsidies, the Politics of Rule-Making, and the Elusive 'Triple Win'." *Environment and Planning A* 45(4): 835–52.

2016. "Fisheries Subsidies, Development and the Global Trade Regime." In *Trade and Environment Review: Fish Trade*. Geneva: UNCTAD: 70–77.

Caporal, Jack. 2017. "WTO Rules Chair Sees Path for Fisheries Agreement as Members Push for Text." *Inside US Trade Daily Report*. March 6, 2017.

Castañeda, Jorge. 2010. "Not Ready for Prime Time: Why Including Emerging Powers at the Helm Would Hurt Global Governance." *Foreign Affairs* 89(5).

Chang, Ha-Joon. 2002. *Kicking Away the Ladder: Development Strategy in Historical Perspective*. London: Anthem Press.

Chen, Stephen. 2017. "China Pledges to Cut Size of Its Massive Fishing Fleet Due to Serious Threat to Nation's Fish Stocks." *South China Morning Post*. June 12, 2017.

Chin, Gregory. 2010. "Remaking the Architecture: The Emerging Powers, Self-Insuring and Regional Insulation." *International Affairs* 86(3): 693–715.

2015. "The State of the Art: Trends in the Study of the BRICS and Multilateral Organizations." In Dries Lesage and Thijs Van de Graaf (eds.) *Rising Powers and Multilateral Institutions*. London: Palgrave: 19–41.

Chin, Gregory, and Carla P. Freeman. 2016. "What Is Next? . . . for World Order and Global Governance." *Global Policy*. November 3, 2016.

Chin, Gregory, and Kevin Gallagher. 2015. "Demise of the US Ex-Im Bank Would Leave the Field to China." *Financial Times*. Beyond BRICS Blog. June 22, 2015.

Chorev, Nitsan. 2008. *Remaking US Trade Policy: From Protectionism to Globalization*. Ithaca, NY: Cornell University Press.

Christoff, Peter. 2016. "The Promissory Note: COP 21 and the Paris Climate Agreement." *Environmental Politics* 25(5): 765–87.

Clapp, Jennifer. 2007. "WTO Agriculture Negotiations and the Global South." In Donna Lee and Rorden Wilkinson (eds.) *The WTO After Hong Kong: Progress in, and Prospects for, the Doha Development Agenda*. New York: Routledge: 37–55.

2015. "Food Security and Contested Agricultural Trade Norms." *Journal of International Law and International Relations* 11: 104–15.

CNN. 2017. "What Is in Our Air." January 13, 2017.

Cooper, Andrew. 2016. *The BRICS: A Very Short Introduction*. Oxford: Oxford University Press.

Coppens, Dominic. 2014. *WTO Disciplines on Subsidies and Countervailing Measures: Balancing Policy Space and Legal Constraints*. Cambridge: Cambridge University Press.

Cox, Michael. 2012. "Power Shifts, Economic Change and the Decline of the West?" *International Relations* 26(4): 369–88.

CRS. (Congressional Research Service) 2017. "Major Agricultural Trade Issues in the 115th Congress." Congressional Research Service. January 30, 2017.

Crutsinger, M. 1999. "Five Nations Call for End to Harmful Fishing Subsidies." Associated Press. March 13, 1999.

Curzon, Gerard, and Victoria Curzon. 1973. "GATT: Traders' Club." In Robert W. Cox and Harold K. Jacobson (eds.) *The Anatomy of Influence: Decision-Making in International Organization.* New Haven, CT: Yale University Press: 298–333.

CUTS. 2017. "*WTO Fisheries Subsidies Negotiations: Main Issues and Interests of Least Developed Countries.*" Geneva: CUTS International.

Dadush, Uri. 2009. "WTO Reform: The Time to Start Is Now." *Carnegie Policy Brief* 80. https://carnegieendowment.org/files/WTO_reform.pdf.

Dalton, Matthew. 2011. "EU Finds China Gives Aid to Huawei, ZTE." *Wall Street Journal.* February 3, 2011. www.wsj.com/articles/SB10001424052748703960804576120012288591074.

Das, Dilip K. 2007. *The Evolving Global Trade Architecture.* Northampton, MA: Edward Elgar.

Deming, Chen, and Liaw Peiru. 2016. *Economic Crisis and Rule Reconstruction.* Singapore: World Scientific.

Department of Energy and Climate Change. 2013. "UK Urges the World to Prepare for Action on Climate Change and Puts Brakes on Coal Fired Power Plants." Department of Energy and Climate Change, Press Release. November 13, 2013.

Doak, N., M. Murai, and F. Douvere. 2016. *Report on the Mission to the Sundarbans World Heritage Site, Bangladesh, from 22 to 28 March 2016.* http://defence.pk/threads/report-on-the-mission-to-the-sundarbans-world-heritage-site-bangladesh-from-22-to-28-march-2016.458823/.

Doumbouya, Alkaly, Ousmane T. Camara, Josephus Mamie, Jeremias F. Intchama, Abdoulie Jarra, Salifu Ceesay, Assane Guèye, Diène Ndiaye, Ely Beibou, Allan Padilla, and Dyhia Belhabib. 2017. "Assessing the Effectiveness of Monitoring Control and Surveillance of Illegal Fishing: The Case of West Africa." *Frontiers in Marine Science* 4(50).

Downs, Erica. 2011. *Inside China, Inc.: China Development Bank's Cross-Border Energy Deals.* Washington, DC: Brookings Institution.

Drache, Daniel. 2004. "Global Trade Politics and the Cycle of Dissent Post-Cancún." *Policy and Society* 24(3): 17–44.

DRC. 2014. "Optimizing and Upgrading Industrial Structure." Development Research Center of the State Council of the People's Republic of China. May 23, 2014.

Drezner, Daniel W. 2007. "The New New World Order." *Foreign Affairs* 86(2): 34–46.

——— 2011. ". . . And China Isn't Beating the US." *Foreign Policy* (184):67.

Drysdale, David. 2015. "Why the OECD Arrangement Works (Even Though It Is Only Soft Law)." In Andreas Klasen and Fiona Bannert (eds.) *The Future of Foreign Trade Support—Setting Global Standards for Export Credit and Political Risk Insurance.* Chichester: Wiley-Blackwell.

*E&E News.* 2015a. "Nations Conflict on Subsidy Rules for Exporting Coal-Fired Power Plants." *E&E News.* November 10, 2015.

2015b. "New Coal-Fired Power Enjoys Support among Bankers in Germany and Asia." *E&E News*. August 13, 2015.

2015c. "US Strikes Deal to Block Coal Plants Worldwide." *E&E News*. November 18, 2015.

2017. "Trump Is Pushing Coal Abroad. Markets May Abide—for Now." *E&E News*. December 13, 2017.

Eagleton-Pierce, Matthew. 2012. *Symbolic Power in the World Trade Organization*. Oxford: Oxford University Press.

Eberlein, Christine, Heike Drillisch, Ercan Ayboga, and Thomas Wenidoppler. 2010. "The Ilisu Dam in Turkey and the Role of Export Credit Agencies and NGO Networks." *Water Alternatives* 3(2): 291–311.

*Eco-Business*. 2017. "Vietnam Makes a Big Push for Coal, While Pledging to Curb Emissions." *Eco-Business*. May 30, 2017.

*Economic Times*. 2016. "Indo-Bangla Forum Writes to PM against Proposed Power Plant." *Economic Times*. October 18, 2016.

*The Economist*. 2012. "Something Old, Something New: A Brief History of State Capitalism." *The Economist*. January 21, 2012.

2017. "All the Fish in the Sea: Ocean Fishing." *The Economist*. May 27, 2017.

Efstathopoulos, Charalampos, and Dominic Kelly. 2014. "India, Developmental Multilateralism and the Doha Ministerial Conference." *Third World Quarterly* 35(6): 1066–81.

Eilperin, Juliet. 2015. "In a Major Step on the Road to Paris, Rich Countries Agree to Slash Export Subsidies for Coal Plants." *Washington Post*. November 18, 2015.

Elsig, Manfred, and Cedric Dupont. 2012. "Persistent Deadlock in Multilateral Trade Negotiations: The Case of Doha." In A. Narlikar, M. Daunton, and R.M. Stern (eds.) *The Oxford Handbook on The World Trade Organization*. Oxford: Oxford University Press: 587–606.

Erickson, Andrew S., and Conor M. Kennedy. 2016. "China's Maritime Militia." *Foreign Affairs Snapshot*. June 23, 2016.

EU (European Union). 2011. "Export Finance Activities by the Chinese Government." Briefing Paper. Directorate-General for External Policies, European Parliament. EXPO/B/INTA/FWC/2009-01/Lot7/15.

2015. "Council Decision on the Position to Be Taken by the European Union within the OECD Export Credit Committees on Modifications of the OECD Arrangement on Officially Supported Export Credits." Brussels. July 20, 2015. COM(2015) 353 final.

2016. "Study on the Subsidies to the Fisheries, Aquaculture, and Marketing and Processing Subsectors in Major Fishing Nations beyond the EU." Brussels, Directorate-General for Maritime Affairs and Fisheries, MARE/2011/01 Lot 2.

European Commission. 2015. "Report from the Commission to the European Parliament and the Council: Annual Report on Negotiations Undertaken by the Commission in the Field of Export Credits, in the Sense of Regulation (EU) No. 1233/2011." Brussels. October 20, 2015. COM(2015) 516.

Evenett, Simon. 2007. "EU Commercial Policy in a Multipolar Trading System." University of St. Gallen Law & Economics Working Paper No. 15. https://ssrn.com/abstract=985514.

Exim. 2006. "Report to US Congress on the Export–Import Bank of the United States and Global Export Credit Competition." US Export–Import Bank, Washington, DC.

——— 2014. "Report to US Congress on the Export–Import Bank of the United States and Global Export Credit Competition." US Export–Import Bank, Washington, DC.

——— 2015. "Report to US Congress on Global Export Credit Competition." US Export–Import Bank, Washington, DC.

——— 2016. "Report to US Congress on Global Export Credit Competition." US Export–Import Bank, Washington, DC.

——— 2018. "Report to US Congress on Global Export Credit Competition." US Export–Import Bank, Washington, DC.

Ezell, Stephen J. 2011. "Understanding the Importance of Export Credit Financing to US Competitiveness." The Information Technology & Innovation Foundation, Washington, DC.

Falkner, Robert. 2005. "American Hegemony and the Global Environment." *International Studies Review* 7(4): 585–99.

FAO. (Food and Agriculture Organization) 2016. *The State of the World's Fisheries and Aquaculture: Contributing to Food Security and Nutrition for All*. Rome: UN Food and Agriculture Organization.

——— 2018. *The State of the World's Fisheries and Aquaculture*. Rome: UN Food and Agriculture Organization.

Ferdinand, Peter. 2016. "Westward Ho—The China Dream and 'One Belt, One Road': Chinese Foreign Policy under Xi Jinping." *International Affairs* 92(4): 941–57.

Fevrier, Stephen, and Manleen Dugal. 2016. "The WTO's Role in Fisheries Subsidies and Its Implications for Africa." *Bridges Africa*. December 20, 2016.

*Financial Times*. 2011. "US to Match Chinese Terms for Train Order." *Financial Times*. January 12, 2011.

——— 2015a. "Export Subsidies for Coal Power Stations Reigned in by OECD." *Financial Times*. November 18, 2015.

——— 2015b. "Rich Nations Assess Plan to Slash Billions from Coal Investment." *Financial Times*. November 9, 2015.

——— 2017. "AIIB Chief Aims to Rival Lenders Such as ADB and World Bank." *Financial Times*. May 4, 2017.

FOE. (Friends of the Earth) 2016. "Strengthening the OECD Coal-Fired Sector Understanding." November 2016.

FOE, OCI, & WWF. 2017. "Financing Climate Disaster: How Export Credit Agencies Are a Boon for Oil and Gas." Friends of the Earth, OilChange International, and World Wide Fund for Nature. https://1bps6437gg8c169ioy1drtgz-wpengine.netdna-ssl.com/wp-content/uploads/2017/10/2017.10.16_FinancingClimateDisaster_final.pdf.

Foot, Rosemary. 2017. "Power Transitions and Great Power Management: Three Decades of China–Japan–US Relations." *Pacific Review* 30(6): 829–84.

Forsythe, Michael. 2016. "China Curbs Plans for More Coal-Fired Power Plants." *New York Times*. April 25, 2016.

Fortnam, Brett. 2017a. "US Rejects Chinese Proposal for Trade Remedy Rules Negotiations at the WTO." *Inside US Trade Daily Report* 35(22).

2017b. "WTO Members Expected to Commit to Continue Fisheries Talks after MC11." *Inside US Trade Daily Report.*

2017c. "WTO Members Fear China Could Link AD and Fisheries Proposals, Sink Ministerial Outcome." *Inside US Trade Daily Report.* May 5, 2017.

Frazier, Mark W. 2013. "Narrowing the Gap: Rural–Urban Inequality in China." *World Politics Review.* September 24, 2013.

Gale, Fred. 2013. "Growth and Evolution in China's Agricultural Support Policies." USDA Economic Research Service Report #153. August.

Gallagher, Kevin P. 2008a. "Trading Away the Ladder? Trade Politics and Economic Development in the Americas." *New Political Economy* 13(1): 37–59.

2008b. "Understanding Developing Country Resistance to the Doha Round." *Review of International Political Economy* 15(1): 62–85.

Gallagher, Kevin P., Amos Irwin, and Katherine Koleski. 2012. "The New Banks in Town: Chinese Finance in Latin America." Inter-American Dialogue Report. March 2012.

Gao, Henry. 2015. "From the Doha Round to the China Round." In Colin B. Picker, Jonathan Greenacre, and Lisa Toohey (eds.) *China in the International Economic Order: New Directions and Changing Paradigms.* Cambridge: Cambridge University Press: 79–97.

GATT. 1994. "Agreement Establishing the WTO." Uruguay Round Agreements, Marrakesh. April 15, 1994.

Gelder, Jan Willem van, Laura German, and Rob Bailis. 2012. "Biofuels Investments in Tropical Forest-Rich Countries: Implications for Responsible Finance." *Sustainability Accounting, Management and Policy Journal* 3(2): 134–60.

Gibbs, Murray. 2000. "Special and Differential Treatment in the Context of Globalization." In *A Positive Agenda for Developing Countries: Issues for Future Trade Negotiations.* Geneva: UNCTAD.

Gilpin, Robert. 1987. *The Political Economy of International Relations.* Princeton, NJ: Princeton University Press.

Godfrey, Mark. 2017. "China Makes Concessions on Eve of WTO Fisheries Talks." *Seafood Source.* December 12, 2017.

2018a. "China Becoming an Environmentalist at Home, While Plundering Abroad." *Seafood Source.* March 28, 2018.

2018b. "China Rushing to Build Global Fishing Bases before Capping Its Fleet Size." *Seafood Source.* January 17, 2018.

Gonter, Michael. 2011. "Premium: The Least Understood Rules of the Arrangement." In *Smart Rules for Fair Trade: 50 Years of Export Credits.* Paris: OECD: 220–24.

Gray, Kevin, and Craig N. Murphy (eds.). 2015. *Rising Powers and the Future of Global Governance* London: Routledge.

Greenpeace. 2015. "Africa's Fisheries Paradise at a Crossroads: Investigating Chinese Companies' Illegal Fishing Practices in West Africa." Greenpeace East Asia and Greenpeace Africa.

2016. "Give a Man a Fish—Five Facts on China's Distant Water Fishing Subsidies." Greenpeace East Asia Briefing. August 8, 2016.

Greenville, Jared. 2017. "Domestic Support to Agriculture and Trade: Implications for Multilateral Reform." Geneva: ICTSD.

*The Guardian.* 2015a. "Japan and South Korea Top List of Biggest Coal Financiers." June 2, 2015.

——— 2015b. "OECD Talks to Phase out Coal Subsidies End in Stalemate." June 12, 2015.

——— 2016. "Greenpeace Sounds Alarm over China's Long-Distance Fishing Fleet." August 9, 2016.

Hall, Steven. 2011. "Managing Tied Aid Competition: Domestic Politics, Credible Threats, and the Helsinki Disciplines." *Review of International Political Economy* 18(5): 646–72.

Hameiri, Shahar, and Lee Jones. 2018. "China Challenges Global Governance? Chinese International Development Finance and the AIIB." *International Affairs* 94(3): 573–93.

Hamilton, Alexander. 1790. *Report on Manufactures.* Philadelphia: Childs and Swaine.

Hampson, Fen Osler, and Paul Heinbecker. 2011. "The 'New' Multilateralism of the Twenty-First Century." *Global Governance: A Review of Multilateralism and International Organizations* 17(3): 299–310.

Hancock, Tom. 2018a. "China's Long-Distance Fishing Fleet Dependent on Subsidies." *Financial Times.* June 13, 2018.

——— 2018b. "China Seeks Bigger Catch from Far-Sea Fishing Fleet." *Financial Times.* February 9, 2018.

Hannah, Erin. 2015. *NGOs and Global Trade: Non-State Voices in EU Trade Policymaking.* Abingdon: Routledge.

Hannah, Erin, Holly Ryan, and James Scott. 2017. "Power, Knowledge and Resistance: Between Co-Optation and Revolution in Global Trade." *Review of International Political Economy* 24(5): 741–75.

Hannah, Erin, and James Scott. 2017. "From Palais de Nations to Centre William Rappard: Raúl Prebisch and UNCTAD as Sources of Ideas in the GATT/WTO." In Matias E. Margulis (ed.) *The Global Political Economy of Raúl Prebisch.* New York: Routledge: 116–34.

Hannah, Erin, James Scott, and Rorden Wilkinson. 2018. "The WTO in Buenos Aires: The Outcome and Its Significance for the Future of the Multilateral Trading System." *The World Economy.* May 6, 2018.

Hannam, Phillip Matthew. 2016. "Contesting Authority: The New Landscape of Power Sector Governance in the Developing World." PhD thesis. Princeton University.

Hao, Feng. 2017. "China's Belt and Road Initiative Still Pushing Coal." *China Dialogue.* May 12, 2017.

Harkell, Louise. 2017. "CNFC: Chinese Squid Fishing Activities Near Argentina up 270%, Peru 515%." *Undercurrent News.* May 26, 2017.

——— 2018. "China Pulls Plug on Subsidies, Licenses of Firms Involved in IUU." *Undercurrent News.* March 9, 2018.

Hart, Melanie, Luke Bassett, and Blaine Johnson. 2017. "Everything You Think You Know about Coal in China Is Wrong." Center for American Progress Blog. May 15, 2017.

Hejazi, Mina, and Mary A. Marchant. 2017. "China's Evolving Agricultural Support Policies." *Choices* 32(2).

Hochstetler, Kathryn, and Manjana Milkoreit. 2015. "Responsibilities in Transition: Emerging Powers in the Climate Change Negotiations." *Global Governance* 21(2): 205–26.

Hoekman, Bernard. 1995. "Assessing the General Agreement on Trade in Services." In Will Martin and L. Alan Winters (eds.) *The Uruguay Round and the Developing Countries*. Washington, DC: World Bank: 326–64.

Hopewell, Kristen. 2015. "Different Paths to Power: The Rise of Brazil, India and China at the WTO." *Review of International Political Economy* 22(2): 311–38.

2016. *Breaking the WTO: How Emerging Powers Disrupted the Neoliberal Project*. Stanford, CA: Stanford University Press.

2017a. "The BRICS—Merely a Fable? Emerging Power Alliances in Global Trade Governance." *International Affairs* 93(6): 1377–96.

2017b. "The Liberal International Economic Order on the Brink." *Current History* 116(793): 303–8.

2017c. "When Market Fundamentalism and Industrial Policy Collide: The Tea Party and the US Export–Import Bank." *Review of International Political Economy* 24(4): 569–98.

2018. "What Is 'Made in China 2025'—and Why Is It a Threat to Trump's Trade Goals?" *Washington Post*. May 3, 2018.

2019. "How Rising Powers Create Governance Gaps: The Case of Export Credit and the Environment." *Global Environmental Politics* 19(1): 34–52.

Hornby, Lucy. 2015. "Beijing Constrained by Record Farm Stockpiles." *Financial Times*. February 3, 2015.

2017. "A Bigger Catch: China's Fishing Fleet Hunts New Ocean Targets." *Financial Times*. March 27, 2017.

Hovi, Jon, Detlef F. Sprinz, and Guri Bang. 2012. "Why the United States Did Not Become a Party to the Kyoto Protocol: German, Norwegian, and US Perspectives." *European Journal of International Relations* 18(1): 129–50.

Hufbauer, Gary, Meera Fickling, and Woan Foong Wong. 2011. "Revitalizing the Export–Import Bank." Peterson Institute for International Economics, Policy Brief No. PB11-6.

Hung, H. F. 2015. *The China Boom: Why China Will Not Rule the World*. New York: Columbia University Press.

Hurrell, Andrew. 2004. "Power, Institutions, and the Production of Inequality." In Michael Barnett and Raymond Duvall (eds.) *Power in Global Governance*. Cambridge: Cambridge University Press: 33–58.

ICAC (International Cotton Advisory Committee). 2016a. "Cotton Report." Presentation by Jose Sette, ICAC Executive Director, WTO 6th Dedicated Discussion of the Relevant Trade-Related Developments on Cotton, Geneva. November 23, 2016.

2016b. "Production and Trade Policies Affecting the Cotton Industry." International Cotton Advisory Committee, Washington, DC.

ICTSD (International Centre for Trade and Sustainable Development). 2013. "Cotton: Trends in Global Production, Trade and Policy." Geneva: ICTSD Programme on Agriculture Trade and Sustainable Development.

2015. "National Agricultural Policies, Trade, and the New Multilateral Agenda." Geneva: ICTSD Programme on Agriculture Trade and Sustainable Development.

IDEAS Centre. 2013. "Cotton Update." *Newsletter* 101. February 21, 2013.

IEA. 2014a. "World Energy Investment Outlook." International Energy Agency. www.iea.org/reports/world-energy-investment-outlook.

2014b. "World Energy Outlook 2014." International Energy Agency, Paris. www.oecd-ilibrary.org/energy/world-energy-outlook-2014_weo-2014-en.

2015. "World Energy Outlook 2015." International Energy Agency, Paris. www.oecd-ilibrary.org/energy/world-energy-outlook-2015_weo-2015-en.

2017a. "World Energy Access Outlook 2017." International Energy Agency, Paris. www.oecd-ilibrary.org/energy/world-energy-outlook-2017_weo-2017-en.

2017b. *International Finance for Coal-Fired Power Plants.* London: IEA Clean Coal Centre.

Ikenberry, G. John. 2011. *Liberal Leviathan: The Origins, Crisis, and Transformation of the American World Order.* Princeton, NJ: Princeton University Press.

2015a. "The Future of Liberal World Order." *Japanese Journal of Political Science* 16(3): 450–55.

2015b. "The Future of Multilateralism: Governing the World in a Post-Hegemonic Era." *Japanese Journal of Political Science* 16(3): 399–413.

Ilcan, Susan, and Anita Lacey. 2006. "Governing through Empowerment: Oxfam's Global Reform and Trade Campaign." *Globalizations* 3(2): 207–25.

Imboden, Nicolas. 2014. "How to Re-invigorate the Cotton Issue at the WTO: Gin Ideas, Spin Proposals, Weave Solutions and Avoid Stocks." In Ricardo Meléndez-Ortiz, Christophe Bellmann, and Jonathan Hepburn (eds.) *Tackling Agriculture in the Post-Bali Context—A Collection of Short Essays.* Geneva: ICTSD.

*Inside US Trade.* 2012. "US, EU Use WTO Policy Review to Critique China's Opaque Trade Regime." June 12, 2012.

2016. "Punke: US Seeks to Conclude EGA By September G20 Leaders Meeting." May 10, 2016.

2019. "China: US Stance on WTO Development Status Shows It Is 'Capricious, Arrogant and Selfish'." July 29, 2019.

*Inside US–China Trade.* 2016a. "Brady, Froman, Obama Link WTO Challenge of China's Ag Support to TPP." 16(37).

2016b. "US Wheat Industry Backtracks on Call for WTO Case on China Subsidies." 16(14).

2016c. "US Wheat Industry Leader: More Steps Needed to Counter Chinese Policies." 16(41).

2017a. "US–China Domestic Agricultural Support Case Moves Toward Panel Stage." 35(4).

2017b. "WTO Members Remain Deadlocked in Ag Talks Despite Flurry of Proposals." 35(30).

ITC (International Trade Commission). 2015. *Rice: Global Competitiveness of the US Industry*. Washington, DC: US International Trade Commission.

Jacobs, Andrew. 2017. "China's Appetite Pushes Fish Stocks to Brink." *New York Times*. April 30, 2017.

Jacques, Martin. 2009. *When China Rules the World: The Rise of the Middle Kingdom and the End of the Western World*. London: Allen Lane.

Jing, Li, and Kwong Man-ki. 2015. "China Unveils Ambitious Plans for 'Made in China' Upgrade within 10 Years." *South China Morning Post* . May 19, 2015.

Jones, Emily, and Clara Weinhardt. 2015. "Echoes of Colonialism in the Negotiation of Economic Partnership Agreements." In Kalypso Nicolaïdis, Berny Sebe, and Gabrielle Maas (eds.) *Echoes of Empire: Memory, Identity and the Legacy of Imperialism*. London: I. B. Tauris.

Kagan, Robert. 2010. "The Perils of Wishful Thinking." *National Interest* 5(3): 14–16.

2012. *The World America Made*. New York: Knopf.

Kahler, Miles. 2010. "Asia and the Reform of Global Governance." *Asian Economic Policy Review* 5(2): 178–93.

2016. "The Global Economic Multilaterals: Will Eighty Years Be Enough?" *Global Governance* 22(1): 1–9.

Kapoor, Ilan. 2006. "Deliberative Democracy and the WTO." *Review of International Political Economy* 11(3): 522–41.

Karkovirta, Pekka. 2011. "Implementing Environmental Common Approaches." In *Smart Rules for Fair Trade: 50 years of Export Credits*. Paris: OECD: 167–71.

Karnitschnig, Matthew. 2017. "Baijing's Balkan Backdoor." *Politico*. July 13, 2017.

Katzenstein, Peter J. 2005. *A World of Regions: Asia and Europe in the American Imperium*. Ithaca, NY: Cornell University Press.

Kelly, Dominic, and Wyn Grant. 2005. "Introduction: Trade Politics in Context." In Dominic Kelly and Wyn Grant (eds.) *The Politics of International Trade in the Twenty-First Century: Actors, Issues, and Regional Dynamics*. New York: Palgrave Macmillan.

Kennedy, Scott. 2015. "Made in China 2025." Center for Strategic and International Studies, Washington, DC. June 1, 2015.

Keohane, Robert. 1982. "The Demand for International Regimes." *International Organization* 36(2): 325–55.

1984. *After Hegemony: Cooperation and Discord in the World Political Economy*. Princeton, NJ: Princeton University Press.

Keohane, Robert, and Joseph S. Nye. 2011. *Power and Interdependence*. New York: Longman.

Kiko Network et al. 2017. "Dirty Coal: Breaking the Myth about Japanese-Funded Coal Plants." Kiko Network, JACSES, Friends of the Earth Japan, CoalSwarm, Friends of the Earth US, and Sierra Club. April 2017.

Kirshner, Jonathan. 2012. "The Tragedy of Offensive Realism: Classical Realism and the Rise of China." *European Journal of International Relations* 18(1): 53–75.

Kong, Bo, and Kevin P. Gallagher. 2017. "Globalizing Chinese Energy Finance: The Role of Policy Banks." *Journal of Contemporary China* 26(108): 834–51.

Konno, Hidehiro. 1998. "From Simple to Sophisticated." In *The Export Credit Arrangement: Achievements and Challenges, 1978–1998*. Paris: OECD.

Koplitz, Shannon N., Daniel J. Jacob, Melissa P. Sulprizio, Lauri Myllyvirta, and Colleen Reid. 2017. "Burden of Disease from Rising Coal-Fired Power Plant Emissions in Southeast Asia." *Environmental Science & Technology* 51(3): 1467–76.

Koremenos, Barbara, Charles Lipson, and Duncan Snidal. 2001. "The Rational Design of International Institutions." *International Organization* 55(4): 761–99.

Krasner, Stephen D. 1979. "The Tokyo Round: Particularistic Interests and Prospects for Stability in the Global Trading System." *International Studies Quarterly* 23(4): 491–531.

2011. "Changing State Structures: Outside In." *Proceedings of the National Academy of Sciences* 108(4): 21302–7.

Kroodsma, David A., Juan Mayorga, Timothy Hochberg, Nathan A. Miller, Kristina Boerder, Francesco Ferretti, Alex Wilson, Bjorn Bergman, Timothy D. White, Barbara A. Block, Paul Woods, Brian Sullivan, Christopher Costello, and Boris Worm. 2018. "Tracking the Global Footprint of Fisheries." *Science* 359(6378): 904–8.

Kupchan, Charles A. 2014. "The Normative Foundations of Hegemony and the Coming Challenge to Pax Americana." *Security Studies* 23(2): 219–57.

Lake, David A. 2009. *Hierarchy in International Relations*. Ithaca, NY: Cornell University Press.

2014. "The Challenge: The Domestic Determinants of International Rivalry between the United States and China." *International Studies Review* 16(3): 442–47.

Lardy, Nicholas R. 2000. "Permanent Normal Trade Relations for China." Brookings Institution, Policy Brief No. 58. May 2000.

2004. *Integrating China into the Global Economy*. Washington, DC: Brookings Institution Press.

Larik, Joris, and Abhijit Singh. 2017. "Sustainability in Oceans Governance: Small Islands, Emerging Powers, and Connecting Regions." *Global Policy* 8(2): 213–15.

Layne, Christopher. 2009. "The Waning of US Hegemony—Myth or Reality? A Review Essay." *International Security* 34(1): 147–72.

2018. "The US–Chinese Power Shift and the End of the Pax Americana." *International Affairs* 94(1): 89–111.

Lazonick, William. 2008. "Entrepreneurial Ventures and the Developmental State." Helsinki: UNU-WIDER, Discussion Paper No. 2008/01.

Lesage, Dries, and Thijs Van de Graaf (eds.) 2015. *Rising Powers and Multilateral Institutions*. Basingstoke: Palgrave Macmillan.

Levit, Janet Koven. 2004. "The Dynamics of International Trade Finance Regulation: The Arrangement on Officially Supported Export Credit." *Harvard International Law Journal* 45:65–182.

Lin, Justin, and Ha-Joon Chang. 2009. "Should Industrial Policy in Developing Countries Conform to Comparative Advantage or Defy it? A Debate between Justin Lin and Ha-Joon Chang." *Development Policy Review* 27(5): 483–502.

Littlecott, Chris. 2015. "Restricting Export Credit Finance for Coal Power Plants." E3G Briefing Paper. November 2015.

Lu, Xiankun. 2015. "Shifting Weights and Balances within the WTO in a Changing Global Trading Landscape." *Bridges Africa* 4(9).

Lundestad, Geir. 1990. *The American "Empire."* Oxford: Oxford University Press.

Lynch, D. 2015. *China's Futures: PRC Elites Debate Economics, Politics, and Foreign Policy.* Stanford, CA: Stanford University Press.

McCauley, Douglas J., Caroline Jablonicky, Edward H. Allison, Christopher D. Golden, Francis H. Joyce, Juan Mayorga, and David Kroodsma. 2018. "Wealthy Countries Dominate Industrial Fishing." *Science Advances* 4(8).

McCright, Aaron M., and Riley E. Dunlap. 2014. "Defeating Kyoto: The Conservative Movement's Impact on US Climate Change Policy." *Social Problems* 50(3): 348–73.

McMichael, Phillip. 2012. *Development and Social Change: A Global Perspective.* Thousand Oaks, CA: Pine Forge Press.

Mahrenbach, Laura Carsten. 2013. *The Trade Policy of Emerging Powers: Strategic Choices of Brazil and India.* New York: Palgrave.

Maier, Charles S. 2002. "An American Empire?" *Harvard Magazine.* November/December 2002.

Mallory, Tabitha Grace. 2013. "China's Distant Water Fishing Industry: Policies and Implications." *Marine Policy* 38: 99–108.

    2015. "Preparing for the Ocean Century: China's Changing Political Institutions for Ocean Governance and Maritime Development." *Issues & Studies* 51(2): 111–38.

    2016. "Fisheries Subsidies in China: Quantitative and Qualitative Assessment of Policy Coherence and Effectiveness." *Marine Policy* 68: 74–82.

Mansfield, Edward D. 2014. "Rising Powers in the Global Economy: Issues and Questions." *International Studies Review* 16(3): 437–42.

Margulis, Matias E. 2010. "Whistling to the Same Tune? The Contest over Future WTO Agricultural Subsidies." In A. Govinda Reddy (ed.) *Agriculture Subsidies and the WTO.* Hyderabad: Amicus Books: 34–44.

    2014. "Trading Out of the Global Food Crisis? The World Trade Organization and the Geopolitics of Food Security." *Geopolitics* 19(2): 322–50.

    2016. "The Forgotten History of Food Security in Multilateral Trade Negotiations." *World Trade Review* 16(1): 25–57.

Margulis, Matias E. (ed.) 2017. *The Global Political Economy of Raúl Prebisch.* New York: Routledge.

    2018. "Negotiating from the Margins: How the UN Shapes the Rules of the WTO." *Review of International Political Economy* 25(3): 364–91.

2019. "A New Grey Zone in Global Trade Governance? Recent Developments on Food Security at the World Trade Organization." In Daniel Drache and Lesley A. Jacobs (eds.) *Crises and Resilience in International Economic Law: Global Governance and Policy Spaces*. Vancouver: University of British Columbia Press.

Margulis, Matias E., and Tony Porter. 2013. "Governing the Global Land Grab: Multipolarity, Ideas, and Complexity in Transnational Governance." *Globalizations* 10(1): 65–86.

Mastanduno, M. 2009. "System Maker and Privilege Taker: US Power and the International Political Economy." *World Politics* 61(1): 121.

Mathiesen, Karl. 2016. "UN Tells Bangladesh to Halt Mangrove-Threatening Coal Plant." *The Guardian*. October 19, 2016.

Maurer, C., and S. Nakhooda. 2003. "Transition from Fossil to Renewable Energy Systems: What Role for Export Credit Agencies?" *World Resources Institute Policy Brief*. December 2003.

Mera, Carlos. 2017. "China's Selling May Keep Food Prices Low This Year." *Financial Times*. Beyond BRICS Blog. January 31, 2017.

Meyer, Gregory, and Emiko Terazono. 2014. "Cotton Farmers Feel a Chill in the Market as Prices Wear Thin." *Financial Times*. December 14, 2014.

MOFCOM (Ministry of Commerce). 2016. "Official of the Department and Treaty and Law Comments on the US Appealing to the WTO against China's Agricultural Support Policies." Ministry of Commerce, China. September 15, 2016.

Moravcsik, Andrew M. 1989. "Disciplining Trade Finance: The OECD Export Credit Arrangement." *International Organization* 43(1): 173–205.

Mortensen, Jens L. 2006. "The WTO and the Governance of Globalization: Dismantling the Compromise of Embedded Liberalism?" In Richard Stubbs and Geoffrey Underhill (eds.) *Political Economy and the Changing Global Order*. Don Mills, Ontario: Oxford University Press: 170–82.

Morton, Katherine. 2017. "Learning by Doing: The Global Governance of Food Security." In Scott Kennedy (ed.) *The Dragon's Learning Curve: Global Governance and China*. London: Routledge.

Muzaka, Valbona, and Matthew Louis Bishop. 2014. "Doha Stalemate: The End of Trade Multilateralism?" *Review of International Studies* 41(2): 383–406.

NAM (National Association of Manufacturers). 2008. "NAMA Sectorals Essential for Balanced Outcomes." Press Release. July 28, 2008.

2014. *The Global Export Credit Dimension: The Size of Foreign Export Credit Agencies Compared to the Export–Import Bank of the United States*. Washington, DC: National Association of Manufacturers. www.nam.org/wp-content/uploads/2019/05/Global-Export-Credit.pdf.

Narlikar, Amrita. 2013. "Negotiating the Rise of New Powers." *International Affairs* 89(3): 561–76.

2017. "India's Role in Global Governance: A Modi-fication?" *International Affairs* 93(1): 132–11.

Narlikar, Amrita, and Diana Tussie. 2004. "The G20 at the Cancun Ministerial: Developing Countries and Their Evolving Coalitions in the WTO." *World Economy* 27(7): 947–66.

2016. "Breakthrough at Bali? Explanations, Aftermath, Implications." *International Negotiation* 21(2): 209–32.

Narlikar, Amrita, and Rorden Wilkinson. 2004. "Collapse at the WTO: A Cancun Post-Mortem." *Third World Quarterly* 25(3): 447–60.

Netherlands. 2014. "Joint Statement by the United States and the Netherlands on Climate Change and Financing the Transition to Low-Carbon Investments Abroad." March 24, 2014.

*New York Times.* 2017. "China Wants Fish, So Africa Goes Hungry." *New York Times.* Editorial. May 3, 2017.

Newman, Jesse, and Patrick McGroarty. 2017. "Plowed Under—The Next Farm Bust Is Upon Us." *Wall Street Journal.* February 8, 2017.

Nölke, Andreas, Tobias ten Brink, Simone Claar, and Christian May. 2015. "Domestic Structures, Foreign Economic Policies and Global Economic Order: Implications from the Rise of Large Emerging Economies." *European Journal of International Relations* 21(3): 538–67.

Norrlof, Carla. 2014. "Dollar Hegemony: A Power Analysis." *Review of International Political Economy* 21(5): 1042–70.

NRDC. 2016a. "Carbon Trap: How International Coal Finance Undermines the Paris Agreement." Natural Resources Defense Council. November 14, 2016.

2016b. "International Coal and Renewables Financing and Climate Change." National Resources Development Council. November 4, 2016.

2017. "Power Shift: Shifting G20 International Public Finance from Coal to Renewables." Natural Resources Defense Council. December 3, 2017.

NRDC, OCI, and WWF. 2015. "Under the Rug: How Governments and International Institutions are Hiding Billions to Support the Coal Industry." National Resources Defense Council, Oil Change International and World Wildlife Fund for Nature. June 2, 2015.

Nye, Joseph S. 2015. *Is the American Century Over?* Cambridge: Polity.

2012. "The Twenty-First Century Will Not Be a 'Post-American' World." *International Studies Quarterly* 56(1): 215–17.

OA. 2010. "Chinese Activities in Eastern Europe—Success through Market-Aggressive Financing Offers." Position Paper. Ost-Ausschuss der Deutschen Wirtschaft (German Eastern Business Association).

OCI and WWF. 2015. "Hidden Costs: Pollution from Coal Power Financed by OECD Countries." Oil Change International and World Wildlife Fund for Nature. November 2015. http://priceofoil.org/content/uploads/2015/11/Hidden-Costs-of-Coal-Economic-Costs-of-OECD-Coal-Finance.pdf.

ODI and Oxfam. 2015. "Speaking Truth to Power: Why Energy Distribution, More than Generation, Is Africa's Poverty Reduction Challenge." Overseas Development Institute and Oxfam. May 2015.

OECD. (Organisation for Economic Co-operation and Development) 2011. *Smart Rules for Fair Trade: 50 Years of Export Credits.* Paris: OECD.

2013. *Perspectives on Global Development 2013: Industrial Policies in a Changing World.* Paris: OECD.

2014a. "Data on Export Credit Support for Fossil Fuel Power Plants and Fossil Fuel Extraction Projects." Room Document No. 1, Paris. October 9, 2014.

2014b. "Revised Sector Understanding on Export Credits for Renewable Energy, Climate Change Mitigation and Adaptation, and Water Projects." (TAD/PG(2014)4).

2015a. "Sector Understanding on Export Credits for Coal-Fired Electricity Generation Projects." (TAD/PG(2015)9/FINAL).

2015b. "Statement from Participants to the Arrangement on Officially Supported Export Credits." November 18, 2015.

2016. "Review of Members' Responses to the Environmental and Social Survey." (TAD/ECG(2015)17/FINAL).

2017a. *Agricultural Policy Monitoring and Evaluation*. Paris: OECD.

2017b. *OECD Review of Fisheries: Policies and Summary Statistics*. Paris: OECD.

2018a. "Arrangement on Officially Supported Export Credits." (TAD/PG (2018)1).

2018b. "Trends in Arrangement Official Export Credits." January 16, 2018.

Orden, D. 2013. "The Changing Implications of Domestic Support and Its Implications for Trade." Canadian Agricultural Trade Policy and Competitiveness Research Network (CATPRN). Commissioned Paper 2013-02. https://ageconsearch.umn.edu/record/146657/files/Commissioned%20paper%202013-02%20Orden%20final.pdf.

Ostry, Sylvia. 2007. "Trade, Development, and the Doha Development Agenda." In Donna Lee and Rorden Wilkinson (eds.) *The WTO after Hong Kong: Progress in, and Prospects for, the Doha Development Agenda*. New York: Routledge: 248–61.

Oxfam. 2002. "Rigged Rules and Double Standards: Trade, Globalization and the Fight against Poverty." Make Trade Fair Campaign. Sustainable Agriculture and Natural Resource Management (SANREM) Knowledgebase. https://vtechworks.lib.vt.edu/handle/10919/65754.

2005. "A Round for Free: How Rich Countries Are Getting a Free Ride on Agricultural Subsidies at the WTO." Oxfam Briefing Paper No. 76. June 15, 2005.

2017. "By the Numbers: Too Many People Still Live in the Dark." October 20, 2017. https://politicsofpoverty.oxfamamerica.org/2017/10/by-the-numbers-too-many-people-still-live-in-the-dark/.

Panich, Leo, and Sam Gindin. 2012. *The Making of Global Capitalism: The Political Economy of American Empire*. New York: Verso.

Patrick, S. 2010. "Irresponsible Stakeholders? The Difficulty of Integrating Rising Powers." *Foreign Affairs* 89(6): 44–55.

Paul, T. V. 2016a. *Accommodating Rising Powers: Past, Present, and Future*. Cambridge: Cambridge University Press.

2016b. "The Accommodation of Rising Powers in World Politics." In T. V. Paul (ed.) *Accommodating Rising Powers: Past, Present, and Future*. Cambridge: Cambridge University Press: 3–32.

Pearson, Margaret. 2019. "China and Global Climate Change Governance." In Ka Zeng (ed.) *Handbook on the International Political Economy of China*. Cheltenham: Edward Elgar: 411–23.

Pinto, Sanjay, Kate Macdonald, and Shelley Marshall. 2011. "Rethinking Global Market Governance." *Politics & Society* 39(3): 299–314.

Pisano, G. P., and W. C. Shih. 2012. *Producing Prosperity: Why America Needs a Manufacturing Renaissance*. Cambridge, MA: Harvard Business Press Books.

Pomfret, John. 2010. "China Invests Heavily in Brazil, Elsewhere in Pursuit of Political Heft." *Washington Post*. July 26, 2010: A01.

Porter, Tony. 2005. "The United States in International Trade Politics: Liberal Leader or Heavy-Handed Hegemon?" in Dominic Kelly and Wyn Grant (eds.) *The Politics of International Trade in the Twenty-First Century*. New York: Palgrave Macmillan: 204–20.

Potts, Jason, Xiankun Lu, Vivek Voora, and Matthew Lynch. 2017. "Greening China's Seafood Value Chain." A Case Study for the CCICED Special Policy Study on China's Role in Greening Global Value Chains.

Quark, Amy A. 2013. *Global Rivalries: Standards Wars and the Transnational Cotton Trade*. Chicago: University of Chicago Press.

Rabobank. 2016. "Rabobank: Global Food Prices Set to Stay Low in 2017." *Global Outlook Report*. November 23, 2016. www.rabobank.com/en/press/search/2016/20161123-rabobank-global-food-prices-set-to-stay-low-in-2017.html.

Rachman, Gideon. 2016. *Easternisation: War and Peace in the Asian Century*. London: Random House.

Raghavan, Chakravathi. 2000. "After Seattle, World Trading System Faces Uncertain Future." *Review of International Political Economy* 7(3): 495–504.

Ravi Kanth, D. 2016. "US Strikes Another Body Blow to WTO System at Rules Talks." *South North Development Monitor* 8274. July 1, 2016.

Reddy, Sudeep. 2011. "US Export Terms Pose Test for Beijing." *Wall Street Journal*. January 12, 2011.

Reinert, Erik S. 2007. *How Rich Countries Got Rich ... And Why Poor Countries Stay Poor*. New York: Carroll & Graf.

Reuters. 2015. "Rich Nations' Fossil Fuel Export Funding Dwarfs Green Spend: Documents." March 30, 2015.

2017a. "China Makes WTO Offer on Fishery Subsidies, But Bait Not Taken." November 1, 2017.

2017b. "Eight Chinese Vessels Detained off West Africa for Illegal Fishing." May 3, 2017.

2017c. "Senegal Detains Seven Chinese Trawling Boats for Illegal Fishing." June 10, 2017.

Ruggie, John Gerard. 1982. "International Regimes, Transactions, and Change: Embedded Liberalism in the Postwar Economic Order." *International Organization* 36(2): 379–415.

1996. *Constructing the World Polity: Essays on International Institutionalization*. London: Routledge.

Ruggie, John Gerard, and Tamaryn Nelson. 2015. "Human Rights and the OECD Guidelines for Multinational Enterprises: Normative Innovations and Implementation Challenges." *Brown Journal of World Affairs* 22(1): 99–127.

Sala, Enric, Juan Mayorga, Christopher Costello, David Kroodsma, Maria L. D. Palomares, Daniel Pauly, U. Rashid Sumaila, and Dirk Zeller. 2018. "The Economics of Fishing the High Seas." *Science Advances* 4(6).

Sanderson, H., and M. Forsythe. 2012. *China's Superbank: Debt, Oil and Influence—How China Development Bank is Rewriting the Rules of Finance.* Singapore: Wiley.

Sauvé, Pierre, and Robert Mitchell Stern. 2010. *GATS 2000: New Directions in Services Trade Liberalization.* Washington, DC: Brookings Institution Press.

Schaper, M. 2007. "Leveraging Green Power: Environmental Rules for Project Finance." *Business & Politics* 9(3): 1–27.

Schewel, Matthew. 2011a. "Ex-Im Chief Sees Chinese Willingness to Adhere to Export Credit Rules." *Inside US–China Trade* 11(20).

2011b. "Hockberg: Ex-Im Matched Chinese Financing in GE Pakistan Train Deal." *Inside US–China Trade* 11(3).

Schrank, Andrew, and Josh Whitford. 2009. "Industrial Policy in the United States: A Neo-Polanyian Interpretation." *Politics & Society* 37(4): 521–53.

Schuhbauer, Anna, Ratana Chuenpagdee, William W. L. Cheung, Krista Greer, and U. Rashid Sumaila. 2017. "How Subsidies Affect the Economic Viability of Small-Scale Fisheries." *Marine Policy* 82: 114–21.

Schvartzman, Milko. 2016. "Argentina's Patience Snaps on China's Illegal Fishing." *China Dialogue.* May 20, 2016.

Schwab, Susan C. 2011. "After Doha: Why the Negotiations Are Doomed and What We Should Do about It." *Foreign Affairs* 90(3): 104–17.

Schweller, Randall. 2011. "Emerging Powers in an Age of Disorder." *Global Governance* 17(3): 285–97.

Scott, James. 2017. "The Future of Agricultural Trade Governance in the World Trade Organization." *International Affairs* 93(5): 1167–84.

Scott, James, and Rorden Wilkinson. 2013. "China Threat? Evidence from the WTO." *Journal of World Trade* 47(4): 761–82.

SEFA. 2017. *Energizing Finance: Scaling and Refining Finance in Countries with Large Energy Access Gaps.* Washington, DC: Sustainable Energy for All.

Sell, Susan. 2002. *Private Power, Public Law.* Cambridge: Cambridge University Press.

2006. "Big Business, the WTO, and Development: Uruguay and Beyond." In Richard Stubbs and Geoffrey Underhill (eds.) *Political Economy and the Changing Global Order.* Don Mills, Ontario: Oxford University Press: 183–96.

Sen, Amiti. 2018. "India, China Warn Members against Hurried Negotiations on Fisheries Subsidies at WTO." *The Hindu.* Business Line. April 23, 2018. www.thehindubusinessline.com/news/world/india-china-warn-members-against-hurried-negotiations-on-fisheries-subsidies-at-wto/article23650220.ece#.

Shadlen, Kennneth C. 2005. "Exchanging Development for Market Access: Deep Integration and Industrial Policy under Multilateral and Regional-Bilateral Trade Agreements." *Review of International Political Economy* 12(5): 750–75.

Shaffer, Gregory. 2018. "A Tragedy in the Making? The Decline of Law and the Return of Power in International Trade Relations." *Yale Journal of International Law* 44(37): 37–53.

Shaffer, Gregory, and Henry Gao. 2018. "China's Rise: How It Took on the US at the WTO." *University of Illinois Law Review* (1): 115–84.

Shaffer, Gregory, Robert Wolfe, and Vinhcent Le. 2015. "Can Informal Law Discipline Subsidies?" *Journal of International Economic Law* 18(4): 711–41.

Shambaugh, David. 2013. *China Goes Global: The Partial Power.* New York: Oxford University Press.

Sharma, Ruchir. 2012. "Broken BRICs: Why the Rest Stopped Rising." *Foreign Affairs* 91(6): 2–7.

Shearer, Christine, Nicole Ghio, Lauri Myllyvirta, Aiqun Yu, and Ted Nace. 2017. *Boom and Bust: Tracking the Global Coal Pipeline.* Coal Swarm, Sierra Club, and Greenpeace USA. March 2017. www.sierraclub.org/sites/www.sierraclub.org/files/uploads-wysiwig/BoomBust2017-English-EMBARGO-MARCH-22.pdf.

Sherwin, Kara. 2016. "China Is Outsourcing Its Pollution." *Foreign Policy.* December 7, 2016.

Singh, J. P. 2014. "The Land of Milk and Cotton: How US Protectionism Distorts Global Trade." *Foreign Affairs.* Snapshot. October 23, 2014.

    2017. *Sweet Talk: Paternalism and Collective Action in North–South Trade Relations.* Stanford, CA: Stanford University Press.

Singh, J. P., and Surupa Gupta. 2016. "Agriculture and Its Discontents: Coalitional Politics at the WTO with Special Reference to India's Food Security Interests." *International Negotiation* 21(2): 295–326.

Skarp, Lennart. 2015. "Chinese Export Credit Policies and Programmes." OECD, Working Party on Export Credits and Credit Guarantees (TAD/ECG(2015) 3). March 16, 2015.

Slaughter, Anne-Marie. 2009. "America's Edge." *Foreign Affairs* 88(1): 94–113.

Sneyd, Adam. 2016. *Cotton.* Cambridge: Polity.

Snyder, Quddus Z. 2011. "Integrating Rising Powers: Liberal Systemic Theory and the Mechanism of Competition." *Review of International Studies* 39(1): 209–31.

Stein, Arthur A. 1982. "Coordination and Collaboration: Regimes in an Anarchic World." *International Organization* 36(2): 299–324.

Steinberg, Richard. 2002. "In the Shadow of Law or Power? Consensus-Based Bargaining in the GATT/WTO." *International Organization* 56(2): 339–74.

Stephen, Matthew D. 2014. "Rising Powers, Global Capitalism and Liberal Global Governance: A Historical Materialist Account of the BRICs Challenge." *European Journal of International Relations* 20(4): 912–38.

Stiglitz, Joseph E., J. Esteban, and J. Y. Lin. 2013. *The Industrial Policy Revolution I: The Role of Government beyond Ideology.* New York: Palgrave Macmillan.

Stiglitz, Joseph E., and Bruce C. Greenwald. 2014. *Creating a Learning Society: A New Approach to Growth, Development, and Social Progress.* New York: Columbia University Press.

Stuenkel, Oliver. 2015. *The BRICS and the Future of Global Order.* London: Lexington Books.

Subacchi, Paola. 2008. "New Power Centres and New Power Brokers: Are They Shaping a New Economic Order?" *International Affairs* 84(3): 485–98.

Subramanian, A. 2011. "The Inevitable Superpower: Why China's Dominance Is a Sure Thing." *Foreign Affairs* 90(5): 66.

Sumaila, U. Rashid, Christophe Bellmann, and Alice Tipping. 2014. "Fishing for the Future: Trends in Global Fisheries Trade." E15 Initiative. ICTSD and World Economic Forum. http://e15initiative.org/wp-content/uploads/2015/02/E15_Fisheries_BP_Sumaila-Bellmann-Tipping_FINAL.pdf.

Sumaila, U. Rashid, Vicky Lam, Frédéric Le Manach, Wilf Swartz, and Daniel Pauly. 2013. *Global Fisheries Subsidies*. Brussels: European Parliament Directorate-General for Internal Policies.

Tabuchi, Hiroko. 2017. "As Beijing Joins Climate Fight, Chinese Companies Build Coal Plants." *New York Times*. July 1, 2017.

Tipping, Alice. 2017. "Tackling Fisheries Subsidies at the WTO: What's in It for LDCs?" *Bridges Africa* 6(8).

———. 2018. "Overview: Building Comprehensive and Effective WTO Rules on Fisheries Subsidies." In *Fisheries Subsidies Rules at the WTO: A Compilation of Evidence and Analysis*. Geneva: International Centre for Trade and Sustainable Development.

*Trade Finance*. 2014. "Asia's Necessary Evil." April 7, 2014. https://tradefinance analytics.com/articles/3328231/asias-necessary-evil.

———. 2015. "New OECD Rule Limits ECA Coal-Fired Power Funding." November 19, 2015. https://tradefinanceanalytics.com/articles/3492282/new-oecd-rule-limits-eca-coal-fired-power-funding.

Trommer, Silke. 2014. *Transformations in Trade Politics: Participatory Trade Politics in West Africa*. London: Routledge.

———. 2017. "The WTO in an Era of Preferential Trade Agreements: Thick and Thin Institutions in Global Trade Governance." *World Trade Review* 16(3): 501–26.

Tvardek, Steven. 2011. "Smart Aid Rules for Development, Not Export Promotion." In *Smart Rules for Fair Trade: 50 Years of Export Credits*. Paris: OECD: 208–14.

Ueno, Takahiro, Miki Yanagi, and Jane Nakano. 2014. "Quantifying Chinese Public Financing for Foreign Coal Power Plants." University of Tokyo, GrasSPP Working Paper.

Umbach, Frank, and Ka-ho Yu. 2016. "China's Expanding Overseas Coal Power Industry: New Strategic Opportunities, Commercial Risks, Climate Challenges and Geopolitical Implications." European Centre for Energy and Resource Security (EUCERS) Strategy Paper 11, Department of War Studies, King's College, London.

UNCTAD. 2016. "The 2014 US Farm Bill and its Implications for Cotton Producers in Low-Income Developing Countries." UN Conference on Trade and Development, Geneva.

UNCTAD-FAO-UNEP. 2016. "Regulating Fisheries Subsidies Must be an Integral Part of the Implementation of the 2030 Sustainable Development Agenda." UNCTAD-FAO-UNEP Joint Statement, Fourteenth Session of the

United Nations Conference on Trade and Development, Nairobi. July 20, 2016.

UNEP. 2011. *Fisheries Subsidies, Sustainable Development and the WTO*. New York: United Nations Environment Programme.

UNESCO. 2016. "Education for People and Planet: Creating Sustainable Futures for All." Global Education Monitoring Report.

United States. 2000a. "China's WTO Accession: Trade Interests, Values and Strategy." Speech by US Trade Representative Charlene Barshefsky, National Conference of State Legislators, Washington, DC. February 4, 2000.

2000b. "A Strategy for the Future: US–China Relations and China's WTO Accession." Speech by Stanley O. Roth, Assistant Secretary for East Asian and Pacific Affairs, US Department of State, Washington State China Relations Council, Washington, DC. April 5, 2000.

2008. "Senate Committee on Finance Press Release: Finance, Ways and Means Leaders Urge President to Stand Firm on Doha Round." December 2, 2008.

2011. "2011 Trade Policy Agenda and 2010 Annual Report." Executive Office of the President. https://ustr.gov/2011_trade_policy_agenda.

2013a. "Export–Import Bank Board Adopts Revised Environmental Guidelines to Reduce Greenhouse Gas Emissions." Press Release, US Export–Import Bank, Washington, DC. December 12, 2013.

2013b. "Guidance for US Positions on MDBs Engaging with Developing Countries on Coal-Fired Power Generation." Department of Treasury. October 29, 2013.

2013c. "Joint Statement by Kingdom of Denmark, Republic of Finland, Republic of Iceland, Kingdom of Norway, Kingdom of Sweden, and the United States of America." White House Press Release. September 4.

2013d. "The President's Climate Action Plan." Executive Office of the President. June 2013.

2015a. "Under Secretary of the US Department of the Treasury Nathan Sheets Written Statement to the House Committee on Oversight and Government Reform, Subcommittee on Health Care, Benefits, and Administrative Rules, and House Financial Services Committee, Subcommittee on Monetary Policy and Trade." US Congress, Washington, DC. April 15, 2015.

2015b. "US–China Joint Presidential Statement on Climate Change." White House Press Release. September 25, 2015.

2016a. "Deputy Assistant Secretary for East Asia Abraham M. Denmark Holds a Press Briefing in the Pentagon Briefing Room." Deputy Assistant Secretary of Defense for East Asia Abraham M. Denmark, US Department of Defense, Transcript. May 13, 2016.

2016b. "United States Challenges Chinese Grain Tariff Rate Quotas for Rice, Wheat, and Corn." US Trade Representative, Press Release. June 26, 2016.

2016c. "United States Challenges Excessive Chinese Support for Rice, Wheat, and Corn." US Trade Representative, Press Release. September 6, 2016.

US Chamber of Commerce. 2016. *Cultivating Opportunity: The Benefits of Increased U.S.–China Agricultural Trade*. Washington, DC.

USDA (United States Department of Agriculture). 2015a. "China Grain and Feed Annual—2015." GAIN Report Number CH15014, Foreign Agricultural Service. May 8, 2015.

2015b. "Cotton Policy in China." Report from the Economic Research Service. CWS-15c-01. March 2015.

2015c. "The Importance of Agriculture Exports to US Trade and the Farm Economy." Financial Conduct Authority Economic Report. September 9, 2015.

2016a. "China and Hong Kong: Challenges and Opportunities." USDA Foreign Agricultural Service, International Agricultural Trade Reports. September 6, 2016.

2016b. "India Agricultural Trade: Expanding Export Opportunities Amid Persistent Limitations." USDA Foreign Agricultural Service, International Agricultural Trade Report. December 21, 2016.

2018. "Northeastern Region 2017 Farms and Land in Farms Summary." Farms and Land in Farms Report. National Agricultural Statistics Service. February 21, 2018

USTR. 2017. *Report to Congress on China's WTO Compliance*. Washington, DC: US Trade Representative.

VanGrasstek, Craig. 2013. *The History and Future of the World Trade Organization*. Geneva: World Trade Organization.

Vassard, Jan. 2015. "A Global Regime for Export Credits in the New World (Dis) Order—Challenges of Multipolarity." In *The Future of Foreign Trade Support—Setting Global Standards for Export Credit and Political Risk Insurance. Global Policy*. e-book. www.globalpolicyjournal.com/blog/author/the-future-of-foreign-trade-support.

Vestergaard, Jakob, and Robert H. Wade. 2015. "Still in the Woods: Gridlock in the IMF and the World Bank Puts Multilateralism at Risk." *Global Policy* 6(1): 1–12.

Wade, Robert H. 2003. "What Strategies are Viable for Developing Countries Today? The World Trade Organization and the Shrinking of 'Development Space'." *Review of International Political Economy* 10(4): 621–44.

2017. "The West Remains on Top, Economically and Politically." In Matias E. Margulis (ed.) *The Global Political Economy of Raúl Prebisch*. New York: Routledge: 135–52.

Walt, Stephen M. 2011. "The End of the American Era." *National Interest* (116): 6–16.

Warwick, Ken. 2013. "Beyond Industrial Policy: Emerging Issues and New Trends." OECD Science, Technology and Industry Policy Papers No. 2, Paris: OECD.

Warwick Commission. 2008. *The Multilateral Trade Regime: Which Way Forward?* Coventry: University of Warwick.

*Washington Post*. 2015. "In a Major Step on the Road to Paris, Rich Countries Agree to Slash Export Subsidies for Coal Plants." November 18, 2015.

WEF (World Economic Forum). 2016. "Renewable Infrastructure Investment Handbook: A Guide for Institutional Investors." December 2016. www3.weforum.org/docs/WEF_Renewable_Infrastructure_Investment_Handbook.pdf.

Weiss, Linda. 2005. "Global Governance, National Strategies: How Industrial States Make Room to Move under the WTO." *Review of International Political Economy* 12(5): 723–49.

2014. *America Inc.? Innovation and Enterprise in the National Security State.* Ithaca, NY: Cornell University Press.

Wilkinson, Rorden. 2011. "Measuring the WTO's Performance: An Alternative Account." *Global Policy* 2(1): 43–52.

Wilkinson, Rorden, Erin Hannah, and James Scott. 2014. "The WTO in Bali: What MC9 Means for the Doha Development Agenda and Why It Matters." *Third World Quarterly* 35(6): 1032–50.

2016. "The WTO in Nairobi: The Demise of the Doha Development Agenda and the Future of the Multilateral Trading System." *Global Policy* 7(2): 247–55.

Wilkinson, Rorden, and James Scott. 2008. "Developing Country Participation in the GATT: A Reassessment." *World Trade Review* 7(3): 473–510.

Williams, F. 1999. "Nations Call for Fishing Subsidy Ban." *Financial Times.* August 2, 1999.

Wilson, Jeffrey D. 2017. "The Evolution of China's Asian Infrastructure Investment Bank: from a Revisionist to Status-Seeking Agenda." *International Relations of the Asia-Pacific* 19(1): 147–76.

Womack, Brantly. 2016. "Asymmetric Parity: US–China Relations in a Multi-nodal World." *International Affairs* 92(6): 1463–80.

Wood, Ellen Meiksins. 2005. *Empire of Capital.* New York: Verso.

World Bank. 1993. *The East Asian Miracle: Economic Growth and Public Policy.* Washington, DC: World Bank.

2009. *The Sunken Billions.* Washington, DC: World Bank.

2013. "The State of the Poor: Where are the Poor and Where are the Poorest." www.worldbank.org/content/dam/Worldbank/document/State_of_the_poor_paper_April17.pdf.

2017. *The Sunken Billions Revisited: Progress and Challenges in Global Marine Fisheries.* Washington, DC: World Bank.

World Bank and WTO. 2015. *The Role of Trade in Ending Poverty.* Geneva: World Trade Organization.

Wright, Christopher. 2011. "Export Credit Agencies and Global Energy: Promoting National Exports in a Changing World." *Global Policy* 2: 133–43.

WTO (World Trade Organization). 2005. "Hong Kong Ministerial Declaration." December 22, 2005. WT/MIN(05)/DEC.

2008. "World Trade Report." Geneva: World Trade Organization.

2015. "Minutes of Meeting, Trade Negotiations Committee." October 5, 2015. TN/C/M/37.

2017a. "Report by Ambassador Stephen Karau to the Committee on Agriculture Special Session." July 25, 2017. JOB/AG/107.

2017b. "World Trade Statistical Review." www.wto.org/english/res_e/statis_e/wts2017_e/wts17_toc_e.htm.

WWF (World Wildlife Fund for Nature). 2007. "Fisheries Subsidies: WWF Statement on the Chairman's Draft." December 12, 2007. Geneva. http://assets.panda.org/downloads/wwf_stmnt_on_fish_subs_text_111207.pdf.

2015. "Coal Finance: Will the OECD Lag behind Emerging Countries Because of Japan?" Briefing Paper. October 2015.

Xiao, Ren. 2013. "Debating China's Rise in China." In R. Friedman, K. Oskanian, and R. P. Pardo (eds.) *After Liberalism? The Future of Liberalism in International Relations*. Basingstoke: Palgrave Macmillan.

Yu, Wusheng. 2017. *How China's Farm Policy Reforms Could Affect Trade and Markets: A Focus on Grains and Cotton*. Geneva: International Centre for Trade and Sustainable Development.

Yue, Li. 2012. "Dynamics of Clean Coal-Fired Power Generation Development in China." *Energy Policy* 51(C):138–42.

Zakaria, Fareed. 2008. *The Post-American World*. New York: Norton.

Zangl, Bernhard, Frederick Heußner, Andreas Kruck, and Xenia Lanzendörfer. 2016. "Imperfect Adaptation: How the WTO and the IMF Adjust to Shifting Power Distributions among Their Members." *Review of International Organizations* 11(2): 171–96.

Zeiler, Thomas W. 1999. *Free Trade, Free World: The Advent of the GATT*: Chapel Hill: University of North Carolina Press.

2012. "The Expanding Mandate of the GATT: The First Seven Rounds." In A. Narlikar, M. Daunton, and R. M. Stern (eds.) *The Oxford Handbook on The World Trade Organization*. Oxford: Oxford University Press.

Zha, Daojiong, and Hongzhou Zhang. 2013. "Food in China's International Relations." *Pacific Review* 26(5): 455–79.

Zhang, Hongzhou. 2016. "Chinese Fishermen in Disputed Waters: Not Quite a 'People's War'." *Marine Policy* 68: 65–73.

Zhang, Hongzhou, and Sam Bateman. 2017. "Fishing Militia, the Securitization of Fishery and the South China Sea Dispute." *Contemporary Southeast Asia: A Journal of International and Strategic Affairs* 39(2): 288–314.

Zhang, Hongzhou, and Fengshi Wu. 2017. "China's Marine Fishery and Global Ocean Governance." *Global Policy* 8(2): 216–26.

Zoellick, Robert. 2010. "The End of the Third World? Modernizing Multilateralism for a Multipolar World." President of the World Bank, Speech at the Woodrow Wilson Center, Washington, DC. April 14, 2010. http://documents .worldbank.org/curated/en/595831521623147298/The-end-of-the-third-world-modernizing-multilateralism-for-a-multipolar-world-by-Robert-B-Zoellick-President-World-Bank-Group.

# Index

Africa
  cotton production in, 87–88
  fisheries subsidies and, Chinese use of, 109–11
  impact of agricultural subsidies on countries in, 85–87
aggregate measure of support (AMS), 76, 80–82
Agreement on Agriculture (AoA), Uruguay Round, 75–76
agricultural subsidies. *See also* cotton subsidies
  aggregate measure of support (AMS), 76, 80–82
  China and. *See* China
  developing countries and, 84–87, 205
    in Africa, 85–87
    China as, 71–76, 84
    political influence on, by China, 85–87
    as victims of subsidies, 62–63
  during Doha 'Development' Round, 63
  EU use of, 61–62
  free trade agreements and, 83–84
  Global North and, 63
  Global South and, 63–64
  impact on developing countries, 85–87
  in international trading system, 61
  overview of, 93
  Oxfam and, 61–62
  reduction of, 60
  U.S. and, 61–62, 68–71
    China's conflict with, 75–76, 82–83
    WTO and, 70–71, 75–76

  WTO and, 61–64
    critiques of rules of, by China, 75–76
    disputes over, 70–71, 75–76
    post-Doha negotiations, 77–84
    Rev4, 77–79
agriculture. *See also* agricultural subsidies
  Agreement on Agriculture (AoA), Uruguay Round, 75–76
  country shares in total agricultural value added, 68
  Duty-Free Quota Free (DFQF) market access, 88–89
  Rev4, 77–79
  tariff rate quotas for, 70–71
  tariffs, in Doha "Development" Round, 46–47
  U.S. exports
    to China, 69–70
    foreign protectionist trade policies as influence on, 69
    global competition as influence on, 69
'American imperium,' 3
AMS. *See* aggregate measure of support
AoA. *See* Agreement on Agriculture
Arrangement on Export Credit (OECD), 11–12, 138–41
  China and, 13–14, 150–51
  Common Approaches for Export Credits and Enviromental and Social Due Diligence, 163–65
  developing countries in, 211
  enforcement mechanisms of, 139–40

241

fisheries subsidies (cont.)
  WTO negotiations influenced by,
    99–102
  World Wildlife Fund and, 100–1
  WTO negotiations on
    post-Doha negotiations, 94
    rationale for, 98–99
    during Seattle Ministerial, 100–1
    U.S. leadership as influence on, 99–102
fishing industry
  in China, 102–4
    in Belt and Road Initiative, 108
    expansion of, 102–4
    fuel subsidies and, 104–5
    as policy goal, 104–5
  economic development and growth
    dependent on, 97–98
  global exports, 103
  global marine capture production, 103
  social dependence on, 97
Food and Agriculture Organization. *See*
  United Nations
food reserves, in China
  agricultural subsidies and, 72–74
  food security policies and, 72–73
  Global Food Crisis and, 66, 73–74
food security, in China, 72–73
Foot, Rosemary, 17
free trade agreements (FTAs), agricultural
  subsidies and, 83–84
Friends of Fish, 209
FTAs. *See* free trade agreements
fuel subsidies, in China, 104–5

G20. *See* Group of 20
G33. *See* Group of 33
GATT. *See* General Agreement on Tariffs
  and Trade
GDP. *See* gross domestic product
General Agreement on Tariffs and Trade
  (GATT), 3–4
  European Economic Community and, 32
  Kennedy Round, 32–33
  principle of reciprocity and, 19–20
  purpose of, 31
  special and differential treatment and,
    19–20
  Tokyo Round, 33
  Uruguay Round, 34–35
  U.S. and, 32
    role in creation of, 31

general input subsidies, in China, 74–75
global cotton subsidies, 89
  elimination of, 92
global economic governance. *See* economic
  governance
global economic institutions. *See specific
  institutions*
global exports, for fishing industry, 103
Global Food Crisis, 66, 73–74
global marine capture production, 103
Global North
  agricultural subsidies and, 63
  China and, 22–23
  liberal international economic order and, 4
Global South
  agricultural subsidies and, 63–64
  China and, 22–23
  liberal international economic order and, 4
global trade governance. *See* trade
  governance
governance. *See specific topics*
Grant, Wyn, 22–23
gross domestic product (GDP), among
  comparative economies, 52–53
Group of 20 (G20)
  China in, 37
  during Doha 'Development' Round, 63
Group of 33 (G33), China in, 37

Hamilton, Alexander, 19–20
Hannam, Phillip, 175
hegemony, of U.S.
  China as threat to, 2–3
    security issues as part of, 17
  fisheries subsidies influenced by
    China and, 130–31
    environmental group's role in, 99–100
    WTO negotiations and, 99–102
  global domination and leadership of, 4
  global economic governance influenced
    by, through redistribution of
    authority, 10
  global economic institutions influenced
    by, 7
  historical development of, 3–4
  liberal international economic order and,
    3–4
  multilateral trading system and, 31–35
    accommodation of rising powers,
      31–33
    creation of, 31